ON GERMANY

GILES MACDONOGH

On Germany

HURST & COMPANY, LONDON

First published in the United Kingdom in 2018 by
C. Hurst & Co. (Publishers) Ltd.,
41 Great Russell Street, London, WC1B 3PL
© Giles MacDonogh, 2018
All rights reserved.

The right of Giles MacDonogh to be identified as the author
of this publication is asserted by him in accordance with the
Copyright, Designs and Patents Act, 1988.

Distributed in the United States, Canada and Latin America by
Oxford University Press, 198 Madison Avenue, New York, NY 10016,
United States of America.

A Cataloguing-in-Publication data record for this book
is available from the British Library.

ISBN: 9781849049450

This book is printed using paper from registered sustainable
and managed sources.

www.hurstpublishers.com

Printed and bound in Great Britain by Bell & Bain Ltd, Glasgow

For Lisa Zirner
Ich denke immer an die alte,
Die alte Frau, die Gott erhalte!

CONTENTS

CONTENTS

PART III
ON THE ROAD

CONTENTS

Map 1

Map 2

PREFACE

German reunification surprised me sunk in *la France profonde*, in Bourg-en-Bresse. On 9 November 1989 I was working in the Departmental Archives and had taken myself out for a quiet dinner with a book. When I returned to my hotel room, I switched on the television to see that the Berlin Wall had been breached: gimcrack Trabi cars were queuing up at the border waiting for a chance to reach the lotus land on the other side; corks were popping from bottles of Sekt on the Wall. It was, without question, politically the most important day of my life. I had grown up in the Cold War, and known nothing else. The shadow of the Second World War had lain over my childhood and youth like a shroud. Quietly, and for a few years now, the other half of Europe had begun to shake off its fetters, but this was the real break-through. I had a book on German opposition to Hitler in production, due to be published in December.[1] As soon as I got back to London, I made plans to go to Germany. I was determined to get to the Wall.

It is now almost thirty years later, and most people have forgotten the euphoria of that time; many others were either not yet born, or too young to understand its significance. The then German Chancellor Helmut Kohl felt he had acquitted the first of two tasks: the first being to unite Germany, the second,

Europe. Now we in Britain stand on the brink of leaving the European Union, and the Cold War, let alone the Second World War, is a distant memory filed under 'history'. Our recall is fickle and short. Of course, some of those who voted for Brexit weren't born in 1989, but we are told that most of them were—indeed, many of them were older than I am.

Reunification occurred a generation ago. After a bumpy ride, Germany is now without question the mightiest nation in Europe. Since West Germany digested the East, the focus of many people's thoughts has been Germany's soft power as exercised via the European Union. The reactions in some quarters have been hysterical, but in Germany itself, there is often a nervous feeling that the country is a bit like Frankenstein's monster: unaware of its own strength, and prone to fits of violence when it veers out of control, it needs to be watched. Framed within the European Union, Germany is contained; should that Union be allowed to break up, Europe could feel that disproportionate might once again—will it always be a force for good?

My interest in Germany goes back to my mid-teens. Unlike many Germanists I have no family links, but my mother does come from Vienna, and I was born into a family with Central European, if not Teutonic, roots. My mother arrived here in Britain with my English grandmother in 1935, so we children did not exactly grow up as refugees, or *Vertriebene*, even if some of our cousins did. We lived away from the bits of London populated by German and Austrian Jews, but I was aware of their culture from the beginning, thanks to periodic visits from and to my godfather: my grandfather's childhood friend, the archaeologist Alphons Barb. Dr Barb would come bearing a large envelope filled with stamps that he had prised off his professional correspondence. He was almost a caricature of a Central European academic. His office in the Warburg Institute—itself a little piece of Germany replanted in London in 1934—reeked of Villiger

Virginia cigars. In it he studied ancient coins and amulets and corresponded with a handful of scholars around the world—chiefly in German, but when that was lacking, in Latin or Ancient Greek.

Dr Barb had moved to Britain in 1939 and died in Croydon in 1979. He never got used to the place. He had been the first director of the Burgenland State Museum in Eisenstadt but, despite his scholarly reputation in Austria, he had worked in a bicycle factory in Leeds until 1949. He found British universities childish and over-obsessed with sport and pleasure. He never got to grips with English literature and invariably returned to Goethe and Schiller. Above all he could not fathom the English fondness for 'low culture'. He was himself the very epitome of *Hochkultur* and, in the occasional sermons he delivered to me, he made it abundantly clear that this was the only thing to strive for.

Dr Barb's model might be a bit worn out now, even in Germany. In 2017 I was driving up from Kempten in the Allgäu to the Alps while a German teacher explained to me how much the *Abitur*—the German school leaving certificate—had been dumbed down in the interests of getting more people into university. It was a familiar story: the classics struck from the list in favour of a smaller number of easier texts. Dr Barb, who died forty years ago, would hardly have recognised the new, global, multicultural Germany.

A few years ago, I handed over my stamp collection to my son, and once again I saw all the stamps that Dr Barb used to put aside for me. Despite everything, the lion's share were German. Growing up in London, I took a keen interest in what was happening in Germany too, from the construction of the Berlin Wall and the student uprising of 1968 to the brutal assassinations carried out by the Baader-Meinhof Gang, *Ostpolitik* and Willy Brandt kneeling before the Monument to the Warsaw Uprising. I observed with interest as Germany rejoined the club of righteous nations and watched the often tardy process of atonement for the crimes of the Second World War, particularly during the '70s, when the left dominated the Bundestag in Bonn. Finally, we waited with bated breath for the two halves of the nation to come back together.

The following pages are the fruit of thirty years of close observation of Germany, and all that that breeds about its heart. They are born of the very long periods I have spent there and the books I have written as a result. Naturally, as an historian, I am keen to see how the past colours the present. In Germany this is particularly true, as Germans cannot escape from their past, and are obliged to relive it every day. Keen observers will see that I spent more time in Germany between 1987 and 1997 than I have since; that I used up a disproportionate amount of that time in Berlin; and have no practical knowledge of the Ruhr or the north-west of the country. I have spent very little time in Hamburg and I sometimes think I am the only person in the world who has never been to Heidelberg. Somebody recently asked me about German cars and I had to explain, not for the first time, that I have never driven in my life. I am also hopeless when it comes to business and did not even kick a football around in my now distant childhood. The only match I have ever seen, on the other hand, was in Berlin-Schöneberg, so I suppose that is a small plea in mitigation.

This book was proposed to me by Michael Dwyer of Hurst. It has been an exciting challenge to summarise my German experience in literary form. I apologise only for my errors and for adding to the growing pile of books that have recently emerged on the subject—albeit with a very different focus from the present volume. I have seen very few of these; only Stephen Green's *Reluctant Meister* of 2014 (which I read in proof) and Peter Watson's *German Genius* of 2010 have come my way. The following list of acknowledgements will do no justice to the real number of people who have educated me over those long years: Sarah Reinke and Uta Janssen of the Stiftung Adam von Trott in Imshausen, Angela Bielenberg, Karl Heinz Bohrer, Stephen Brockman, Sebastian Cody, Jennifer Fay, Lara Feigel of King's College London, Baron Green of Hurstpierpoint (Stephen Green), Iris Guske of the Institut für Fremdsprachenberufe in Kempten, Ursula Heinzelmann, Jan Johnsen, Paula Kirby, Werner Pfeiffer, Clarita and Urs Müller-Plantenberg, Hilke Nagel from the VDP in Mainz, Verena Onken-von Trott, Stuart Pigott, Ned Richardson-Little, Christopher Wentworth-Stanley, and Lara Weisweiller-Wu, Farhaana Arefin and Daisy Leitch from Hurst. I thank my family too, once again, for dealing with my moods and obsessions.

Giles MacDonogh, London

PART I

GERMANY SINCE 1945

INTRODUCTION

In modern history at least, no country has fallen quite as low as Germany did in 1945. Poland disappeared politically as a result of the eighteenth-century Partitions, but its people remained very much in place and agitated when they could. The nearest parallel to the destruction of Germany would be the Thirty Years' War (1618–48), where once again the chief sufferers were the Germans, but then they were the victims, pawns in a power game played out by Austrians, French, Danes and Swedes. Germans could not make the same claim at the end of the Second World War—not only had they caused it, but they had wrought havoc throughout Europe and the world. They deserved to lose, and they knew a retribution would be enacted of Carthaginian proportions. The punishment was dictated by Stalin, Roosevelt and Churchill at Yalta in February 1945: Germany would be occupied for as long as was deemed necessary. To make the victors happy, the German cake would be cut into three unequal slices. Later it was decided that France would have its zone too, but cut from the ribs of the British and US territories. Berlin was likewise to be chopped up into four 'Sectors'.

The figures are disputed, debunked and revised, sometimes in the interests of scoring points, but it is safe to say that around 5 million German soldiers died in the war, and in the ensuing months and years perhaps as many as another million died as POWs. The last bedraggled prisoners, the 'latest home-comers', were not released before 1956. Nor was it just the Russians keeping them incarcerated. Although they were open for only a few months, the Rhine Meadow camps administered by the US Army saw thousands of German POWs perish. Possibly the best account of the camps is to be found in the book written by Josef Nowak,[1] a Swabian playwright and opponent of the Nazis who had been conscripted onto an anti-aircraft battery. As an Italian speaker, he had acted as an interpreter between the German commander and his largely Italian team. In the spring of 1945 he was taken prisoner by the Americans.

I have written about the Rhine Meadow camps, but I did not know of Nowak's account until recently. During one of the bitterest late winters and springs in recent history, the prisoners—essentially anyone apprehended wearing uniform—were obliged to sleep on the naked earth dressed in rags. Some of them dug foxholes with any implements they could lay their hands on. These holes often collapsed, burying and frequently killing their inmates. They were also beaten and robbed by their guards. Like many other former POWs, Nowak says that the black American troops guarding them behaved with more decency than the whites.

Food was occasionally tossed into the pens—sometimes American rations in tins, or raw lentils and haricot beans which had the most catastrophic effects on digestion. Quite often, the prisoners went for days without receiving anything at all. Naturally, they perished in droves. Particularly bittersweet was the moment, after weeks of waiting, when the Germans received their first bread. They were hoping for some dark rye, or a crispy wholemeal loaf—the excellent, filling bread for which their country is still so famous. Instead they got a half-inch-thick slice of American Wonderloaf. It was a painful anticlimax.

Once the Allied Zones came into force in July 1945, the camp passed into the hands of the British, who administered it with greater fairness. The food improved, and prisoners were even allowed to attend Mass. They were not completely out of the woods, even then. Some 8 million German citizens had been members of the Nazi Party, and that required rehabilitation. Leading Nazis were imprisoned. Others who were only slightly implicated were let off more lightly.

The cure to be administered in each case was decided by the *Fragebogen*, or questionnaire, with its list of almost impossible questions. The *Fragebogen* determined whether you would be able to work again in the near future. As almost all teachers, doctors, lawyers and judges had been obliged to join the Party, this meant that, for the time being, the leading elements of German society were pushed out into the wilderness. Many crept back quite quickly, however, and German politicians turned a blind eye. It was not always that the latter sympathised with the Nazis: in some cases, they were only too aware that the country could not do without its cadre.

After the humiliation of the *Fragebogen* and interrogation chiefly by German Jews in British uniforms—not many British officers spoke German—the small fry, Nowak included, were discharged from the POW camps into the jagged remnants of their land. For a while Germany had been a country without men, and the women had fallen prey to its conquerors.[2] During the war, at least a further 400,000 German civilians had been killed by Allied bombardment. Between the end of the European war and the creation of the Republics in 1949, 2.25 million more were cut off and perished in the east, or expired trying to reach the country's new borders. All in all, 16.5 million Germans were estimated to have undertaken the perilous trek back to the Fatherland.[3]

The Potsdam Conference in August 1945 was an attempt to define German territory. On the agenda were also denazification,

demilitarisation, and decentralisation. The Western Allies settled on the pre-1937 borders, while Stalin held to a bizarre
formula of 'Germany is what it is now'. It was already clear at
Yalta that Germany would receive a new eastern border and that
the fate of its easternmost stretches would be decided quickly.
Stalin wanted another ice-free port; that meant Königsberg in
the Baltic, and half of East Prussia—the other half he was happy
to award to the Poles.

He also wanted all of Poland east of the Curzon Line, which
meant evicting the 1.7 million Poles who lived there. In fact the
Poles had acquired that territory from Russia only in 1921, and
just a quarter of its inhabitants were Polish. Poland would be
compensated with German land and the 8 million Germans there
would be deported.[4] In fact, many had been already, as Stalin
knew only too well. He held all the cards at Potsdam, and no
matter how hard the Western leaders tried, he yielded on nothing. Despite Truman, Churchill and Attlee, Germany lost
21 per cent of the territory it had possessed before Hitler started
his rampage. Although officially nothing was hard or fast until
the 'peace conference', which only eventually happened at the
Two-Plus-Four talks in 1990, the Poles annexed the former
German territories in 1949.[5]

RECONSTRUCTION

Within this shrunken space called Germany, much had been
destroyed: homes, offices, and a very large number of factories.
Four foreign armies settled down among the more habitable
ruins. Although Germany was allowed to form its own government as early as 1949, foreign armies remained in garrison on
their land for a further forty years, and some small units of
British and American troops are still there.

Like characters from a Heinrich Böll story, the men returned home with bandaged feet. They included many mere boys who had been fighting with the grown-ups, or who, aged fourteen or fifteen, had been called up as *Flakhelfer* and assigned to anti-aircraft batteries. The teenage warriors would later be 'outed', particularly the novelist Günter Grass, who had forgotten to admit after the war that he had been in the Waffen SS. The *Flakhelfer* had much less to be ashamed of. One was the young Helmut Kohl, who had been a Hitler Youth *Pimpf* (cub-scout). In April 1943, he had been sworn in as a *Flakhelfer* in the Bavarian Alps by Artur Axmann, head of the Hitler Youth. In 1945 Kohl walked home to Ludwigshafen on the Rhine—or rather to Mannheim, because he could not get across the river. When his mother located him, she brought him a precious jar of peach jam, 'which he scoffed greedily.'[6] Not much was left of ugly Ludwigshafen. There hadn't been much to lose: it was largely a base for the chemical producer BASF and other industries, and had only been bumped up to urban status in 1859.[7]

For the next few years the young Kohl had to mind his step with the forces of the French occupation, who were stripping the land with something near the avidity of the Soviets on the other side of Germany. In 1946, there was even a hunger strike organised in protest. Kohl rapidly assailed all the requisite political fortresses: he was a party member of the right-wing CDU (Christian Democratic Union) from sixteen, Germany's youngest ever regional president when he took over in Rheinland-Pfalz, and at forty-seven became leader of the party and the opposition in Bonn, West Germany's capital. In the meantime he had married his childhood sweetheart, Hannelore Renner, whose gruelling experiences as a 12-year-old girl embodied what had happened when the Soviet (and other) soldiers entered Germany in 1945.

The CDU remained nominally a Christian party. Before leadership elections, an ecumenical service was held, presumably a chance for the Holy Spirit to inspire choices.[8] Another who made his way back from the war, but this time as a thirty-year-old Wehrmacht *Oberleutnant*, was Franz Josef Strauss. Like Kohl, he made his way into 'Christian' politics at once. The field was empty, and people were anxious to fill the political vacuum left by the Nazis. The big man in Bavaria was Josef 'Ochsensepp' Müller: an exemplary figure of the Nazi-era opposition, he was a Catholic lawyer who had acted as an emissary between the 20 July Plotters and the Pope and narrowly escaped death as a result.[9] Müller did not get on with the big beast in Cologne, Konrad Adenauer, and established his own base at his Munich home. The Catholic-dominated CSU (Christian Social Union in Bavaria) was formed in November 1945, and its aspiring politicians were known, after Müller's street address, as the Gedonstrasse Circle.[10]

* * *

The Soviet Union had received the largest slice of the cake: the chunk of the Reich that lay between the Elbe and Oder rivers. The Russians stripped it bare and took everything home, down to the railway tracks, light bulbs and lavatory bowls. The removal of so many train lines had a catastrophic effect on local transport in East Germany that was still noticeable as late as 1992. After the Allies fell out over money in 1948, the Russian Zone developed into the DDR: a separate, quasi-one-party socialist state dominated by the SED (Socialist Unity Party), a fusion of the pre-war socialists and communists. It was still essentially German, but much more austerely so. The party was relatively popular at first—some 50 per cent of the Russian Zone's citizens had voted for left-wing parties before 1933—but they were also scarred by the events of 1945: rape, theft, murder and the deportations to the Soviet Union. Some half a million went through the mill of denazification. Former Nazis were not allowed to teach in Kindergartens or universities.[11]

Until the Volksarmee was created in response to a militarised West Germany, East Germany was heavy on paramilitaries. There was the elite regiment of Felix Dzerzhinsky Guards: 10,000 men trained to protect the SED and 47,000 border guards whose job was hardly to keep the West out—there were no attempted incursions—but rather to keep their own people in. Added to that were the People's Police or Vopos, and the paramilitary Kasernierte Vopos, a further fighting force. The Ministry for State Security had 97,000 employees, not including the IMs. These 173,000 unofficial informants—compared with 7,000 in the Third Reich—were awarded the task of sneaking on a population of 17 million—one nark for every sixty-three people. With all of their filed, copied and annotated reports, there were more paper files in the DDR than had been amassed in Germany from the end of the Middle Ages to the collapse of the Reich in 1945.[12]

> The Stasi was the internal army by which the government kept control. Its job was to know everything about everyone, using any means it chose. It knew who your visitors were, it knew whom you telephoned, and it knew if your wife slept around. It was a bureaucracy metastasised through East German society: overt or covert, there was someone reporting to the Stasi on their fellows and friends in every school, every factory, every apartment block, every pub.[13]

Many people observed that not a lot had changed between Nazi and SED rule. Attitudes towards the Church—in East Germany this meant almost exclusively the Lutheran Evangelical Church—continued to echo the impatience and intolerance of the Nazis; psychologists rejected Freud, much as their Nazi predecessors had done; children were still indoctrinated by party organisations. Chiefly, however, what the DDR carried over from the Nazis was this apparatus of terror—only it might be said to have done it better.

One of the first measures in constructing the DDR was Land Reform, with the big landowners seeing their land removed and redistributed. An all-out attack on the nobility was unlikely to be unpopular with the East Germans, as it promised more land for small farmers. This proved a delusion, however; by the early '50s it became clear that no one other than the state would benefit from Land Reform. The most you could aspire to was between 1 and 2 acres, which might have been enough to provide a little more for the family, but rendered a career in farming a non-starter in the so-called 'State of Workers and Peasants'.

When I met Prince Georg zur Lippe at Schloss Proschwitz on the Elbe opposite Meissen a few years ago, he recounted his father's plight. The Lippes were a minor branch of a former ruling family who had become major industrialists and employers in Saxony. They also owned a largeish wine estate. Naturally, both business and vineyard were lost under the DDR and Prince Georg's parents were sent to one of the handful of camps for the deposed aristocracy or gentry. That they survived the first months was largely due to their elder children, who passed them food through the barbed wire. When they were released, they had not a penny to their names. They had to stay with the princely Castells in Franconia, where Prince Christian earned his bread as a delivery man. The Lippes' story has a happy ending, however, for after the *Wende*—the turn or change, as the fall of the Iron Curtain is known—Prince Christian's son Georg began, bit by bit, to buy back the estate and Schloss, ending up with some 500 acres of vineyard and one of the most reputable wines in Saxony.

* * *

It wasn't always so easy across the border in the Western Zones, either. The Trotts' Imshausen manor house in North Hesse was crammed with refugees, as was pretty well always the case throughout the war and its immediate aftermath. One day soon after the end of the war in 1945, an American NCO drove up and told the inhabitants that they would all have to leave, as the house was being requisitioned by the Army. Clarita von Trott explained to the man that, less than a year before, her husband and his friends had been strung up on meat hooks in Berlin's Plötzensee Prison for trying to kill the tyrant. The American went away and returned later that day. He had enquired in the local town of Bebra, and the people there had confirmed Clarita's story. The family and the refugees were allowed to stay. In many more places, however, the Western Allied armies had far less compassion for the homeless Germans, the vast majority of whom were in their zones.

West Germany's revival was remarkably swift. Following defeat, there was a period of no currency, when the country survived on a barter system called the 'cigarette economy.' It sounds inauspicious, but this was the beginning of a number of fortunes, including for the founders of the supermarket Aldi. The value of a cigarette was fixed: in October 1945, for instance, it was equivalent to 4 oz of bread. American Lucky Strikes were the favoured brand and the centres of the trade were railway stations.[14] When the new Deutsche Mark was introduced on 25 June 1948, everyone got a bit of cash to spend, and suddenly there were shops again—but this proved the straw that broke the camel's back in Moscow, leading directly to Soviet attempts to cut Berlin off from the West. In preparation for the Blockade, the Russians had walked out of the Four-Power Kommandatura on 17 June and ended all cooperation between the Allies. That situation was to persist in the imperial capital until the four Sectors were wound up after the *Wende*.

Böll's short stories, written at this time, tell of wounded men who emerge from Allied internment and take their first steps in business. *Mein Onkel Fred* deals with a former soldier who rolls off a friend's sofa he had been sleeping on, buys a handful of buckets and begins trading in flowers. From 1948 onwards, after the currency reform, the future was rosy—but it had not always been thus. Another of Böll's stories tells the tragic character of Lohengrin (*Lohengrins Tod*), a little boy shot by American troops for stealing coal from a railway truck. Such larceny was called *fringsen*, because it was claimed Cardinal Frings, the archbishop of Cologne, had condoned it.

Soon, the Cold War broke out and came to the rescue in the Western Zones. Germans in the Soviet Zone had no choice but to do what they were told, but with the possibility of another war breaking out between the victors, the West German people had to be won over. The Berlin Airlift provoked by currency reform was a massively successful propaganda exercise. The Americans, and to some extent the British, risked their lives to feed the stranded people of the old capital. Several films were made of the incident, to show how bravely the Americans had defended the defeated Germans against their Soviet occupiers. The best was *The Big Lift* starring Montgomery Clift.

The Basic Law or *Grundgesetz* established the West German republic on 23 May 1949, and elections were called for August. The CDU and CSU 'Union' parties won by the narrowest of margins, and Konrad Adenauer was elected chancellor by one vote—his own. Theodor Heuss, leader of the Free Democrats, became the first, largely ceremonial, president. In the Soviet Zone, the SED responded by creating its German Democratic Republic (DDR or GDR) on 7 October.

After this, West Germany had to be hurried through the remaining process of atonement for the sins of the Third Reich. There was no time or desire to arraign the remnants of the Party, and they crawled out of the woodwork again after perfunctory denazification. The cunning Rhinelander Adenauer cosied up to General de Gaulle over a bottle of Château Margaux, and in 1951 the seeds of the future Common Market were planted. War-torn nations would no longer fight over resources, but share the little they had. In 1957, West Germany became a founder member of the new European Community, together with France, Italy, Belgium, Holland and Luxembourg. On the Mainland at least, bygones were going to be bygones.

The East was another country now. After Land Reform, first big business and then small businesses were mopped up by the state, leaving the state-owned HO as the sole retailer. When the DDR was created, it was perceived as a temporary measure: sooner or later, the 'unity' implicit in the ruling SED's name would become reality. The DDR wasn't quite a sovereign state, as the four-power-controlled Berlin remained an island in the middle, but it was recognised by the USSR at the same time as it recognised all the other Soviet satellites. For the time being, Berliners had freedom of movement within the city. That was only stopped when the Berlin Wall went up in 1961.

UNITY OR DIVISION

The two Germanys were headed in two very different ideological directions: one to the East, swallowing all the criteria required for membership of the Soviet-led Eastern Bloc; and the other to the West, where the path lay towards NATO and opposition to the spread of communism.

In the West at least, Adenauer was not looking to reunify Germany. The first test of Western resolve came with the 'Stalin note' of 10 March 1952, which called for a peace treaty for all Germany, as prescribed by the Potsdam Conference in the summer of 1945. Plans for a further 'Peace Conference' to end the Second World War had been cancelled, but Stalin was offering Adenauer the chance to bring the two halves together. The former mayor of Cologne consulted his Western partners, who replied on 23 March that this would be a possibility, if the UN approved free elections for the whole of Germany. The Soviet demand for neutrality was considered out of the question. The German East was sacrificed to expediency.

Adenauer would not be deflected from his 'Western orientation'.[15] Like many others on the right, his young collaborator Franz Josef Strauss was convinced that the offer was just a trick, a manoeuvre to disturb 'progressive Western integration.' In May the USA, Britain, France and West Germany signed the German Treaty, which prepared the country for remilitarisation and Western integration and slammed the door on reunification. The DDR responded by declaring a 5-kilometre buffer zone behind the border, which required the resettling of hundreds of families. The rhetoric became aggressive once again: 'The toppling of the Bonn vassal regime is a precondition for the resurrection of German unity.'[16] When Austria accepted the same package three years later in 1955, Strauss decided that it had only taken the offer to be rid of four-power control.[17]

* * *

On 5 March 1953, Stalin died. In the three months since December 1952, the numbers emigrating from East to West Germany had almost tripled, from 22,000 to 58,000. Under pressure from their Soviet masters in Berlin-Karlshorst, the ruling SED had also moved against the larger farms and farmers, arresting thousands in the interests of collectivisation. On Stalin's death, East Germans expected the sort of change in direction that was taking place within the USSR. The result was a series of strikes in East Berlin and Saxony-Anhalt, in and around Halle and Magdeburg. Calls were made for the government to resign and for free elections, and the DDR became the first country in the Eastern Bloc to rise up against the Soviet Army, three years before Hungary and fifteen before Czechoslovakia.

Part of the problem was higher prices, and the escalating cost of schnapps in particular. Another part of the problem lay in the increasingly draconian sentences for minor acts of larceny. A third was the persecution of the churches—the DDR was 94.3% Christian, of which 81.6% were Protestant[18]—a fourth low wages. A mass protest took place on the Strausberger Platz on 17 June; that day, getting on for 1 million East Germans went on strike or demonstrated. In many places, government, Party or Stasi offices were sacked and files destroyed. The East Prussian journalist Marion Gräfin Dönhoff was one of those excited by these developments: 'without weapons, with sticks and stones, the workers launched themselves against Russian tanks. The Leuna Works were burned down in Leipzig, in Magdeburg they stormed the prison, there were strikes in the docks, a strike at Zeiss in Jena, on the railways, in the coal and uranium mines.'[19]

The Magdeburg police laid down their weapons, but the workers' victory proved short-lived. Tanks were sent in, even if violence was minimised. By 30 June there had been 6,171 arrests. The number of dead is reckoned at fifty-one: seven were sentenced to execution by Soviet courts and three by DDR judges; six were members of the security forces; two crushed by tanks; and the rest caught in the shooting. There was serious retribution in the DDR following the uprising, and 'Red' Hilde Benjamin—sister-in-law of the writer Walter Benjamin—became justice minister with a mission to purge the bench.

The sole political response from the West came from the mayor of West Berlin, Ernst Reuter. He accommodated those who fled from East Berlin that day in the courtyard of the Bendler Block where Stauffenberg and his fellow plotters had been shot on the night of 20 July 1944. This was surely no accident; from 1948, there had been an annual commemoration of the men who had risen up against Nazi tyranny there. Beyond this gesture, however, despite all the rhetoric that had spurned the Stalin Note of a year before, there was not one attempt to use this uprising to the West's advantage.

Meanwhile, the Eastern Bloc looked firm in its resolve to adhere to its path and continue to push for socialism.[20] The Soviet Union's detonation of its first hydrogen bomb on 12 August 1953 turned up the heat under the Cold War. The West's negative response to the Stalin Note of the previous year meant that the Soviet Union refused to talk further about reunification. On 5 May 1955, West Germany became a sovereign state and joined NATO the following day, thereby graduating to grown-up membership of the Western alliance, trusted with soldiers, tanks, fighters and warships. Adenauer's golden boy, the cigar-puffing Minister of Defence Franz Josef Strauss, set to work with his chequebook.

The Soviets responded by creating the Warsaw Pact and making the DDR a member on 14 May. With time, the DDR too would have an impressive fighting force, and Germans were armed against Germans. The creation of a West German army had a curious knock-on effect in the East: the appointment of chaplains from the umbrella Evangelical Church created a grey area, whereby the dominant segment of the Church in West Germany might have been said to have infiltrated the East. Arguments could thus be made that NATO padres had some authority over East Germany's army chaplains, a situation that might have proved catastrophic in time of war. Pastors in the DDR adopted a Pauline view of the controversy and fell in behind the state. The socialists were winning anyhow, with more and more young people choosing an atheist coming-of-age ceremony over a religious one.[21]

* * *

The Eastern Bloc coagulated, and the time for unity was deferred, seemingly forever. The DDR remained a covert one-party state ruled by the SED. The collection of state-supporting parties was known as the 'National Front'. Elections followed the old Hitlerian system of plebiscites, and government-backed representatives were returned with over 99 per cent of the vote. Other parties continued to exist, right up to 1989, but had no say in government, and were often, as with the Ost-CDU, riddled with informers.

In the West, meanwhile, political parties came back to life. The socialists rallied to the Social Democratic Party (SPD) as their rank and file emerged from Nazi prisons and concentration camps. After two bad electoral campaigns and only 30 per cent of the vote, in 1959 in Bad Godesberg they decided to drop their socialist policies and fully participate in the politics of the Economic Miracle.[22] In the early years of the Western republic, there was also a profusion of small right-wing parties that exhibited sympathy for the Nazis, and others that sought the return of Germany's lost provinces in the east.

Adenauer proved remarkably persistent. He held on to power in West Germany for fourteen years, standing down only on 5 October 1963 at the age of eighty-seven, forty-six years after entering the Prussian House of Lords as mayor of Cologne. Given the prevailing attitudes to Germany in May 1945, Adenauer's success in fumigating his country was phenomenal. In April 1953 he flew to Washington and was received as head of government of a state that would shortly become an equal partner of the United States, Britain and France. 'Germany was the pariah among nations, the Germans had been banished from world history, criminals in the game of politics ... That marked the beginning of the Adenauer Era.'[23]

Closer to home, the meeting of minds between Adenauer and de Gaulle meant more than just the Common Market; it meant an abiding relationship that would be the rock on which the Market and later the European Union was and is still founded. The French relationship was just as important to other German chancellors, not least Helmut Kohl, the right-wing Catholic from the Pfalz who found particular support in left-wing French President François Mitterand (1981–95). This was not merely surprising given their very different political attitudes. Kohl had grown up in the French Zone, and as a teenager suffered the French occupiers' harshness and rapacious desire to appropriate all that they could find.[24] But Mitterrand's Jewish counsellor, Jacques Attali, was refreshed to find that Kohl never entertained a shadow of doubt about Germany's guilt. In 1985 Kohl made a spectacular gesture in standing on the battlefield at Verdun, hand-in-hand with the much shorter and slighter Mitterrand. The writer Ernst Jünger, whom both men admired, was also in the wings.[25] By then he was the oldest remaining holder of Germany's highest medal for gallantry, the *Pour le Mérite*.

ATONEMENT

No one spoke too much during the Adenauer years about what had happened to the Jews. In Britain and the United States, '50s war films showed the Germans to have been the same enemy as in the First World War: square-headed Prussian martinets, with the occasional decent old-fashioned nobleman among them, bullied by some common SS 'oik' in a leather coat. Concentration camp survivors now based in Israel were encouraged to keep quiet: the new Jewish state proclaimed strength and ruthlessness, and was not prepared to support what it perceived as weakness. Things began to change in the late '50s. The Eichmann trial in Jerusalem reopened old wounds, as did the Israeli decision to trade with West Germany, which led to protests in the streets.

A spate of books on the camps had been published just after the war, works like Eugen Kogon's *Der SS-Staat* (1946) and Gerald Reitlinger's *Final Solution* (1952). In 1961 came the first edition of Raul Hilberg's magisterial *Destruction of the European Jews*. It was largely ignored in Germany, although it is true that a number of German books on the subject were published from 1960 onwards.[26] When it came to cinema, Hollywood picked up the ball long after Germany, where *The Murderers Are Among Us* was released as early as 1946. *Exodus*, Leon Uris's book on the creation of the State of Israel, brought up the subject of the death camps in 1958, and was adapted in 1960 into a successful film starring Paul Newman. Three years later, the director Stanley Kramer tackled the theme head on. In his *Judgment at Nuremberg*, Spencer Tracy, playing a judge from Maine, is appointed to try the Nazi bench, but a crisis breaks out with the Berlin Airlift and he is warned by a US general not to be too harsh: 'We need the help of the Germans.' The judge refuses to be cowed. Sentencing Burt Lancaster's repentant former justice minister, he reminds him that the justice system went awry in Germany the moment it condemned someone known to be innocent.

THE WALL

The DDR was more troubled by the present than the past. By 1960 the situation in Berlin was causing alarm within the ruling SED. In that year alone, East Berliners bought 9 million tickets to cultural events in the Western half of the city.[27] With Berliners and other Easterners free to travel from one Sector to another, some got lost and never returned. Political prisoners could also be bought out by 1962. It was all too easy to defect: as Rita demonstrates in the East German film *Divided Heaven*, all you needed was 20 pfennigs to take the S-Bahn to the West—though the goody-goody Rita bought a return. More than half the émigrés from the East escaped that way. This hole in the net led to a substantial drain on the Soviet Sector, with its best and most highly qualified citizens disappearing into the West.

The SED had long had the means to stop its citizens from slipping through the net, including the support of its friends in the Soviet Union. Only a decade after the Berlin Airlift, Khrushchev began to squeeze the former German capital again. On 27 November 1958, after a further snub on the subject of a peace treaty, the Soviet leader declared that Berlin would be newly regulated. The Sectors would go, and the Western powers would act as guarantors for a 'free' demilitarised city. In the West, withdrawing the Western Allied garrisons meant removing the protection that had sustained their Sectors since the successful Airlift. Once again, the West was under pressure to sign a peace treaty.[28] Meanwhile, the Cold War was heating up: first came the Bay of Pigs episode in April 1961, when the US funded a botched invasion of Cuba, followed by abortive talks in June between Khrushchev and Kennedy. After this Vienna summit, Kennedy made a televised speech affirming that Berlin's status was not for changing.

The governing mayor of Berlin, Willy Brandt, was the man of the moment. Born Herbert Frahm in Lübeck, he was an illegitimate child who grew up in a militant socialist milieu. He was elected to the first German Bundestag in 1950, and became Berlin's governing mayor in 1957, shortly before Khrushchev dropped his bombshell in November 1958. He was affectionately known as 'Weinbrand-Willy' (Brandy Bill) and welcomed Marlene Dietrich back to her home town for the first time since her move to the US during the Third Reich—a significant moment for someone who had sung of having 'a suitcase still in Berlin'. Brandt tried not to be a socialist mayor, but rather the 'Mayor of all Berliners',[29] choosing to forge a coalition with the centre-right CDU even when the socialist SPD formed the majority in the city parliament.

But hundreds continued to leave daily through the Berlin drain. East German production suffered, and debts to the West rose. There was fear that Bonn was leading an economic war against the East. It had too great an influence on the DDR's industrial output, supplying both machines and spare parts. By 1961, East Germany had a certain Soviet style. If you did well at work there were few privileges: a trip to one of the state's little treasures, a theatrical performance in Weimar, or a civic reception if your work team had been particularly productive. Otherwise, quality of life was not great. Coffee was made from malt and cigarettes were both cheap and foul-smelling. Anyone who was anyone arranged deliveries of both from relatives in the West. There was a special vocabulary for flight that signified the desire to escape: verbs like *abhauen*, *weggehen* and *abrufen*. Some committed Party ideologues remained untempted, but they were a small number: for the majority, West Germany was an increasingly strange and enticing foreign country.

Marion Dönhoff pointed out at the time that the USSR had effectively handed its Sector of Berlin over to the DDR. The 49-year-old Erich Honecker was responsible for the construction of the Wall. As with Land Reform, this was accompanied by an attack on the rustics; the number of permitted smallholders was reduced by two thirds, and the gesture sent many into emigration. Above all, however, the flight to the West remained a brain drain, with sizable percentages of science and technology graduates emigrating with their qualifications, like Manfred, Rita's beloved chemist in *Divided Heaven*. Despite rigorous checks on the U- and S-Bahn trains, 30,442 East Germans fled to the West in July 1961.

On 8 August, 1,741 refugees registered at the West Berlin centre in Marienfelde, the highest number in a single-day period since 1953.[30] The next day, the figure rose to 1,900. On 12 August it was 2,400. Volksarmee leave had been cancelled on 4 August, and on 6 or 7 August a 14,000-man force had been assembled in Potsdam. On Sunday 13, the 'Anti-Fascist Defence Wall' went up overnight, marking the second phase of the so-called Democratic Republic.

West Germany was outraged: Mayor Brandt, who had been brought back from a campaign trip to Kiel at 5 a.m., lost heart, calling the DDR a 'gigantic prison'.[31] He observed that it had taken the West twenty hours to react to the construction of the Wall and for troops to appear on the borders of the Western Sectors. It was another twenty before they lodged a protest at the Western Allied Kommandatura, and a total of seventy-two hours before a mild protest was delivered in Moscow. Kennedy was known to be sailing his yacht, de Gaulle was relaxing in Colombey-les-Deux-Églises, and Harold Macmillan was clearing the moors of grouse. West Berliners had been 'betrayed and sold down the river.'[32] Brandt was hopping mad. 'These shits,' he fumed, 'they should send some patrols to the Sector borders at least, so the Berliners don't think they have already been deserted.'[33] Apart from removing the means by which most East Germans had achieved freedom from all over the DDR, the Wall had serious effects in West Berlin in particular, where many people lost not only their friends and relations, but also, often, their cleaners.

A NEW GENERATION COMES OF AGE

At first there had been several possible crossings between West and East Berlin, but with the Wall that total was reduced to eight for pedestrians, with one—Checkpoint Charlie—reserved for foreigners and diplomats. Crossings were also restricted to one direction, West to East, because East Germans were now stopped from visiting friends and relatives in the West. Brandt likened this move by the DDR to Hitler's entering the Demilitarised Zone of the Rhineland in 1936. The Wall, he said, was the 'perimeter fence of a concentration camp'. The Allies had been quietly assured it would not affect them, although the

Americans did eventually send a further detachment of 1,500 men to reinforce their garrison. There was hope among the SED that the Union parties in the Western capital of Bonn would be weakened by the promise of more economic help from Moscow, and in a sense this wasn't wrong. In the elections of 17 September 1961, the Union parties lost their absolute majority for the first time, though they were able to hang onto power.

Meanwhile, with more secure borders, the DDR moved into a more positive stage: between 1960 and 1970, the number of families possessing a television increased from 17% to 69%; fridge-owners from 6% to 14%. In 1970, sixteen out of every hundred families drove a Trabi, for 8,000 Ostmarks and an eight-year wait, or a Wartburg. Others had Czech Skodas or Soviet Moskvitches or Zhigulis.[34] Luxury goods remained expensive, and the best food and drink was only obtainable in foreign currency. At the same time, there were moves against 'decadent' Western culture; in 1965, after a Rolling Stones concert at West Berlin's Waldbühne,[35] thousands of Marks were required to repair the damage. Had the Stones played in East Germany, the culprits would more likely have been dispatched to labour camps.

* * *

The West affirmed its determination to resist any change to Berlin's status in President Kennedy's speech from Schöneberg Town Hall on 26 June 1963.[36] When one considers the calibre of American presidents who have followed since, Kennedy's address was both slick and moving: he paid tribute to the veteran Cold Warrior Lucius Clay, who was present in the audience with Adenauer and Brandt. 'Civis Romanus sum!' declared Kennedy, 'Ich bin ein Berliner ... we are all Berliners'. It was a propaganda tour de force in the spirit of the 1948 Airlift, and of course foreshadowed Reagan's speech of 1987, when he told Gorbachev to 'tear down this wall'. Kennedy's popularity in West Germany was real enough. When he was assassinated in Dallas on 1963, the 'grief was hardly any less [felt] than in America.'[37]

Politics continued to develop in the West. Ludwig Erhard, architect of the Economic Miracle, replaced Adenauer as chancellor in 1963 and was followed in 1966 by another CDU man, Kurt Georg Kiesinger, who continued to lead a grand coalition until 1969, when Willy Brandt brought the Socialists to power for the first time since the war. By the '60s, the war babies were also coming of age. Many took exception to the subliminal Nazi culture they encountered in the streets, schools and lecture theatres, but a large number of Germans were still not prepared to accept the defeat of 1945. The ethnic German refugees from across the Oder had regrouped in the Bund der Heimatvertriebenen (Union of Expellees from their Homelands). In 1950 they had won 23 per cent of the vote in Schleswig-Holstein, and that year in Stuttgart they produced a Charter of the German Expellees. A year later, they boasted seventy-eight deputies in six German state parliaments. The right offered a number of newspapers, such as the *Deutsche National-Zeitung* founded in 1951, the *Soldaten-Zeitung* until it ceased publication in 1969, or the *Sudetendeutsche*, which is still published today.[38]

The police force was full of minor Nazis, many of whom had been Party members before 1945, or had fought in the SS. I recall myself as a teenager lying in Cologne's Friedenspark in 1971, peacefully reading my book. A police car drove right up to me across the grass: 'Grosser Denker (great thinker)!' barked the officer from the window with evident contempt, and drove off again. I told my host—Heinrich Böll's brother—who had shot himself in the foot to get out of the army during the war. His response was short and sharp: 'Verdammte Nazis (damned Nazis)!'

The ultimate retort to this backward-looking tendency in the West was 1968. Hitler had hated the universities and had starved them of air, if not actually shutting them down. Thus, after

1945, they appeared to be free from guilt. Nazi scholars (if that is not oxymoronic), even those like Hans 'Rassen' Günther who had spouted eliminatory racial theory, worked their way back into the faculties as if nothing had happened. According to the former student leader Urs Müller-Plantenberg, the atmosphere was suffocating. By 1968, the Vietnam War was entering a new phase, with the Tet Offensive beginning that January. The death on 2 June 1967 of the 27-year-old demonstrator Benno Ohnesorg in the course of a demonstration against a state visit by the Iranian Shah was the overture to the uprising. The rebels later took their cue from Paris, but hopes of any alteration in the European alignment were dashed by the brutal crushing of the Prague Spring in August.

Nevertheless, the revolt achieved momentum and led to radical change in the way Germans studied. In West Berlin at least, Germans ceased to wear ties and their professors put aside their elaborate gowns and mobcaps. The air was heavy with insult. The old guard was still running the newspapers, for example, and was detested by junior journalists, who wrote them off as 'fascistoid'. Marxism was all the rage, but few looked across the wire to the DDR for a radical solution to West Germany's problems. According to Karl Heinz Bohrer, instead they sought out the factory workers, with a preference for those in Northern Italy.[39] Despite the absurdities of '68, there were positive results. As the future president Richard von Weizsäcker put it, 'it forced out a new, upright attitude to the Brown past and altered the relation-ship between the people and the state and authority for evermore, so that middle-class democratic society received a new quality.'[40]

Helmut Schmidt thought much the same: 'Many of these young people seriously believe that they need to demonstrate for the cause of freedom, they also believe their fathers did not do enough about this.'[41] Nazis in the higher ranks of the police stood down. The younger policemen had not been Nazis, but nonetheless had strong ideas of law and order and right and wrong that were anathema to West Germany's students. The student revolt also achieved a bloody dimension through the militant far-left Baader-Meinhof Gang/Red Army Faction, which carried out political assassinations well into the '90s. Some of their victims were the sort of fat-cat businessmen the students hated most, and there was sympathy for the gangs, despite the carnage. When the culprits were brought to trial, money was raised in left-leaning milieus to pay for their lawyers.

The '60s were not only the time when authority in all its forms was overturned; there were also radical changes to society that marked the end of post war austerity. Men went into outer space, largely put there by German scientists working in the Soviet Union (kidnapped and under duress) and the United States (initially kidnapped and later bought over with dollars). The contraceptive pill was marketed. The changes were also shown in the arts, where Joseph Beuys was telling his pupils that anyone had it in him or her to be a painter, and in music, the reform movement was led by Hans Werner Henze. English pop music was all the rage and the Beatles and the Rolling Stones performed in West Germany, challenging traditional German music for the first time. A new group of cinematographers came to the fore, led by Werner Herzog, Rainer Werner Fassbinder and Volker Schlöndorff.

OSTPOLITIK

In 1969, Willy Brandt ended twenty years of rule by the Union parties. He wanted détente, in response to Khrushchev's sabre-rattling and the erection of the Berlin Wall. This would mean the abandonment of the Hallstein Doctrine that had until then been a principle of West German foreign policy: West Germany would have no relations with any country that recognised the DDR, with the exception of the Soviet Union, which was one of its guarantors. Brandt had come away from the Wall debacle with the realisation that the West would not defend Berlin if the Soviet Union were to move into their Sectors of the city: 'The curtain was drawn back, and look: the stage was empty.'[42] As mayor, Brandt made changes. He negotiated the right of West Berliners to spend a day with their families in the East at Christmas. Nearly 800,000 availed themselves of the chance in the 1960s–80s. The Berlin Senate came to the conclusion that small steps were better than big words.

The '70s were also the time of Ostpolitik. A quarter of a century after Germany's defeat, Willy Brandt, the first Socialist chancellor since Hermann Müller in 1930, decided now was the moment to look for friends in the east. In this he was assisted by his secretary of state, Egon Bahr. Brandt proceeded to negotiate the 1970 Moscow and Warsaw Treaties. In March 1970, he took the momentous step of meeting the East German First Minister Willi Stoph in Erfurt, and in August he signed the Moscow Treaty. His government's recognition of the Oder-Neisse Line in 1971 dashed the hopes of millions of Germans who had still harboured a desperate hope that they might one day return to their homelands further east.

Brandt also made a highly public apology to the Poles for the crimes of the Second World War. What had so often been swept under the carpet now came from the lips of a German chancellor; as Brandt told the Poles, 'Names like Auschwitz will accompany both our nations for a long time and will remind us that it is possible to have hell on earth.' As Brandt made his way to the monument commemorating victims of the Warsaw Ghetto, he fell to his knees: 'under the burden of recent history I did what people do when words fail them, provoked by the thought of the millions of murders.'[43] He told Günter Grass that his gesture was 'tied up with the desire to begin a new phase in the history of our nations, which has been so tragic up to now.'[44] However, the border treaty signed with Poland in the Palais Radziwill on 7 December 1970 was provisional. When it was ratified nearly eighteen months later by the Bundestag, it was stipulated that 'Article IV (the Polish Border)' could only be settled by a peace treaty that had yet to be organised. Nevertheless, many Germans believed that they were hearing the requiem for the lost provinces of the Silesia, Pomerania and East Prussia, which had become Poland's 'Recovered Territories'.

Brandt enjoyed the support of many artists and writers, such as Heinrich Böll, Hans Hellmut Kirst, and Günter Grass, with whom he had a long correspondence. But his journey to 'Canossa' angered both ordinary Germans and Bavarian First Minister Franz Josef Strauss, who called it 'capitulation'.[45] There was considerable rejoicing in 1974 when Brandt was brought down by the Stasi agent Günter Guillaume, whom the chancellor had taken into his confidence.

As one of his more recent biographers points out, Brandt is a huge figure in post war German history. When he died in 1992, his state funeral was an event that could only be compared with those of Walther Rathenau or Gustav Stresemann in the Weimar Republic; and yet he was loathed too. I recall when I was writing about Adam von Trott—who met Brandt in exile in Sweden during the war—I came across a clutch of vituperative pamphlets written by right-wing Germans who never forgave him for fleeing Nazi Germany, or for recognising the Oder-Neisse Line that marked the East German-Polish border agreed at Potsdam (see above). He was 'a traitor to his country'. [46] More recently, I had a long chat with a lady from Lübeck who affirmed the extreme levels of hatred that Brandt could engender when it came to right-wing Germans like her mother.

BACK IN THE DDR

Anyone growing up in 1950s East Germany had to make allowances for ideology, and the construction of the Berlin Wall was the ultimate test. It formed the background to Christa Wolf's classic East German novel *Divided Heaven*, whose heroine's loyalty to the state proves greater than the love she bears for her fiancé. For Angela Merkel's father and mother in Brandenburg, Pastor Horst and Herlind Kasner, the Wall struck like thunder. Although Horst Kasner seems to have approved of the DDR's central tenets, most of his family was beyond the wire in the West—now, they were cut off in 'the Zone'.[47] The next test came in 1968 with the Prague Spring. The teenage Angela's father hoped that socialism might adopt a human face in Germany too, but that bubble burst all too quickly.[48]

Just as the Hitler Youth had been the test of conformity for Germans growing up between 1933 and 1945, in Cold War East Germany the bullet you need to bite in order to succeed was the FDJ (Free German Youth), with its 'friendship' salute, and its junior branch, the Young Pioneers. Lip service had to be paid to the Soviet Union and its role in liberating Germany from the fascist yoke; successful children were therefore introduced to the USSR as a matter of course. They learned Russian, and the best of them were allowed to experience the Soviet regime firsthand. Angela Kasner was one of these. She was very good at Russian and won a Silver Lessing Medal at the age of fifteen. Later she also triumphed in an 'Olympiade' and was able to go to Moscow as part of her prize.[49] When asked about the trip years afterwards, she said she'd bought a Beatles record while she was there—but later admitted it might have been the Stones.

After a contretemps with the authorities at her school in Templin, Angela began studying at Leipzig University in 1973. Once again she had to mind her Ps and Qs. Following the demolition of the old university, most faculties had been rehoused in a skyscraper designed in the form of an open book. There were some seventy or eighty places available for physics, but ideological education had by no means ceased. There were compulsory modules in Marxism-Leninism—known to some as 'Marxism-Senilism' because it was personified by a group of very old men—and sporting ability counted towards her degree. She continued to do her bit in the FDJ for many years to come. The Russians were never far away either—young Angela had to iron Soviet soldiers' shirts. Her father, Pastor Kasner, thought this was no big deal: 'You'll recover,' he said.[50] She travelled to Moscow again, this time with her fellow physics student Ulrich Merkel, who became her first husband in 1977.

Before the war Leipzig had been one of Germany's top universities. It was recognisably the same place until the 1960s. The university church dating from 1409 had survived the war unscathed, with the body of the university there beside it. But the buildings had been dynamited in 1968 after Walter Ulbricht, head of the SED, had ruled that 'the thing must go'.[51] He made it clear he didn't want to see a church when coming out of the opera. There was a perceptible desire to eliminate the past on both sides of the Iron Curtain: in Brunswick or Braunschweig, the grand ducal palace was replaced by a supermarket, while the other palaces and churches that formed the remnants of German culture were swept away. Even in the historic towns and cities that had been spared wartime bombardment, bulldozers moved in. What remained was altered—or cunningly disguised to look modern.

The West German police force may have been filled with ex-Nazis until around 1968, but there was no question about freedom of thought. Across the wire, it was another story: anyone who had succeeded even a little in the DDR was likely to be asked to become an IM (unofficial informer) for the Ministry for

State Security—in other words, to spy on friends and colleagues. According to Angela Merkel's own revelations, that moment came when she was at the Technical University in Ilmenau, Thuringia, but she had been prepared by her father, who had equipped her with the replying argument that she was incapable of keeping her mouth shut.[52] She went to work at the DDR's Academy of Sciences in Berlin-Adlershof, where the neighbourhood of the Stasi's own Felix Dzerzhinsky Guards would concentrate her mind. But she does not appear to have suffered. She had no contact with the world of dissidents, although she is alleged to have come back from a trip to Poland filled with enthusiasm for Solidarność. She was not impressed with the religious socialism expounded by rebels in the Zionskirche and the Gethsemanekirche.[53] A Stasi report on the Academy staff describes her as having a 'clean political attitude.'[54] In all probability, it was a matter of what they called *Anpassung*: fitting in, adapting. As the daughter of a pastor in a state that generally distrusted the clergy, this would have been second nature to her. In the eastern part of Germany people had been 'fitting in' since 1933. A rumour that Angela Merkel was in charge of promotion and propaganda for the FDJ has always been vehemently denied. When she was asked in a television interview about her service in the FDJ, she admitted that it was 70 per cent opportunism.

Angela Merkel achieved her majority in the golden age of the DDR. Willy Brandt's recognition of both the Oder-Neisse Line and the DDR, as well as the fall of Walter Ulbricht in 1971, led to a new confidence in the viability of the eastern state. Erich Honecker succeeded Ulbricht and duly recognised West Germany in turn; in 1971 both Germanys became members of the UN. In 1975 they signed the Helsinki Accords aimed at improving relations between Western countries and the Eastern Bloc. It was here that Chancellor Schmidt met General Secretary Honecker for the first time. There were even the inevitable jokes told behind closed doors: why does *Pravda* cost 4 kopecks while *Neues Deutschland* is so much more? Because you need to factor in the cost of translation. What is the most important letter in the DDR? W—because without W, Walter Ulbricht would be 'Alter Ulbricht' (old Ulbricht) and the Waffenbrüderschaft (brotherhood in arms) would become the Affenbrüderschaft (brotherhood of apes).

The building of the Berlin Wall in 1961 had to some degree staunched the permanent leakage of talent to the West. By Western standards, the DDR was not rich, but it towered over the rest of the Eastern Bloc, and now the Easterners could enjoy holidays in relatively poor Hungary and Romania. The student revolution of 1968 had had a knock-on effect in the East. Instead of the formal address *Sie*, most people now used the familiar *du*; there was more camaraderie in Party offices after the departure of Ulbricht on 3 May 1971, and Honecker looked younger than his fifty-eight years in his light-coloured suits and fashionable ties.[55] East Germany remained a repressive society, but the Soviet Union had now taken the back seat, allowing the largely Saxon elite to manage its own affairs.

* * *

After a week-long interregnum under Walter Scheel of the liberal FDP,[56] Brandt was succeeded by Helmut Schmidt (1974–82). The chess- and piano-playing chancellor proved a popular figure with almost everyone; he appears to have got on far better with Mrs Thatcher than his right-wing successor, Helmut Kohl. Possibly this had something to do with the bar Schmidt had installed in his house in Hamburg-Langenhorn, where he regularly entertained foreign heads of state. But his great bugbear was the revival of terrorism; 1977 would prove to be quite the bloodiest year in recent German history.

Across the border in West Germany, in the spring of 1977 it might have appeared that the Baader-Meinhof threat had been contained, and that its leaders—Andreas Baader, Ulrike Meinhof and Gudrun Ensslin—were safely under lock and key. There had been hiccups, such as the November 1974 killing of Günter von Drenkmann, head of West Berlin's higher court, and in April 1975 members of the Gang had taken hostages at the German Embassy in Stockholm, which resulted in two deaths on each side. The pretext for the new wave of violence in 1977 was the court conviction of Baader, Ensslin and Jan-Carl Raspe (Ulrike Meinhof had already killed herself). It began in April when the state prosecutor, former Nazi Siegfried Buback, was 'executed' with his chauffeur and bodyguard. On 30 July it was the turn of the head of the Dresden Bank, Jürgen Ponto, a man who had made his first fortune in the cigarette economy of the immediate postwar years. Hanns Martin Schleyer, president of the German Employers' Association and another man with a Nazi past, was kidnapped. Chancellor Schmidt signed an undertaking at his office that were he or his wife Loki to be seized, there was to be no exchange or ransom.[57] A photograph shows Schmidt sitting between Schleyer's wife and son at his funeral, apparently crying.

On 13 October the Lufthansa aircraft *Landshut* was hijacked on its way from Palma de Mallorca to Frankfurt, the hijackers demanding that the Baader-Meinhof chiefs be released from prison. They killed the pilot and flew the airplane to Mogadishu, where it was successfully stormed by German Special Forces on 18 October, killing three out of four hijackers. That day, Schleyer was killed by his captors, and Baader, Ensslin and Raspe all committed suicide in their cells. A fourth member of the gang, Irmgard Möller, bungled the attempt and survived. She was released from prison in 1994. Some Baader-Meinhof members quailed at the violence. Silke Maier-Witt discovered that the Zurich bank customer killed during a robbery in which she had taken part was a Jewess: 'Now I'm like my father, the SS-Mann.' She could go no further and fled with nine other

terrorists to the DDR. There she was retrained and assigned
with the others to Stasi offices up and down the land. As the
Wall teetered, Maier-Witt demonstrated. Western justice caught
up with her in 1989, and she was sentenced to ten years, par-
doned after five. She claimed in 2017 that she was willing to
speak to Schleyer's family.[58]

The right was excluded from power throughout the '70s. Its
charismatic leader was the Bavarian CSU politician Franz Josef
Strauss. Strauss remained the most powerful voice in opposition,
wielding his 'Sonthofen Strategy' of giving no quarter to
Schmidt's government (1974–82).[59] Naturally, the lawlessness of
Schmidt's time in office was a boon to Strauss, who tried to make
political capital of the crisis. As it was, he failed to win the 1980
election, and retired hurt to his power base in Bavaria. The leader
of the Union parties and candidate for the chancellorship was
now Helmut Kohl.

KOHL REUNITES GERMANY

By the '80s there was a consumer society in the East, and more
and more goods were available, although some of them only for
Western currency. The DDR now had the leisure, and some of
the money, to begin rebuilding. Although it had destroyed the
palaces in Berlin and Potsdam and the Garrison Church was
flattened for being the 'Temple of Prussianism', the SED became
sensitive to the need to rebuild the 'Florence on the Elbe' that
was Dresden and create the Disney-fied quarter of Nikolaiviertel
in Berlin. There they assembled a collection of ancient buildings,
part old, part borrowed, part new. On the Prenzlauer Berg, many
pubs and little restaurants began to thrive in the largely surviving
late-nineteenth-century *Mietshäuser* or blocks of flats. In some
of them you might even have heard a whiff of political dissent. In

August 1987, the Interhotel chain opened its flagship in East Berlin's Friedrichstrasse. It was a proper five-star hotel with an excellent restaurant, but the guests were unlikely to be from the DDR itself, as everything had to be paid for in hard currency.

This confidence allowed East Germany to participate in international sporting competitions, creating an elite with access to the spare parts and blood stockpiled in Berlin's Charité Hospital. In the borough of Pankow, the *nomenklatura* built their villas behind high walls, and special sites were selected so that they might spend their holidays in dachas, sloshing Saale-Unstrutt wine away from the prying eyes of a people deprived of the luxuries they enjoyed: perks available to them alone by dint of their station.

* * *

West Germans had not finished with the past. They had their noses rubbed in it. *Vergangenheitsbewältigung*—managing, or coming to terms with the past—was still on everybody's lips. Local historians and schools uncovered the unpleasant details of what took place in their villages and towns during the Third Reich. The *Historikerstreit* emerged towards the end of the decade: an acrimonious dispute among historians as to whether it was possible to see the Nazi period as closed, or whether it was required of all Germans to atone for it for years to come. The historians who favoured drinking the chalice down to the dregs appear to have won. Some distinguished scholars retired hurt. The '80s was also the time of *Heimat*, a thirty-two-episode series of films exploring the history of a village in the Hunsrück, above the Mosel Valley. The series naturally afforded the chance to see how Nazism had affected individual families and how far they had been able to put it behind them after the war.

There had been considerable opposition to the idea of the CSU's Strauss achieving power, not least from the weekly *Spiegel* magazine. In 1980 the journalist Bernt Engelmann, a particular thorn in Strauss's side, wrote an entire book detailing the politician's infamies, his abuse of power and the many scandals that had blown up along the way. These included the mean-spirited denunciation of the novelist Hans Hellmut Kirst as a 'werewolf' in Goebbels's largely imaginary 1945 resistance force; Kirst spent seven months in American internment in Garmisch as a result. Engelmann warned that the book would have been 'unnecessary, had the CSU leader not allowed himself to be named candidate for the Union in the summer of 1979.'[60] Following the CSU/CDU's defeat in the October federal elections, Strauss retired to his stronghold of Bavaria, becoming first minister of that state in 1982. Here, at least, he could indeed be 'duke'. One of his recent biographers hastens to point out that Strauss was not a Bavarian nationalist and never tried to pass himself off as a stock peasant. He was an urban Munichois.[61]

If the '70s had been dominated by the Socialists Brandt and Schmidt, the '80s—and to some extent the '90s—were the Helmut Kohl years, with government in the hands of the centre-right CDU (1982–98) and Kohl nudging the wave towards reunification. Above all, he was credible to foreign heads of state. Ronald Reagan liked him despite what looked like a farcical arrangement made at Bitburg on 8 May 1985 to celebrate the fortieth anniversary of the end of the Second World War, where both leaders had agreed to make a speech at a cemetery containing the bones of no fewer than forty-nine members of the Waffen-SS. This ceremony created a storm—they should have gone to a concentration camp (Belsen was later added to the itinerary). Reagan was not put off. He confided to his diary: 'We were very moved. Helmut swore eternal friendship.'[62]

The Helmut and Ronnie Show was back on the road again in Berlin on 12 June 1987. Not to be outdone by his Democrat predecessor, Reagan made a speech to 40,000 West Berliners with Kohl at his side, in which he called out to 'Mr Gorbachev' to 'tear down this wall.'[63] Reagan was starving the Eastern Bloc. When the cry was echoed by DDR radicals, the regime responded by banning the more liberal Soviet magazines. Kurt Hager, a member of the DDR's Politburo, explained to citizens, 'If your neighbour re-carpets his flat, you do not need to feel duty bound to lay new carpets in your own flats as well.'[64] Kohl met General Secretary Honecker three times in Moscow and Bonn, and credit was extended to the DDR. The main action in this period, however, was neither in Berlin or Moscow, but in Hungary, although Solidarność and the Polish Pope also played their part.

Since the early '80s, Hungary had become increasingly relaxed about its form of socialism. In January 1988 the regime announced that anyone had the right to obtain a passport and to travel to the West. In March the Hungarian government signed the Geneva Convention for Refugees: no refugee might be turned back.[65] On 2 May, Hungarian border guards began removing barbed wire on the Austrian frontier. On 27 June, the Hungarian and Austrian foreign ministers, Gyula Horn and Alois Mock, removed sections of the wire themselves before news cameramen.[66] In September, West German Foreign Minister Hans-Dietrich Genscher was able to give the good news to a group of East German refugees holed up in Prague's West German Embassy: they could proceed into West Germany itself.

By then, the borders were fully open, and tens of thousands of DDR citizens were able to make their way to Austria. An East German opposition movement called the Neues Forum was founded by the widow of the dissident chemist Robert Havemann, and notable campaigners such as Bärbel Bohley and Jens Reich joined up. In Luther's Wittenberg, Pastor Friedrich Schorlemmer remained a fierce critic of the regime. The presence of Protestant clergymen in the opposition may have justified the regime's profound distrust of them. Stasi Minister Erich Mielke was furious and accused Hungary of betraying socialism, but the USSR refused to intervene.[67] When he came to East Berlin to celebrate the fortieth anniversary of the DDR, Gorbachev could not understand why Honecker was not prepared to broach reforms like the other countries of the Eastern Bloc.

Gorbachev was hedging his bets. Even in December 1989, after demolition of the Wall had begun, he was still keen to maintain the two Germanys. Kohl had been working on him. There had been positive talks in Moscow: in Gorbachev's words, 'We didn't quote Bismarck, but he was present for all that.'[68] In June 1989, Gorbachev had returned the visit and seen Kohl at his Bonn bungalow. The two men went down to the Rhine and Kohl pointed at the water: 'Look at this river. The Rhine flows into the sea. You can dam the Rhine, but then it will find another route and pursue it with all its might; and so will it be with German unity...'[69] Gorbachev listened, but intimated that he would 'help'—by which he meant he needed money.

The events in Hungary and the growing awareness that the Soviet Union would not step in to save the DDR caused concern among the *nomenklatura*. On 11 September 1989 Stasi chief Mielke asked if they were witnessing another 17 June (1953).[70] In Prague and Warsaw, the West German embassies filled up with refugees. The DDR responded by imposing visas on its citizens wanting to travel to Prague. The ferment began to bubble when there was rioting in Dresden on 4 October. This occurred shortly before the celebrations arranged for the fortieth anniversary of the DDR (6–9 October); Gorbachev was lukewarm about coming. The demonstrations continued on 7 October, when 15–20,000 people gathered in the Alex in Berlin, chanting, 'Gorbi! Gorbi!' Two days later in Leipzig, tanks were ready to move in to disperse 70,000 demonstrators. The Soviets advised against bloodshed. A week later, the number of protesters at the Monday event reached 100,000. On 17 October Honecker was ousted under pressure from Politburo member Günter Schabowski, former editor of *Neues Deutschland*. He was replaced by Egon Krenz, leading protesters to pun that they wanted '*unbekrenzte Freiheit.*'[71]

Kohl did not let up. He had won round Bush Senior and had support in the Bundestag. French President Mitterrand advised him to 'avoid an explosion'.[72] On 26 October, he made a fourteen-minute telephone call to Krenz, the first man to talk of the 'change' in SED policy: 'however, change does not mean collapse.'[73] On 4 November there were 700,000 protesters in the Alex calling for '*Blumen statt Krenze*' (flowers not wreaths—another pun on Krenz's name). They wanted freedom and reform, but the protesters did not mention the reunification of Germany. The DDR owed $26.5 milliard to the Western powers and was running a deficit of $12.1 milliard.[74] No one seemed ready for the event when it happened, and clearly not Helmut Kohl, who had flown to Warsaw on 8 November.

The Damascene moment came during a televised interview with Schabowski, an unofficial spokesman for the regime. He was asked if permission was still needed to travel to the West. He replied no. Asked when this new liberty would come into force, he replied, '*Sofort ... ich habe nichts Gegenteiliges gehört*' (at once ... I've heard nothing to the contrary). Angela Merkel was meeting a friend to go to the sauna—when she emerged, she heard the news and called her mother to say, 'When the Wall comes down we'll go to Kempinki [in West Berlin] and eat oysters'. The whole atmosphere had changed. She decided not to wait for her mother. With her bathing costume under her arm, she crossed the border at Bornholmer Strasse and went to the West.

Meanwhile, this was Kohl's first visit to Poland. He wanted to go to the Annaberg in Silesia and attend a peace Mass at Kreisau, the former home of 20 July Plotter Helmuth James von Moltke, near Wrocław (Breslau). At 6 p.m., he met Lech Walesa, who told him that the DDR needed to apply the brakes. That was fifty-seven minutes before Schabowski dropped his bombshell in Berlin. Kohl then went to a banquet at the Palace of the Polish Ministerial Council. These were the days before mobiles and he was cut off from his advisors. When the news reached the Bundestag in Bonn, the deputies sang the national anthem. Wolfgang Schäuble, president of the federal Bundestag from 2017, called it 'for me the most moving moment in the whole story of the years 1989 to 1990 ... Many simply wept, the older ones in particular ... but it was clear, now this horrible thing together with the monster started by Hitler was coming to an end.'[75] From the Chancellery Eduard Ackermann was finally able to reach Kohl on the telephone: 'Herr Chancellor, at this precise moment the Wall is falling!' Kohl couldn't believe his ears: 'Herr Ackermann, are you sure?'; 'That is incredible!'[76] President Richard von Weizsäcker was travelling in South Germany: 'Never before or since have I experienced an event taking place on German soil where literally the entire world celebrated with us Germans from the depth of their hearts.'[77]

Kohl was aware that he was needed in Berlin, and that would mean interrupting the state visit—the Polish president, Wojciech Jaruzelski, was not pleased. Kohl could not fly directly to West Berlin, as West German chancellors required Allied permission to visit Allied Sectors, so he flew to Hamburg, where US Ambassador Vernon Walters provided him with an American military aircraft to get him to Berlin. There Kohl found that Weizsäcker had stolen a march on him. He had been to Potsdam across the Glienicke Bridge and gone to the Potsdamer Platz—the very hub of Berlin's old city—where he had decided to walk across to the Soviet Sector. An East German police lieutenant-colonel saluted him, saying, 'Herr Bundespräsident! Nothing to report.'[78] Kohl's 10 November speech at the Schöneberg Town Hall, however, was not a success: he was shouted down by the crowd, whom he dismissed as 'plebeian Berlin lefties.'

Despite this inauspicious beginning, Kohl soon caught up. There were 400,000 Soviet troops in East Germany, but Gorbachev ensured they were confined to barracks. At 10 p.m. that night, Kohl called Mrs Thatcher to explain the situation. Half an hour later he called Bush. Mitterrand's call had to wait until 9.15 on the morning of the eleventh. The French president said the fall of the Wall was 'a great moment in history'.[79] The following day, Kohl returned to Poland, visiting Auschwitz on 14 November.

Kohl travelled to East Berlin on 22 December, and after Christmas he visited Dresden to hold talks with Hans Modrow, who had taken over as first minister of the DDR on 18 November.[80] I was in Leipzig a week later, and listened to Modrow's defiant speech on the wireless as I lay in my bath in a skyscraper Interhotel near the Central Station. My destination was Berlin, of course, and I was there on New Year's Eve. I was travelling with a friend, and we were ill prepared for the crush. The restaurants in the West were offering expensive menus to celebrate the end of the year. There was not a hotel room to be had or even a locker where we might lodge a bag or suitcase.

We went to the Wall via Friedrichstrasse, where the inhabitants of the flats on either side pelted us with fireworks. People were chipping away at the Wall with chisels. One man had doused it with petrol and successfully set fire to a long stretch of it, which burned festively until the Western police arrived to spoil his fun. The Vopos, for their part, were still ostensibly checking papers at the Brandenburg Gate, but no one heeded them: they shook the officers' hands instead. There was a huge street party going on, with much singing, and bottles of sparkling Sekt were being passed round. A middle-aged Ossi lady offered me a bed in her flat, which I foolishly declined—the bed can't have been any harder or colder than the tiled floor at U-Bahn Zoo where I finally got a couple of hours' sleep. That was after the party was called to a halt when a man died climbing the Gate. The Vopos used the accident as an excuse to clear the Pariser Platz.

* * *

I suspect that the chancellor did not waver; he thought he had done the right thing. Kohl, the hack politician, could now consider himself one of the most successful figures in the history of Germany. He went about merrily collapsing 'the post-war order that Stalin had imposed on the peoples of Europe.'[81] He demonstrated both impatience and realism when it came to its political elite. Many of the emerging politicians were suspicious. Prominent lawyer Manfred Stolpe, though he would look like a possible East German leader after the DDR's first and last free election in March 1990, was discounted on such grounds. His contacts with the Stasi had been too many and too conciliatory. The same judgement befell Lothar de Maizière, who would become East Germany's last, and only democratically elected, leader following the March vote.

Kohl's problems were not just dealing with the *nomenklatura* of the East and the sceptics in the West who wanted to exclude the East from the new Federal Republic. He had also to square the Western leaders, of whom by far the most obstinate was Margaret Thatcher. Her attempts to delay German unity Kohl branded as 'hysterical'. By his reckoning, Mrs Thatcher was able to spike German reunification until February 1990. They were not on the same wavelength, with Mrs Thatcher expressing an 'emotional enmity towards Germany', and she bore a grudge towards Kohl from a time at St Gilgen in Austria when he had broken up a meeting claiming important business, but was later found by Mrs Thatcher in a café, tucking into a large cream cake. 'That, she never forgave me for,' he wrote.[82]

But if Kohl had no charm for Mrs Thatcher, he had a good relationship with the others. Bush Senior did not oppose reunification, and although Gorbachev was reluctant to see the end of the DDR, he agreed in the end. Kohl was closest to Mitterrand; on 22 June 1990 they went on a boat trip on the Middle Rhine, steering clear of the Lorelei rock, and dined at the Hotel Krone in Assmannshausen. On the way back to Bonn, Kohl gave his friend a Merian map of Kaub. Mitterrand was aware that this was where Blücher had crossed the Rhine in the new year of 1813–14 on his way to Paris. Kohl was already discussing the next challenge before him: 'the unification of Europe.'[83] Another project was the European Army, which would be agreed in 1992 at the 59th Franco-German Summit in La Rochelle and ratified before Maastricht. A planning-staff was appointed in July that year, and the unit based in Strasbourg. The corps was to have 35,000 men and be operational by October 1995.

* * *

The Oder-Neisse issue was not dead, despite Willy Brandt's concessions in 1971. It was back on the table before the Two-Plus-Four talks of 1990: on 8 and 9 December 1989 it was raised again. Could it be possible to regain some of the eastern territory lost to Poland at Potsdam? Mrs Thatcher opposed that with all her might. It was, however, Kohl's 'friend' Mitterrand who did his utmost to scotch it, by inviting the Polish leaders to France and making common cause with them. The existing Polish border was guaranteed on 8 March 1990, half a year before the two Germanys signed the Two-Plus-Four Agreement. Foreign Minister Genscher affirmed that the German people had no territorial demands, other than the unity that was the will of the German people. On 17 June 1991 a treaty of friendship would be signed between Germany and Poland, which, among other things, stopped the persecution of Poland's small German minority.

At the Two-Plus-Four talks, the Soviet delegation had to accept that East Germany would become part of NATO; this was only agreed once Germany promised to reduce the size of its army. Until 1994, there were some 400,000 Soviet troops garrisoned between the Elbe and the Oder. Kohl was aware that he would have to buy them out. He originally proposed 8 milliard Marks, but Gorbachev stuck at eleven, and in the end he got fifteen. Another decision, much criticised at the time, was to accept parity between the eastern and western Marks: on 1 July that issue was settled as well. At the London Summit held that month, the time of confrontation was officially deemed to be over: 'we stood at the beginning of an epoch of cooperation.'[84] On 31 August 1990, the Second World War officially ended.

THE CAPITAL RETURNS EAST

On 3 October 1990, the DDR was formally wound up. Its death was a moment to celebrate—there was a great party in Berlin that night. At the Schauspielhaus they played Beethoven's Ninth, and half a million people stood on the Gendarmenmarkt to hear Brahms and Mendelssohn. Across the old border, the Liberty Bell tolled at the Schöneberger Rathaus, where West Berlin Mayor Ernst Reuter and President Kennedy had extolled the idea of freedom after 1945. The West German president, Richard von Weizsäcker, spoke: 'There are moments in life where your own past actually flashes across your inward eye, as in a speeded-up film sequence.'[85] A former mayor of Berlin himself, Weizsäcker suppressed his antipathy towards Kohl, although it was well known.[86]

The aftermath of reunification was a time when I was often in Berlin; indeed I was there on the day that it became Germany's capital again. I remember the PR woman from East Berlin's only, and heavily bugged, five-star hotel, who told me she had never been to West Germany and she was never intending to go. I also recall the crimson-faced drunks who hung around the

Friedrichstrasse S-Bahn station singing the *Horst-Wessel-Lied.* When there was a coup d'état in Moscow on 19 August 1991, I was in Frankfurt an der Oder on the Polish border. I had heard something just before I left Berlin, but it had failed to sink in; then a man stopped me in the street with a petition of support for Gorbachev and still the penny didn't drop. When I went up to my hotel room, I switched on the television to see Boris Yeltsin riding around on his tank with a KGB general.

The next morning, I walked straight over the Friedensbrücke into Poland. No one bothered to look at my papers. As I wrote at the time, 'I was just one of a hundred Germans crossing the bridge to buy cheap fruit and vegetables.. And it was cheap. A *Wechselstube* [currency exchange] quoted 17,000 złotys to the pound. A cabbage cost 2,000, or 7p, a kilo of tomatoes perhaps 12p.' I took a bus north to Kostrzyn (Küstrin), the fortress where Frederick the Great was incarcerated by his father. Out of the window I observed 'villages [that] had a perfect, timeless quality to them; ducks and geese wandering around by millponds. The houses with their half-timbered barns were perfect representations of Brandenburg architecture. If you closed your ears to the Polish spoken around you, you were back in pre-war Prussia.'[87] The fort had been blown up by the SS in 1945, but a bastion survived. I caught a glimpse of it only when my bus took me back to Słubice.

The situation was still frail that night, when I had dinner in the House of German-Soviet Friendship. It was next door to the building in which, in 1951, the DDR had accepted the Oder-Neisse Line as its Polish border. I observed the Soviet soldiers wondering whether they would be ordered back to Russia to put down the coup. Soviet forces remained in the East right up to August 1994, and until then had nowhere to go. From within their compounds they perpetrated astonishing acts of larceny, stealing all the new cars in showrooms and loading them onto cargo planes bound for Moscow. The impotent German authorities were reduced to paying them to leave, sometimes by building hospitals for them back home. The Western armies remained in their barracks for the time being too; I met friends in the British Army of the Rhine until 1994. I also watched polo on the Maifeld—constructed for Hitler's Olympiade—and went to drinks Parties on the site of Hess's Spandau prison or at the Marlborough Club on the Theodor-Heuss-Platz. Of all the occupying army messes, the French Sunday lunch at the Pavillon du Lac in Tegel was considered the best. No one wanted the American offering: waffles.

* * *

The division of Germany into two states and the building of the Wall had ripped the heart out of Berlin. I used to work in the Staatsbibliothek in what had once been the busiest place in the old city. Not far away was the junction of the Potsdamer Strasse with the Potsdamer Platz, which was formerly Berlin's answer to Piccadilly Circus. When I looked out of the window, all I could see were acres of scrubby sand and the multitude of rabbits that were its sole inhabitants. Only two structures had survived: the Weinhaus Huth—a café formerly with some literary pretentions—and a few fragments of Berlin's grandest hotel, the Esplanade, including the Kaisersaal, one of its sumptuous public rooms.

After reunification, the site was acquired by Sony, which took the decision to scoop up the Kaisersaal and move it elsewhere once the Potsdamer Platz was redeveloped. When it reopened in the mid-90s, a copy of Max Koner's portrait of the last Kaiser was hung over the chimneypiece—the one that had allegedly left the French ambassador incandescent with rage, exclaiming: 'That's not a portrait, it's a declaration of war!' Apart from the small bust in the rebuilt Hotel Adlon's Louis Adlon Restaurant, this was the first time that the Kaiser's features had been officially exposed to the Berlin public since 1945. It is significant that both imperial likenesses were aired in private spaces. Reunification must have made fortunes for many lawyers: there was a scruffy-looking Café Adlon in the Kurfürstendamm where I used to drink; once the Hotel returned to the Pariser Platz, it was obliged to change its name. The Western incarnation of Lutter und Wegner in Charlottenburg, on the other hand, appears to have ridden the storm: today there are two, east and west of the now missing Wall.

For a decade and more, the centre of Berlin was a building site. In some areas, this is still true today. For the new high-rise developments grouped around the Potsdamer and Leipziger Plätze, for example, the planners had to be aware that the water table lies only 4 metres below the ubiquitous sand, and the buildings need to go down twenty. Concrete rafts were prepared as foundations, something that Albert Speer had known, and practised, when he built the New Chancellery for Hitler in 1938.[88] The first and most politically sensitive of the new developments was the rebuilding of the Pariser Platz behind the Brandenburg Gate. The Russians had cleared away all the old buildings, turning the place into a great dusty parade ground. The Pariser, Leipziger and Mehring Plätze were the old 'Square,' 'Octagon' and 'Circus' dating back to the urban improvements of Frederick William I, father of Frederick the Great. Restoring the Pariser Platz was particularly sensitive, as it involved recreating embassy buildings that had been on the site before 1939—including the French Embassy in the north-east corner, and the Americans' in the south–west. The debate went back and forth as to whether or not they would opt for a pastiche; the eventual solution was a vague suggestion in scale and design of the buildings that had been there before. The British opted out of this and became part of the same development as the Adlon, stretching back to the Wilhelmstrasse, while the Americans tried to hold out for a 'compound' that would afford them greater security. A similar sort of small-scale modernism became the model for the Leipziger Platz, dashing all hopes of rebuilding Alfred Messel's modernist Wertheim Department Store, or the Warenhaus Tietz by Alfred Sehring in the Leipziger Strasse.

The reconstruction post-1989 has had architectural 'pretensions'. All sorts of very famous architects were pulled in to do a building on the Potsdamer Platz, although it is not always true that they did their best work there. Norman Foster successfully transformed the gutted Reichstag building, and Nicholas Grimshaw designed the Gürteltier or Armadillo building off the Kurfürstendamm, which might be my personal favourite. The development of the eastern Wilhelmstrasse, which occurred at the very end of the SED's time in office, would not make the shortlist of avant-garde Berlin buildings. The Russians demolished the eastern side of the street together with the ruins of Hitler's Chancellery soon after the war. In the early '90s, both sides of the road were lined with jerrybuilt blocks of flats in the most execrable taste. My only hope is that they fall down soon. At the place where visitors entered Albert Speer's 1939 new Chancellery, a Kindergarten has been constructed; you now see tiny children disporting in their playground where the entrance to the tyrant's palace once stood. For a long time it was also possible to see the way into part of Hitler's Bunker. For some unexplained reason, a number of tomato plants were growing and fruiting on the small, sandy hill.

* * *

Probably the most emotional experience I had of German reunification was when I was invited to the party to reopen the Hotel Adlon in August 1996. In just thirty-eight years of its existence, the Adlon had achieved the status of being not only the city's grandest hotels but also an indispensable social pole, its bar and dining room playing vital roles in the history of those times. Even during the darkest days of the war, it kept going, dishing out rooms and whatever good food was available to whoever could wangle it. Of the rebuilt Adlon as architecture I had my doubts. The outside had been fashioned in a muted classical style, but the interior was fussy, putting emphasis on 'glitz' and more worthy of the Emirates than Berlin. The worst innovation was to make an open-plan bar beside the lobby, rather than recreate the dark, panelled space where people had huddled in corners to leak stories in the heyday of the Weimar Republic or in the grimmer times under the swastika. This new bar was a place to enjoy a swift half while you waited for your wife to change her shoes.

There was compensation in the view from my room on the sixth floor. It looked out over the Gate, and the houses left and right had now been rebuilt in what was a far better imitation than the hotel itself. 'Suddenly you are in the old heart of Berlin again, overlooking the Gate from a luxury hotel for the first time in fifty years.'[89] Later I admired the replica of the old courtyard fountain and the plans to revive the Parisian-style terrace on the Pariser Platz. There were bits of Schinkel here and there, even in the suites, and a copy of Menzel's *Balsouper*. The party went on for most of the day. There was a press conference at lunchtime, featuring President Roman Herzog, former Brandenburg First Minister Stolpe, Mayor Eberhard Diepgen and others. Left-wing friends had grumbled about the fact the square was to be cordoned off while the president and various ministers attended the party that night; but there was something marvellous about milling around the Pariser Platz in a dinner jacket with a glass of champagne in my hand, only eight years after the Wall had come down. We spilled out of dinner at about 10.30, and then it was the cue to set off the fireworks. We could see the gaps where the American and French embassies were to go, and there was the site of the house where Max Liebermann had watched the parade on 30 January 1933 and remarked, '*Ich kann nicht so viel fressen, wie ich kotzen möchte.*'[90] I sat down with two Grafs and ended the day toping with another brace of Junkers in the Adlon Bar. The grim, unlovely landscape of *The Spy Who Came in from the Cold*, of the wars hot and cold, was most decidedly gone.

STITCHING TOGETHER THE TWO HALVES

Germany was now once again a unified state, although a lot smaller than its previous incarnation. There were 87.7 million Germans distributed over some 108,300 square kilometres. The elections held on 2 December 1990 were the first to take place throughout Germany for fifty-eight years. In 1991, the Bundestag held a free vote on where to situate the capital of reunited Germany. By a majority of just eighteen, the deputies voted for Berlin. Speaking as a simple member of the Bundestag, Kohl called Berlin the 'focal point of German division and longing for German unity.'[91] Verities dictated by propaganda or the practical necessities of Cold War, such as Prussia's responsibility for Germany's evil past, were now re-examined in a new light. A decision needed to be taken about the old *nomenklatura*, particularly those who, like Honecker and Mielke, had been responsible for murderous decisions. From December 1991, Erich Honecker sought refuge in the Chilean Embassy in Moscow, but the Chileans refused to grant him asylum. He returned to Berlin but was deemed too ill to stand trial and the charges were dropped. He died in Chile on 29 May 1994.

No one doubted that putting Humpty Dumpty back together again would be a task anything less than Herculean. Everywhere muscle sinews truncated by the Cold War had to be restitched to their counterparts higher up the limb. Railway lines terminated at the border, leaving little towns like Bebra in Hesse in a sort of limbo. The frustration of travelling from former East to West or West to East was immense. I recall it took me two or three attempts to get from West Berlin to the little palace at Rheinsberg in which Frederick the Great had lived as crown prince. Once I got no further than Oranienburg, and had to make do with the sad remnants of the royal palace, and Sachsenhausen concentration camp.[92] You had to go east first; then suffer the consequences of the fact that the Russians had made off with the railway track after 1945. There was usually a stretch of *Pendelverkehr*: getting out of the train and waiting for the incoming train to use the same, sole set of tracks.

One of the first questions was the matter of ownership. The East German state no longer existed, and West Germany had no desire to own everything east of the Elbe, from hotels to grocers' shops. If there was no claimant, the property could be sold for profit. The Treuhand agency responsible for reprivatising East German businesses moved into Hermann Göring's old Air Ministry on the Wilhelmstrasse, and a small army of people were employed on short-term contracts to work out who owned what. I had a friend who was there at the time. I met him for a drink on the Savignyplatz one evening. He told me there was a scattering of Prussian Junkers—Arnims, Zitzewitzes, Bredows and Bismarcks; a hangover, maybe from the old tradition of service to the state—but Ossis predominated by two-thirds to a third. At 4.30, he said, the Easterners all went home. I wrote in my diary in August 1992 of 'One of his Ossi colleagues [who] had been sacked that day. The Gauck Commission had established that he was a Stasi IM.'[93] I visited my friend at the Treuhand, and still remember its paternoster lifts, which had no doors and were in perpetual motion. You needed to be brave enough to jump down or up, as the case required. The friend, I might add, did not stay long. He acquired a porcelain factory for himself and went into business.

For some prosperous Westerners, 'Ossis' from the DDR were not welcome. Many hoped that they would remain in a separate state and not become a burden to the West. The last thing they wanted to hear was that there would be higher taxes to pay for reunification. I had my ear twisted about this by a Munich-born banker at a dinner party off the King's Road in London. To add to this, the Ossis were easily categorised as 'losers', political backwoodsmen who now gravitated towards the extreme right, got drunk and started singing Nazi songs, beating up Africans or Vietnamese cigarette-peddlers or burning down asylum hostels. They had not enjoyed the same style of ideological scrutiny or the education in guilt that had been so widespread in the West. Worse perhaps was that, when they did behave with decorum, they stood by the political principles of the DDR, abiding by the authoritarian socialism that had been their governing ideology. For the time being their representatives continued to sit in the Bundestag and represent constituencies east of the Elbe, where they were elected by Easterners who resented the superior, patronising attitude of the 'Wessis'.

* * *

Many changes had to be made in the East, and very little has remained of its character, bar the jaunty little Ampelmann in his hat who tells you when to cross the road. The DDR's monuments went one by one, from the Wall to the Palace of the Republic. Streets were reawarded their original names, such as the Platz der Republik, which is now once again the Gendarmenmarkt; out went Thälmann, Pieck, Ackermann and Clara Zetkin. The Communist leader Ernst Thälmann, murdered by the Nazis, was the most popular and has proved the most resilient of these Marxists. There are still more than 600 Thälmann streets and squares. Also still popular are the Plätze der Einheit (celebrating the hoped-for fusion of the two German republics) and

Freundschaft (Friendship) Strassen, alluding to the greeting used by the FDJ.[94]

East Germany had been constructed out of the rump of Prussian Brandenburg that was not ceded to Poland, its arch-enemy Saxony, Mecklenburg, and Thuringia. Many people liked to maintain that there was a Spartan, Prussian spirit to the DDR, but where the rank and file might have been Prussians, the Saxons were mostly in charge. As we have seen, as soon as the DDR had had a government, it had set to work purging it self of the pre-1945 past: palaces and churches were dynamited and manor houses bulldozed or turned into asylums; the former nobility were incarcerated in concentration camps—some old, some new—and their country estates and castles confiscated, before they were cast out to the Western Zones. By the '70s, many of the war-scarred buildings had been cleared away, making room for proper socialist monuments like the Palace of the Republic or the 365-metre-high Television Tower in Berlin, which opened with great fanfare in 1969. It was taller than anything in West Germany. Skyscrapers announced a new Interhotel chain of hotels designed to receive the tourists from the socialist world who came to see the Nikolaiviertel or the Museumsinsel in Berlin, Sanssouci in Potsdam or the Zwinger in Dresden. Much of the eastern end of the Linden had been put back up, but in an unscholarly way, as I discovered when I went to a party in the Kronprinzenpalais in 1991.

For much of its forty-year life, East Germany had remained poor and proud.[95] It could not boast the gaudy splendour of West Berlin, but it was still the richest country in the Eastern Bloc, and its citizens lorded it over Hungarians, Bulgarians and Romanians when they went on their annual holidays. It had all been going with a swing when the leaders of the regime were taken by surprise by Gorbachev's 'transparent' glasnost. East Germany collapsed like a house of cards. After 1989, many 'Ossis' were treated with scarce-concealed disdain when they queued up for menial jobs in the West. The border had been fairly porous before the Berlin Wall went up, and even later on East Germans could be 'bought out' by relations in the West, so that those who were left in 1989 were either the *nomenklatura*—officials who had a vested interest in maintaining the regime—or the 'detritus', inferior in the eyes of West Germans purified through denazification and fattened by the Economic Miracle. Some of these Easterners began to rue their incorporation into the reunified Federal Republic, and wondered why they couldn't carry on as they were, albeit in a post-socialist state.

* * *

One East German who seems to have seen the new possibilities immediately was Angela Merkel. To her, the events of 9 November were a real eye-opener: 'freedom was the biggest surprise of my life ... All roads led to the Wall.'[96] Almost as soon as the frontier was breached, she chose a political party with an eye to the future, non-socialist state. The Ost-CDU led by Lothar de Maizière was politically tainted despite its 130,000-strong membership, so she joined the centre-right Democratic Awakening, founded by Pastor Friedrich Schorlemmer and Wolfgang Schnur. It turned out to be a less than wise decision, as Schnur was soon unmasked as an IM. For the time being, however, Dr Merkel had a new vocation. She busied herself in the centre-right party's Friedrichstrasse offices in her standard brown cords, a '*Mädchen für alles*' (Girl Friday) or, less politely, a 'grey mouse'. She was good with computers and became the press spokeswoman who announced the unfortunate truth about Schnur, before going over to the Ost-CDU to help de Maizière prepare to hitch the DDR to the West.

It was Helmut Kohl's decision to take 'das Mädsche'[97] as he called her, into his fourth administration on 3 October 1991. This epithet, 'the girl', suggests slightly more than just 'a girl'.

For some it means the 'tomboy'.[98] At their first meeting Kohl asked her if she 'understood women': as she put it later, 'as a woman you certainly do a bit, don't you?' The question was not as peculiar as it sounded: he was clearly planning to appoint her as minister for women and youth. Later, she was Kohl's minister for the environment, picking up on the policies that had been at the heart of the Democratic Awakening.[99] Kohl admired her for what a contemporary called her 'naturalness and realism'; or, as he put it, a 'directness and straightforwardness [that] lacked the petulance which is often hard to bear in so many women.'[100] Dr Merkel also brought together the two halves of Germany in her own self: she was the Christian of the Christian Democrats, and a former FDJ officer of the DDR. She was born in Hamburg, but grew up across the border in the historically Prussian region of the Uckermark. Her father supported the system as a pastor, but as a pastor's wife, her mother could not work as teacher; and their daughter was seen as slightly suspicious by the Stasi.

The fact that the Stasi slur never clung to Angela Merkel was good news for her. The Stasi's tentacles stretched far further than the Gestapo's had. Even a fleeting connection with the organisation was the death of several promising politicians' careers after 1989—not just the unfortunate Wolfgang Schnur, but also the best of all to emerge just after the Wall collapsed, Manfred Stolpe. He became first minister of the state of Brandenburg in 1990 and was then federal housing minister in Gerhard Schröder's administration in 2002–5, but his contacts with the Stasi eroded trust in him. Lothar de Maizière was also destroyed by such contacts and quit his position 'in tears' on 3 October 1990.[101] He was cleared, and returned as Kohl's deputy, but new evidence was found and he stood down again, to be replaced by Merkel, on 30 September 1991.

By this time, Germany had achieved its natural weight. The test came at Maastricht on 9–10 December that year, when the European Community was transmogrified into the European

Union. 'The economic and currency union were clearly sketched out and irrevocably established.' But Germany effected the changes, and despite much ill will from within and without, the West digested the East. In 1998, after sixteen years in the saddle, Helmut Kohl lost power to the Socialists led by Gerhard Schröder. Kohl had it coming to him. The arrest of the CDU's treasurer, Walther Leisler Kiep, on 4 November 1999 revealed that the party had been receiving millions of Deutsche Marks in undeclared donations from shady businessmen. On 2 December a parliamentary commission was appointed to investigate the affair. On 22 December Angela Merkel wrote an opinion piece in the *Frankfurter Allgemeine Zeitung* that must have felt like the final stab in the back, a message to the party to distance itself from the 'Übervater': 'The party needs to learn how to go without its old warhorse'. In this 'Emancipation letter',[102] Merkel argued that Kohl must stand down from all his offices.[103] He eventually took full responsibility for the episode, and bowed out of politics. Party leader Wolfgang Schäuble was also touched by the scandal, even if he was hardly responsible.

In the end, the disappearance of the two most important figures in the CDU of the 1990s meant that Angela Merkel was able to slip through and achieve leadership of the party. In 2005 she managed to elbow the smooth-talking Schröder and the SPD from power, and, at the time of writing, remains German chancellor to this day. Despite her mildly controversial past in the East, she has proven the same safe pair of hands that Kohl was too in his time, and is now widely perceived as the leader of the Western world. Germany naturally basks in that reflected light.

Her popularity has also remedied, to some extent, the perceived inferiority of East Germans, but the East remains much poorer than the West. An average Hamburger is between twice and three times as rich as a Berliner—and that includes West Berliners—twenty times richer than a Saxon, and thirty times wealthier than a Thuringian. Building land is most expensive in

Bavaria, and yet two-and-a-half times more Ossis go west than Wessis go east.[104] Westerners also have a higher disposable income and there are fewer unemployed. All Germans are old, with a national average age of 44.85, but in the east they are older—47.3 in Saxony-Anhalt. The compensation for residents of that state is that property around the state capital of Magdeburg is the cheapest in Germany. The east also has almost double the amount of woodland.

* * *

Merkel's most controversial decision to date has been to allow up to a million Middle Eastern, African and Asian refugees to enter the country in 2016, thereby not only causing widespread fear and protest in Germany, but also leading to strong reactions in other lands. It can certainly be argued, for example, that the panic generated in certain quarters by this decision contributed to the British vote to leave the EU on 23 June that year. Nor has the policy been a comfortable one for Germans. The liberal critic Karl Heinz Bohrer speaks of the 'civilisatory and psychological explosives the refugees had in their knapsacks.' For him, Merkel had 'No thought for the Western culture that would remain strange to the strangers. And what would happen then?'[105] Despite the Christian message in welcoming the refugees, he argued, the excuse was one of globalisation; a humanitarian gesture, but also justified with reference to the extra manpower these migrants would offer Germany. As for the dangers, Bohrer asked, would re-education—of the kind that Germany had successfully applied to its own 'native' population after both 1945 and 1990—be sufficient to turn the refugees into people with Western values?

Meanwhile, Europe is lurching to the right. At the time of writing, there are very few social democratic regimes on the continent. At first, it was the old DDR left that made waves in the pan-German Bundestag; chiefly Gregor Gysi's PDS, the ancestor

ON GERMANY

of today's Die Linke (Left Party). However, since Merkel first became chancellor in 2005, that pendulum has swung to the right. The shock-horror news at the elections of 24 September 2017 was the success of the extreme-right AfD. This anti-immigrant and anti-EU party, a sort of brighter and sharper version of Britain's UKIP, won 12.6 per cent of the national vote. It did best within the borders of the old DDR—proving that, politically as well as economically, the East continues to do its own thing. The AfD became the main party in Saxony with a 27 per cent vote share, scooping up ballots from the old DDR socialists of Die Linke.

The AfD had exploited the usual fears: 46% of Germans were worried about the growth of Islam, and 38% resented the numbers of foreigners in Germany. Others voiced concern about crime and terrorism.[106] Chancellor Merkel has promised to listen to right-wing Germans a bit more in the future. Overall, these elections proved a setback for her: the Union parties' share of the vote dropped to 33%, with the Social Democratic Party (SPD) limping in behind them at 20.5%. The liberal FDP, once a major force in postwar politics, had since suffered a decline in popularity—but now saw improved fortunes once more. It came in fourth with 10.7% of the vote, closely followed by Die Linke (9.2%) and the Greens with 8.9%. Generally it was richer people with higher levels of education who voted for the FDP, while significant numbers of younger people chose Green.[107] Despite losing 420,000 votes to the AfD, Die Linke won votes from both the SPD and the Greens.[108] Hard-left SPD supporters are demanding an end to the moderate Bad Godesberg definition of the party, and some proper socialism for a change.[109] To deal with the new geography of the Bundestag, Finance Minister Wolfgang Schäuble of Merkel's CDU has been dropped from government and made president of the chamber.

* * *

The past is always the present in Germany, and most right-thinking Germans are terrified of military commitment. According to highly vociferous elements in the population, Germany's military may only be used to promote peace, and there is strong resistance to deployment abroad. The airbase at Büchel near Cochem-Zell in the Mosel is a particularly sore point. The French handed it over to the German Luftwaffe in 1955, and it is now the home of the Tornados of Squadron 33, armed with B61 nuclear bombs. These are the only nuclear weapons in Germany, and are maintained by the USAAF under a dual key arrangement. Neither side may use them without the other's permission. The base is near the Skagerrak Bridge over the River Mosel, built in 1927 to commemorate Germany's 1916 'victory' over the Royal Navy in the battle we call Jutland. In Germany itself, the Skagerrak Bridge is no longer controversial, but people are still fuming over the one currently being built between Ürzig and Zeltingen, which threatens to cast its shadow over the precious vines of the Middle Mosel.

During the 2017 election campaign, Chancellor Merkel chose not to talk about Germany's relations with the EU, possibly so as to avoid debating with the AfD. She failed thereby to answer calls from President Emmanuel Macron of France and Jean-Claude Juncker in Brussels to refound and federalise the EU. To most thinking Germans, the European Union, now much derided elsewhere, is a vital institution, because it allows Germany to sink its national persona (and its past) into a modern, supernational institution. Any threat to the EU is a threat to the foundations of the reunified Federal Republic. That Germany takes on the role of leadership unwillingly is a commonplace—even seventy-two years on, Germany is still frightened of its shadow.

PART II

THE GERMAN PEOPLE

THE PRUSSIAN SPIRIT

In August 1991, the German Federal Republic was suffering from another of its traumas, occasioned once again by the need to come to terms with its past. This time King Frederick the Great of Prussia was rocking the boat. Arriving in Berlin on the 15 August, I found a stack of magazines in a bar in the Uhlandstrasse. *Der Spiegel* had a Frederick the Great issue, with an essay by its founder-editor, Rudolf Augstein. *Stern* countered with a piece by Sebastian Haffner, who had previously been known as a defender of Prussia. Now he appeared to have changed his mind. *Spiegel* carried out a survey on when people thought 'Fritz' had lived: 10 per cent of Germans believed him a contemporary of Martin Luther.

Prussia's most famous ruler had been dead 205 years, but he had yet to be laid to rest in the simple 'philosopher's grave' he had intended for himself—buried beside his favourite whippets on the terrace of his summer palace, Sanssouci in Potsdam. After his death his nephew and successor, Frederick William II, countermanded his orders and had him buried in the Postdam Garrison Church vault that had been constructed for Frederick's stern and temperamental father, the 'Soldier King' Frederick William I (r. 1713–40). In this disagreeable company, what was left of Frederick the Great was obliged to make do until the closing months of the Second World War.

As German victory began to look unlikely, even to leading Nazis, Prussia's first minister Hermann Göring issued instructions to have Frederick and his father removed from their vault. He feared what might happen to them should they fall into the hands of the Red Army. The two kings took off on a macabre journey, eventually coming to rest on Burg Hohenzollern in Swabia, in south-west Germany. On 14 April 1945, RAF bombers destroyed much of the centre of Potsdam, gutting the Garrison Church; a few days later, Russian tanks were seen among the ruins. The substantial remains of the church were demolished in 1968. Instead of the famous bell peal that had rung in the hearts of so many generations of Prussians, a Glockenspiel was erected on concrete piers, beside a huge dusty parade ground. Great concrete slabs of residential buildings went up all around. Socialist Potsdam was decidedly no place for the bones of Frederick the Great.

In 1989, the DDR first tottered, then tumbled and in 1990 the process of reunifying East and West began in earnest. The then Prussian pretender, Prince Louis Ferdinand of Hohenzollern, saw his chance and began to agitate for the return of his ancestors' bodies to their *Residenz* in Potsdam. The Garrison Church was no more, but there was room for Frederick William in the Italianate Friedenskirche down the hill from Sanssouci, where the short-lived Emperor Fritz (r. 1888) was buried with his wife, Queen Victoria's eldest daughter Vicky, in a luxurious tomb. As for the 'Philosopher King', was not the solution to put him in the grave he had always intended for himself, on the vineyard terrace of his favourite retreat?

In itself, the decision to return Frederick the Great to Sanssouci would hardly have caused more than a grumble. In fact, the storm that greeted the reburial on 17 August 1990 was occasioned by Federal Chancellor Helmut Kohl's desire to attend the ceremony and join in the singing of the Leuthen Chorale with sundry members of the old royal family. Even worse, the story went round that the Bundeswehr, Germany's politically correct army, was to present arms to the dead warlord. Was this not the cue, the press asked, for the revival of Prussian militarism? Was Prussia, that allegedly stone-dead monster, about to rise up from an unmarked grave?

There was mortal dread in Berlin and elsewhere that skinheads and neo-Nazis would gather in Potsdam for the reburial. I went myself, as I was in Berlin, together with an old friend and her husband, a major in the British Garrison. At the Voltaireweg, the road was blocked by police paramilitaries. At that point:

> we got out and walked up the road behind Sanssouci. It was 11.20. There must have been a few hundred spectators and a few hundred police holding them back. Occasionally police vans rumbled past. Journalists were allowed right up to the gate on presentation of a 'Presse-Ausweis.' The crowd looked orderly: nothing but curious, middle-aged people; and not a skinhead or neo-fascist among them.

> Further along, G reported a loquacious policeman who was telling stories of what had happened earlier that day. I went along and listened: there had been a military parade, the man said, but no more. At about 11.45, Kohl arrived in a black Mercedes. As I later discovered, he had been at the Friedenskirche burying the Soldatenkönig, Frederick William I. The press surged forward but there was scant time to observe his belly before he was inside the gates. After Kohl's arrival, the police allowed the crowd to break ranks. We went over to the fence but could see little beyond the black catafalque. We heard the march composed by Prince Louis Ferdinand and later the great Leuthen hymn: *Nun danket alle Gott!* The Major joined in: he said they'd sung it at school. Then we left.[1]

On 18 August I learned from the *Berliner Morgenpost* that the military presence at the church had been more or less reduced to the pallbearers. There was a party at the Neues Palais and Brandenburg First Minister Manfred Stolpe, together with the historian Christian Graf von Krockow, had made speeches defining Frederick's legacy. The only non-Hohenzollern to attend the reburial had been Kohl.

The German papers I found in that bar had taken it upon themselves to examine the legacy of Frederick the Great and Prussia in general. Were there no positive aspects of Frederick's forty-six-year rule (1740–86)? Was Prussia just an excuse for black-hearted militarism? Were there concealed Prussian elements lurking in the cogs of the Federal Republic itself? This was not the first time the embers had been raked over. Even in the old East, the decision in 1980 to return Christian Daniel Rauch's equestrian statue of the king to Unter den Linden had not been taken lightly.[2]

While the Bundesrepublik had been limited to the western half of the country, Prussia had been easy to forget. But the new power base of the reunified Federal Republic, the Rhineland, had been a Prussian province from 1815 to 1945. When the former mayor of Cologne, Konrad Adenauer, became the West's first Chancellor in 1949, he was happy to shut Prussia out of his field of vision. He had been a member of the Prussian House of Lords, but had never liked it much. In his mind, Germany was going to wed itself to Western Europe, starting by forging a firm bond with Charles de Gaulle's France. Prussia proved a practical scapegoat, especially as the victorious Allies had already cast it onto the dung heap of history on 25 February 1947. On that day, the Allied Control Council, the four-power governing body of the postwar occupation, issued Control Council Law no. 46, formally abolishing Prussia as an entity: 'The Prussian state which from early days has been a bearer of militarism and reaction in Germany has de facto ceased to exist.' The dissolution of its remaining agencies and institutions was guided by 'the interests of preservation of peace and security of peoples and with the desire to assure further reconstruction of the political life of Germany on a democratic basis.'

Britain in particular blamed Prussia for the First World War. When a second conflagration broke out in 1939, the 'pike was in the pond' again and needed to be 'netted to save the other fish'. Despite their origins in Catholic Bavaria, the Nazis, for the British, were somehow 'Prussian', and so they were remained until the 1960s at least. In some quarters—the British popular press for example—the Germans are still Prussian militarists today, prone to donning their *Pickelhauben* and going to war at the drop of a helmet. Naturally, anyone who upsets the British—particularly the Luxembourgeois president of the EU Commission, Jean-Claude Juncker—is an honorary Prussian.

The inhabitants of the lands west of the Oder knew from bitter experience what it meant to live under Russian occupation. Those who could fled in 1945; they expected more humane treatment from the British, French and Americans. The arrival of 11 million Germans from across the Oder in the shattered towns and villages of western and southern Germany did not pass without comment from the natives. In Schleswig-Holstein, on the Danish border, émigré Prussians found a decent enough welcome in a flat land not dissimilar from the one they had left behind. Similarly, the people of Westphalia and the Rhineland were used to Prussians, having put up with more than a century of Prussian rule. In Swabia and Bavaria, however, the local Catholic population treated the refugees with ill-concealed contempt.

For the soldiers and civilians in uniform who worked for the Allied Control Council, the bad blood between the southern Germans and the easterners was hard to understand: '*So is' es*,' a Catholic southern German told the Englishman James Stern. 'It might well be compared, I think, with that of the French towards the Germans. And the war has greatly increased the hostility.'[3] The Bavarians showed their dislike for the bedraggled Prussian refugees by making them as unwelcome as possible. One man from Elbing on the Baltic ran into Stern while looking for a bed for himself, his wife and their half-starved child. He had been turned away from the houses in the town. 'Get out, you swine from East Prussia,' he had been told, 'you can damn well bring your own beds.'[4]

In the Soviet Zone too, and later in the DDR, there was a similar ideological need to stamp out the Prussian legacy. At the first, the urban proletariat and the farm workers responded warmly to the measures that drove the middle classes, the Junkers and other landowners across the border to safety in the West. Meanwhile, any positive contribution to German history that Prussia might have made was expunged from the books. The exception, strangely enough, was the 'über-Junker' Bismarck, still venerated in the West because he had united Germany, and the Western republic was committed by its constitution to do the same.

Older historians tried to maintain Prussia's reputation while all about them the worthies were torn to shreds. Frederick the Great was a monstrous militarist, his father Frederick William a Nazi. The other kings were not much better, the very worst being 'Kaiser Bill'. The historians Hans-Joachim Schoeps, Walther Hubatsch and Gerhard Ritter fought a valiant rearguard action, pointing out that Prussian rule meant tolerance and the rule of law. Ritter had excellent credentials, having been imprisoned by the Nazis. On East German television in 1978, Dieter Panse presented a documentary called *The History of Prussia is a Part of Our Own History*. Two years later, Ingrid Mittenzwei wrote an apologetic biography of Frederick the Great, and denounced the linear interpretation of German history. In 1980, General Secretary Honecker sanctioned the return of Old Fritz's statue to the Linden. Prussia's pre-*Wende* rehabilitation culminated in the exhibition at West Berlin's Gropius-Bau, which ran from 15 August to 15 November 1981.

Even before this, a few little Prussian fetishes had emerged in the East German army: they adopted the slow march or 'goosestep' invented by Leopold of Anhalt-Dessau, the *'alte Dessauer'*. Soldiers wore acanthus leaf shoulder flashes and were decorated with the Scharnhorst Order. The centenary of Carl von Clausewitz was celebrated on both sides of the wire, but the DDR was able to lean on its friends in Poland to have the great military theorist's remains transferred from Wrocław (formerly Breslau) to his birthplace, Burg bei Magdeburg.

On 7 August 1994 I took a copy of my book on Prussia to Clarita von Trott in Dahlem. After some negative comments about the cover, she expressed the opinions of the 'Hanseat' she was: 'she could not understand that it had somehow "gone". She was brought up in Schleswig-Hostein: i.e. Prussia; and at school she sang *Üb' immer Treu und Redlichkeit bis an Dein kühles Grab*.[5] She didn't like the idea of Prussia but admitted that corruption was impossible in the Prussian context.' By this time—the mid-90s—Prussia was no longer a dirty word. The bookshops were full of reminiscences and firms seemed happy to use the name. An insurance company I came across in Potsdam was called 'Preussenwacht', a 'Preussischer Hof' hotel had opened, and in Pritzwalk, they were brewing 'Preussenpils' again. Potsdam, of course, had always been a bit keen on Prussian memorabilia: evil-smelling brandy in bottles emblazoned with pictures of Old Fritz, Potsdamer Rex Pils, maps from imperial times and much, much more.

Berlin hotels seem to have led the change in attitudes: at the Brandenburger Hof there were portraits of Frederick William I and Frederick William IV in the foyer and Queen Louise and her sister in the bar. When the new 'gourmet' restaurant opened in the Adlon there was a bust of William II, who had patronised the old hotel and known Louis Adlon since the days he had run a popular restaurant in the Zoo. When William's daughter married in 1913, the guests had been put up at the Adlon. Now, after the *Wende*, the hotel was the first semi-public space to honour its earliest patron.

In a memorable statement, Angela Merkel said, 'My life was not as grey as the DDR was as a state.' Although I knew East Berlin a little before the Wall came down, my first visits to the East German countryside occurred in 1991. Only the state was grey, and in some parts the landscape was better preserved than in West Germany. In many places it was charming, filled with lakes, pine forests and redbrick medieval churches. Typical of Prussia is Templin, the small, walled town where Angela Merkel went to school. East Germany was largely made up of Prussian Brandenburg, Saxony, Thuringia and Mecklenburg. Although its leaders were the Saxon Ulbricht and the Saarländer Honecker, the rank and file were Prussians, and many people saw the DDR as an essentially Prussian state: stark, austere and Spartan.

Angela Merkel strikes me as a very Prussian person, true to the elder Moltke's motto '*mehr Sein als Schein*'—more in reality than appearance. For most of her life she has sported a pudding-bowl haircut, and she appears to have learned about lipstick on or after the *Wende*. She is said to have a portrait in her office of Catherine the Great—a German princess from Anhalt-Zerbst, a territory that sided with Prussia in its many wars. One of Chancellor Merkel's few pleasures seems to be opera and she likes to go to Bayreuth with her second husband, the physicist Joachim Sauer, whose fondness for the art form and self-deprecating style have caused him to be known as the 'Phantom of the Opera'. Besides Bayreuth, Merkel's pleasures and demands are the simplest: the couple live in Sauer's small old flat, admittedly in a wonderful spot opposite Museum Island, and the chancellor drives an old car and does her own shopping. When they go out they prefer a French restaurant—Zur alten Gaslaterne in Prenzlauer Berg—over Borchardt in the Französische Strasse, a favourite among other politicians with expense accounts.[6]

THE GERMAN PEOPLE

VERGANGENHEITSBEWÄLTIGUNG

At the fag end of summer 2017, I spent an illuminating few days at a conference in Imshausen, North Hesse, a tranquil spot not far from the old Iron Curtain. Here was the manor house of one branch of the von Trott zu Solz family. They no longer live there now; after the war the manor was turned into a foundation that, among other things, celebrates Adam von Trott, one of the most important members of the group that conspired to kill Hitler on 20 July 1944, who was hanged on 26 August that same year. Above the house are the rolling hills and woods Adam loved so much and the quasi-monastic community with its base in the Tannenhof. There is also an organic farm, leased to a young man with an appropriate missionary zeal. At the highest point above the village is the impressive cross that Adam's brothers Werner and Heinrich erected in his honour. In 2013, Adam's widow Clarita was buried there in accordance with her dying wishes.

Clarita died more than sixty-nine years after her husband, and 17 September 2017 would have been her hundredth birthday. The aim of the conference was in part to evaluate her role in preserving her husband's memory through the difficult years after the war, in the face of deep-rooted scepticism about the attempt to kill Hitler. Many had seen Trott and his fellow conspirators first and foremost as traitors. It took a long time to change people's attitudes, particularly in rural areas like North Hesse. This was not only seen in Germany itself: Trott had been a Rhodes scholar at Balliol College, Oxford between 1931 and 1933, and made friends there with a large number of men and some women who later went on to become public figures. During the war many of these turned against him. Fortunately for Trott, he died in almost total ignorance of how many of his attempts to seek British or American support were scuppered by people he would have been pleased to call friends.

Clarita's dedication to the task of rehabilitating her late husband was astonishing, and was rightly celebrated at the conference. It was an example of that very special thing: *Vergangenheitsbewältigung*, or the debate to come to terms with the dark side of the German past. Clarita was described as a *Zeitzeugin*,[7] a witness to her time. The term encompasses a rather wider meaning in German, because the *Zeitzeuge* is an established accessory to learning—a man or woman who visits schools in order to describe what they experienced in the past, with a view to preventing it from happening again. Children not only hear from *Zeitzeugen*; since the '80s they have also completed projects on what Nazism meant in their communities, and gone on school visits to museums and concentration camps. Two more words associated with this management of the past came up while I was in Imshausen: one was *der Abgrund*, the abyss, referring to the emotional void or trauma that many people felt at the end of the War; the other was *die Versöhnung*, reconciliation, which encompasses the rather broader sense of repairing the damage done by National Socialism.

Much of our first day was spent at the Adam von Trott Schule in nearby Sontra. The school has a pier decorated with photographs of Adam, but on this occasion the hall had also been turned over to an exhibition on Clarita's life. There is a concern that young Germans are no longer listening to the siren voices of people like Clarita, and that the stories of National Socialism and the resistance are beginning to lose their bite—the survivors of that time are mostly dead. The worry is that some of these young people will drift towards the extreme right, which is now doing increasingly well at the polls, winning more than 10 per cent of the vote in September 2017, and over ninety seats in the Bundestag. I took over a class for a couple of hours. Most of the children seemed impressively motivated, even if a few were too shy to speak. At the end of the school day we watched Hava

Kohav Beller's painfully moving film *The Restless Conscience*. If children need to see anything to understand the evil of Nazism, it is this film. I had the honour of sitting next to Hava herself during the screening, and later helped her up to the memorial cross to see Clarita's grave.

* * *

As we know, after May 1945, the Allies banned Nazi Party members from public life until they had filled in an extensive *Fragebogen* or questionnaire. This was the prelude to 'denazification'. Regional courts then examined each case and decided to what degree the petitioner was 'incriminated', and whether or not they might rejoin the fold of white sheep. The purge took different forms in the different Occupation Zones. The Allies tried the big fish, putting many of them behind bars with impressive tariffs, and a smallish number were hanged. After 1949, however, those who were still in prison were very quickly released. In East Germany, too, the process of denazification was not pursued for long, and society was fairly haunted by Nazi ghosts. Virtually all men below and above a certain age had been soldiers, and some of them would have been happiest to gloss over what they did in those years, particularly those who had occupied positions of command. In Christa Wolf's *Divided Heaven* (1963), Manfred has complete contempt for his father, who wore an SA uniform after 1933; other characters are blighted by their roles in the war and their captivity after it.

The rule of thumb devised by the Armies of Occupation after 1945 suggested that the Wehrmacht had behaved more or less honourably in the Second World War, but that the SS was a no-no. Later this rule was modified to exempt most of the Waffen-SS, its armed wing, from prosecution. This neat moral division was blown sky high by a 1995 exhibition entitled 'Vernichtungskrieg—Verbrechen der Wehrmacht' (War of

Annihilation—The Wehrmacht's Crimes),[8] which revealed that regular army soldiers, too, had participated in wartime atrocities. Conversely, not all members of the Waffen-SS were implicated. Some were simply brave soldiers who had joined Himmler's army because it was better equipped, or, after July 1944, because they had no choice. Despite this, the revelation that Günter Grass had fought with the SS as a teenager at the end of the war caused uproar, and once again focused attention on the writers of the so-called *Flakhelfer* generation. One who came under particular fire was Martin Walser, who had had the temerity to tilt at one of West Germany's sacred cows, the Jewish critic Marcel Reich-Ranicki.

* * *

Part of our discussion in Imshausen concerned the Western republic during the Adenauer years (1949–63) and its reluctance to prosecute former Nazis. Until 1968 or so, the older generation was still profoundly stained by their activity within, or acquiescence to, the Third Reich. Just after the war, it is said that as many as 80 per cent of West Germans wanted to see all leading Nazis answer for their crimes. By 1950, that number had dwindled to 38 per cent. People were worried it might be their turn next. Everywhere they talked of 'drawing a line' under the events of the past.[9] In the early years of the Western republic, there were a number of statutes introduced to inhibit trials against Nazi criminals.[10] It should be recalled that the sentences against resistance members like Adam von Trott, Helmuth James Graf von Moltke and Peter Graf Yorck von Wartenburg were still in force, lending legal authority to a view still shared by many Germans after the war: that these men had been rightfully condemned to death.

On the other hand, there were undoubtedly problems facing Adenauer's government when it came to denazification. Was there the time, and were there the right sort of people, to form a new, post-Nazi cadre? In 1945 the Nazi Party had 8 million members and the United Nations had drawn up a list of 34,270 German war criminals.[11] Under the Reich accession to certain offices and the practising of important professions would have been quasi-impossible without membership of the Party or an affiliated organisation. A total postwar ban, then, would have meant no lawyers, doctors or teachers. Despite good intentions at the beginning, very soon they all crawled back, the judges in particular.[12] That Konrad Adenauer was pragmatic about prose-cuting Nazis is an understatement, but there were trials, and they continue to this day. Indeed, more than once I have been called in to comment on Sky News on the sentencing of nonagenarian SS men.

Between 1945 and 2005, there were 36,393 recorded individual trials or instances of joint enterprise such as the Auschwitz or Majdanek trials. This figure represents a minimum, because it transpires that some records are missing.[13] Some 172,294 people came before the courts, and of these around 140,000 were judged guilty. There have been sixteen death sentences handed out by Federal German courts—as opposed to the Allied tribunals—of which only four were carried out. Three of the executions took place in Berlin: two women from a sanatorium who had killed handicapped patients in their care, and a minor Nazi from Friedenau who murdered a man who had already been injured by other cronies. The fourth was a Nazi bigwig executed in Solingen. In most cases, the accused received a sentence of between six months and a year. Perhaps the most sensational trials that took place in the earlier period happened in the DDR, in the little Saxon town of Waldheim. The Soviet authorities were anxious to close the concentration camps at Bautzen, Buchenwald and Sachsenhausen, which they had put back to work after May 1945. To this end 3,342 prisoners were handed over to the courts. The vast majority of them were then imprisoned, but twenty-three were sentenced to death. They were strangled, as no hangman could be found on the day. Sentences for participation in the mass murder of the Jews only became the lion's share of judicial condemnations from the '60s onwards.[14]

Not only were many judges biased against anti-Nazis, there were problems producing witnesses when so many people were dead, missing, or could conceal themselves in other Zones.[15] While I was in Imshausen, Adam and Clarita von Trott's younger daughter, Clarita Müller-Plantenberg, quite rightly drew our attention to two important trials that took place at the beginning of the Adenauer era. The first of these was against Wolfgang Hedler, a fanatical former Nazi Party member who had been elected to West Germany's first Bundestag to represent the right-wing Deutsche Partei. During his election campaign he continued to malign the 20 July Plotters as 'traitors to the fatherland.' His speech made waves after the *Frankfurter Rundschau* published a piece about it, leading to Hedler's trial for defamation at the end of January 1950.[16] Hedler had sounded off on a number of other matters too, such as the killing of the Jews and the German responsibility for starting the war, which he naturally denied.[17]

Two weeks later the judge, another former Nazi Party member, dismissed the charges. An appeal was launched which finally saw Hedler go down for nine months. Annedore Leber, one of the 20 July widows, had alerted Clarita von Trott to the case, and Clarita asked her father Max Tiefenbacher, a prominent Hamburg lawyer, to represent them and a number of other widows. The case presented the crimes of the Nazi regime and contrasted them against the definition of a state governed by law as set out by the Kreisau Circle dissident group, of which Adam von Trott, Julius Leber and Moltke had been prominent members. It was the first West German case against the defamers of the 20 July Plotters, and Hedler's eventual conviction came as both a relief and a milestone in the reestablishment of responsible government in the Western republic.

The second case was against Otto Ernst Remer of the Guard Battalion Grossdeutschland, the generalmajor—a major until he put down the Plot—who had played a central role in scotching the 20 July plans. Like Hedler, Remer had defamed the Plotters, calling them traitors, in a political speech during his electoral campaign in Lower Saxony. Remer was standing for the extreme-right Socialist Reich Party. The case against him was brought by the Jewish lawyer Fritz Bauer, the state prosecutor in Braunschweig who had been in a concentration camp during the Third Reich but had escaped, first to Denmark and then to Sweden. Here Clarita joined Marion Yorck, widow of Peter Graf Yorck von Wartenburg, as a witness for the prosecution. Remer's defence was constructed around the fact that he had sworn an oath of loyalty to Hitler, but this was thrown out and he was sentenced to three months in prison. The court had pronounced that the Nazi state did not abide by the rule of law and a lawless state cannot be betrayed. This verdict was extremely important in changing attitudes among Germans towards the Nazi regime.[18] Such court cases finally succeeded in convincing more people that the regime had not only been illegitimate, but that it was within the rights of man to seek to topple it.

So long as the 20 July Plotters were still officially perceived as traitors, their wives were ineligible for the widows' pensions handed out more routinely to the relicts of the judges who had ordered their hanging. I recalled Clarita von Trott being asked at Hofgeismar in August 1994 when she had first received a pension. It was an emotional moment. She had waited a long time, but good friends had made sure that she had not wanted for herself or her children. Charlotte von der Schulenburg—widow of Fritz-Dietlof Graf von der Schulenburg, who had also perished in Plötzensee—had waited until 1949 before petitioning the courts for financial support. It was not until 1952 that she finally received a pension, and only then because her husband had been a Third Reich civil servant—not because he had lost his life trying to bring down the regime.[19]

Many of these widows who fought so fiercely for their husbands' memory lived on into their nineties, like Clarita or Freya Gräfin von Moltke, whose husband Helmuth James was hanged in January 1945. Freya too was active in the late '50s, drawing attention to the work of the Kreisau Circle, which was named after the Moltkes' house in Silesia. On 11 March 2011, the centenary of her husband's birth, she was received by Chancellor Merkel. Marion Gräfin Yorck von Wartenburg, the widow of Peter, lived to 102. She was probably the woman who participated most in the discussions of the Kreisau Circle. After the war she was elected to the bench, but proved such a draconian judge that she was popularly known as 'Judge Merciless'. She was particularly fierce in her judgements on homosexuals, as homosexuality continued to be illegal under Article 175 of the Penal Code until 1969. Not only did she award the maximum sentences, she even cited jurisprudence from Nazi times in her sentencing. Her attitude led to condemnation by Berlin liberals.[20]

* * *

Adenauer may have found himself in an invidious position. He was watching his back, he was watching the West; he was watching former soldiers, because he desperately wanted to rearm, to please his new friends. The Bundeswehr did not honour the men of 20 July until 1959. Adenauer was also watching the Bundestag, which was in favour of rehabilitating the former soldiers. He made no meaningful comment about the men of 20 July. Even the president, Theodor Heuss (1949–59), was mealy-mouthed, at first at least. It was not until 1952 that he made a clear and unequivocal statement about his disgust at the men who called the Plotters' sacrifice into question.[21] There was a powerful lobby seeking to amnesty the remaining war criminals sitting in Landsberg Prison.

In May 1957, East Germany stole a march on the Bonn administration when it began exposing Nazis in the West German legal system as 'hanging judges [*Blutrichter*] in the service of Adenauer'. For the next three years, there were revelations every six months or so, and around 1,000 civil servants and court officials were named as being implicated in political or racially motivated death sentences. West Germany largely ignored the taunts.[22] The situation began to change in the autumn of 1958, partly as a result of a growing scepticism overseas when it came to the Western republic's claim to be a country abiding by the rule of law. At that point an office for the investigation of Nazi war crimes was established at Ludwigsburg. The process of prosecution was centralised and resulted in a breakthrough. There were now 500 committal proceedings, and another 700 went forward by 1964.

Now the gruesome stories came spilling out at last: Auschwitz, Chełmno, Treblinka, Gross-Rosen; the ghettos of Łodz and Warsaw; forced labourers and death marches; not to mention the massacres of Eastern European civilians by ethnic German units, and the roles played by Sipos (security police), Orpos (uniformed police), and the SD (intelligence). The Auschwitz Trial took place between 1963 and 1966, and the Frankfurt Diplomat Trial in 1966–7. Often impetus came from the lawyer Fritz Bauer.[23] In the middle of this reawakening of justice in West Germany came the Eichmann Trial in Jerusalem, more based on witness testimony than on the documents that took pride of place in German proceedings. The final Majdanek Trial did not take place until 1976, and lasted nearly six years. All the while the Bundestag was pressed to end the statute of limitations for Nazi crimes.

* * *

As a result of *Vergangenheitsbewältigung*, Germans like now to face their uglier past head on. As recently as April 2017, I was invited to address students in Kempten on my family's experience in the Third Reich. They listened intently and asked no questions. It would be hard to imagine Germans challenging lecturers who presented the facts in this way, and yet at one time David Irving enjoyed huge support from an educationally neglected element in Germany that was still angry about the way their past was portrayed; and only recently a spokesman for the extreme-right AfD party described the Holocaust Memorial in Berlin as 'the disgraceful monument'. Listening into conversations in small-town pubs can be illuminating, but few Germans today would have the courage to voice their anger openly. Naturally there is very little criticism of Jews or Israel.

There has been a mild controversy over the placing of the commemorative *Stolpersteine* that have marked European streets with the names and details of Nazi victims since 1992—but much of the debate has been based on the price of these 'stones' and the fact that one sole producer, their inventor, has 'cornered' the market. The idea is that you 'stumble' upon these cobblestone-sized pieces of brass, which record the details of Jews who were deported or murdered, set into the pavement directly in front of the commemorated person's former residence. I have often stopped to read the stones when I have encountered them in Berlin or Vienna. They can be at best incomplete, as the bombing of German cities was so draconian that whole areas have lost their previous street plans. Critics complain that the stones are a monopoly of the artist Gunter Demnig and that they are expensive at €120 each. Munich has taken the decision to ban the cobbles, with the backing of the former president of the Jewish Council Charlotte Knobloch, who objected to the fact that people not only walked on the stones, but failed even to notice that something was written on them. In other parts of

Germany, there have been fewer hitches. The British wine merchant Peter Hallgarten told me that he had been to the ceremony in Oestrich-Winkel in the Rheingau to commemorate several members of his own family.[24] He had spent his early childhood in the Rheingau before emigrating to England with his famous father Fritz.

'Militarism' is still taboo. When Germany created its postwar Bundeswehr and joined NATO in 1955, it was important to fashion an army that was non-militaristic. As a boy I marvelled at the sight of German soldiers with their long hair tucked up into their berets. As a long-haired and distinctly reluctant member of my school cadet corps, I was acutely envious. To some extent after 1945, Germany revisited the prescriptions issued at Versailles—there were, for example, to be no smart regiments. For all that, however, one or two somehow managed to attract the social elite, much as IR 9 did between 1920 and 1945. One young royal prince, for example, told me that he was joining a particular regiment to do his national service, because 'it was the nearest thing to an old cavalry regiment.' And, despite these precautions, Germany's military is perpetually in trouble domestically. Any form of involvement in foreign peace-keeping missions brings with it a deal of opposition—the army can do nothing right. In 2017 Defence Minister Ursula von der Leyen had to face another problem common to armies: bullying. In reunified Germany's politically and socially responsible military, this was not to be tolerated. The brigadier responsible for training was dismissed.

Historical political violence, on the other hand, is not always perceived as a bad thing. The youthful Edelweiss Pirates, who managed to rise up against the Nazi police in Düsseldorf during the war, are well remembered. Too many soldiers used obedience to higher command to excuse their behaviour during the war. There has also been a limited respect, particularly among students, for certain revolutionary groups such as the Baader-Meinhofs or Red Army Faction in 1968 and the '70s—they were fighting fascism, or so it was maintained, and their victims were often hard-nosed capitalists and former Nazis. No such respect is exhibited towards the Islamist terrorists who have shown their colours since 2015.

* * *

The DDR had its own ways of dealing with recent history: chiefly, it was buttoned up in the straitjacket of Marxism-Leninism. The past was allowed to exist, and could be excused within the framework of this dialectic—in stark opposition to political correctness. Until fairly recently, the Museum of Brandenburg-Prussian History in Potsdam still regaled its visitors with the Marxist phases of history: feudalism, absolutism, the aspiring middle classes, a lot on the Revolution of 1848, and so on. There was no mention, on the contrary, of the bombing of Potsdam, the destruction of the town, or indeed the Russians in general. The Soviets were only to be thanked for liberating the Germans from Hitler. After the *Wende*, these East German versions of history were gradually thrown out; outside the Humboldt University of Berlin on the Linden, there were piles of remaindered volumes penned by great worthies such as Engels, Grotewohl, Pieck, Becher and Ackermann.

After 1989, the adoption of Hitlerite values in East Germany was part spite, part letting off steam. There was not going to be any more serious punishment. In the first months after the Wall fell, I quit Friedrichstrasse Station with a friend and sat down for a beer. The next table was occupied by drunken East Berliners:

> two old boys with blotchy faces who probably remembered Adolf
> from their youth; four drunken teenagers with red faces who looked
> as if they could not stand much more than half an hour before they
> slipped under the table spread with cheap Ossi wine. One of the old

boys lumbered to his feet and began to sing *Die Wacht am Rhein*, but he gave up when he discovered he had forgotten the words. The youths nonetheless showed their appreciation for his performance by stumbling to their feet and giving a rather limp Hitler 'Grüss'.[25]

What was absent from the East, and omnipresent in the West, was the feeling of collective guilt. This had been used as a weapon to subdue the Germans after 1945, and by the '60s was to some extent ingrained. All Germans—every man, woman and child born before May 1945—were responsible for Hitler and the atrocities committed in his name, not just the 37.4% or 33.1% who voted for him in the last two free elections in 1932, or indeed the 43% that gave him the thumbs-up in the less-than-free elections of March 1933. To some extent, this guilt was passed on to subsequent generations. By this time, of course, it was no longer being imposed by the Western Allies, but by the Germans themselves, as a kind of atonement for their sins. In East Germany, however, Germans not only applied it less rigorously, but also blamed it on unrepentant fascists in the West.

Reunification marked a change in attitudes in both East and West. On 20 July 1994, Helmut Kohl—now chancellor of a united Federal Republic—was on hand to celebrate the fiftieth anniversary of the July Plot. One of the twelve names he cited was Adam von Trott. A month later, I played my own small role at a conference dedicated to his memory in Hofgeismar, Hesse—a precursor to the 2017 gathering. The intentions and credentials of the 20 July Plotters were re-examined—there was still no room for heroes, but there was less sniffing about the Plotters' motives. The new Germany was less dismissive than the students of '60 had been, or indeed the unreformed or part-reformed Nazis after 1945. Nor was this revision limited to the Nazi period. The DDR's history, its use of sneaks and repressive policies, the slaying of 327 people who tried unsuccessfully to reach the West—all were subjected to a handwringing commission, presided over by Pastor Joachim Gauck and dominated by the same Lutheran clerics who had become the prime movers in the liberation of the East.

LAND UND LEUTE

Germany is a rich and varied landscape. In one of the country's earliest published cookery books, the medieval author evokes its different terrains: the north-east with its forests, the vines in the south-west, the mountains in the Alps and the lesser ranges in the Giant Mountains (Riesengebirge) and the Harz, the rolling hills of Hesse, and the two 'Switzerlands' in Brandenburg and Saxony.[26] Olives don't grow in Germany, nor do lemons or oranges or figs, but most other things do. There is wonderful fruit in the south of Württemberg and Baden, and a wealth of produce in the Black Forest. There are good cattle in the Black Forest too, sheep in North Hesse and pigs just about everywhere. And there is game in profusion: wild boars regularly trash suburban gardens in Berlin and elsewhere. Other, non-edible animals have recently joined the throng: wolves have made a comeback forming packs in a few dozen places, and there was the sad tale of Bruno the Bear in Bavaria who ate thirty-three sheep, four domestic rabbits and a guinea pig together with some hens and wild rabbits and the contents of several beehives. Bruno was famously described by the CSU leader Edmund Stoiber as a 'Problembär'.

Pork is of course the standard German food—sausages, they joke, are the German answer to vegetables. Being Germany, there is a heavy stress placed on organic farming, and biodynamism was more or less a German creation, founded on Rudolf Steiner's views on how to grow potatoes. I visited an organic German potato farm recently. I have no idea whether the farmer followed Steiner's prescriptions to the letter and buried cow horns filled with dung in the corners of the fields, but the soil was tilled by horse and the farmer did not even possess a car. He was linked by association to many other local farmers who could provide a broad palate of produce to make it more interesting to his customers. There is even a federal programme, BÖLN (Network of Federal Ecological Agriculture), which has been set up to unite 240 registered organic domains that sell their produce direct to the consumer.

I got to know the German-speaking world relatively late. My first visit was as a 15-year-old. With time I explored the land and its people, the varied terrain from Bavaria to the Mecklenburg Lakes, the Rhine and the sandbox of Brandenburg and experienced the huge variety of language that passes for German too. Germany was unified only in 1871, which means that people continue to have strong regional affiliations: when one man opens his mouth to venture an opinion, another will put him down with the exclamation, '*Typisch Bayrisch!*' (Typical Bavarian!) Attitudes are apparently formed on the tip of your tongue. Those contrary opinions are frequently expressed in dialects. Above the 'Benrath Line' (north of Düsseldorf) there are various species of Platt, or Low German. In the surviving German part of Pomerania, now mostly Polish, it is easy to guess the meaning of 'Wat is o klock?' In Mecklenburg, 'Good morning to you too' is rendered as 'Gun-dag-ook'. The nineteenth-century novelist Theodor Fontane, who came from Neuruppin in the Mark Brandenburg, delighted in replicating the various Platt dialects of north-eastern Germany in his novels and stories.

Platt has many variations, from the Dutch border to Schleswig-Holstein, to Mecklenburg and German Pomerania. The original dialect of Berlin and Brandenburg, with its hard 'chs' that make 'ick' and 'icke', derives from Platt. A Mecklenburger will not understand an Allgäuer any more than a Viennese speaking

Wienerisch will be comprehensible to a Berliner—whether he speaks Berlinisch or not. Many northern and eastern dialects are marked by soft 'G's that sound like English 'Y's: *Yorg hat die yanze Yans yeyessen.*[27] Berlinisch combines a dialect pronunciation with a great many local slang words, some of which originated in Platt. Some also come from the French Huguenots, who arrived in great profusion in the seventeenth century. It is now more like big city slang, resembling Parigot or Cockney. There was an excellent book and print seller in the Potsdamer Strasse from whom I bought a small stash of Menzels in my time. An Ossi, he used to tell me his life story in broad Berlinisch. I met two brothers in Mecklenburg. One was a university professor in Hanover and spoke Hochdeutsch; his brother was an out-of-work electrician with a passion for Haydn who lived in Oranienburg, north of Berlin. They came out of the same egg, so to speak. As little boys, they had trekked from Tilsit with their mother in 1945 and endured Lord knows what hardships on the way. I had no problem with the German spoken by one, but I was utterly defeated by the other. Sometimes I have amused myself watching how dialects distort the language. In Swabia, a cultural region straddling Baden-Württemberg, *habe* became 'habé', *klingt* 'glingkt', *sagt* 'sackt'. In the Rhineland *Bier* is 'Pier'. In Austrian Styria 'L's are diphthongs—*alt* becomes 'oit', *kalt* 'koit', and so on.

Again the Rhenish dialects form a family, although they say Moselaner was influenced by the French occupation in Napoleonic times. In Trier, they are proud of this French connection. There is a band crossing Germany from the Allgäu to Alsace, where the same Alemannic German is spoken as in Switzerland and the Austrian Vorarlberg. It is a separate language, and as old as German itself. Germans lump all Alemannic speakers together and call them 'Schwäbisch', or Swabian. Bavarian German is vaguely reminiscent of Austrian German, and gets more difficult the further you get from Munich and the big towns. Saxon is universally condemned as a barbaric deformation of the language, and is famous for its nasal twang, which makes Saxons sound as if they have permanently blocked noses. The Saxons are considered slightly malevolent figures of fun, and other Germans howl in pleasure or in pain as soon as they open their mouths. Part of their sinister reputation comes from the fact that they ruled the roost in the old DDR.

The best German, they say, is that spoken in the centre around the Harz Mountains, and most particularly in Brunswick or Braunschweig. Until recently, the only people who spoke the formal, standardised Hochdeutsch I learned at school were Herr and Frau Doktors. Hochdeutsch serves as a lingua franca: a language used when speaking to strangers. I recall, a long time ago, a winemaker asking my driver in dialect if I understood German, to which I replied directly, 'Nur wenn du Deutsch sprichst'— 'only if you speak German'.

German is not the only language spoken in Germany. Apart from Turkish, the principal foreign language is Sorbisch or Wendisch, which is used by the original Slavic inhabitants of Transelbian Germany, though it is now largely confined to the Spreewald and some pockets of Saxony. The number of Wendisch speakers has certainly declined, despite the government's well-meaning policy of putting up bilingual signposts outside their villages. In the eighteenth century, seven of the roughly 100 Prussian army regiments communicated in Wendisch. There were other regional languages before 1945, such as the Wasserpolnisch spoken in Upper Silesia and the Kassubian around Danzig. Both were essentially 'patois', combining elements of both German and Slavic languages. In the Ruhr, many Polish miners naturally spoke Polish. Then there was Yiddish, spoken by the poorer Jews in most of the big cities. The richer Jews did their best to speak Hochdeutsch.

To foreigners, German with its compound nouns is famously ungainly and unwittingly comic, too. When Twitter announced that they were going to double the permitted character count to 280, the German Foreign Office tweeted, 'That's four German words': *Rindfleischetikettierungsüberwachungsaufgabenübertragungs gesetz*. This is an example of the ugliest form of German: 'Beamtendeutsch', or civil service German, although it might be said in mitigation that bureaucrats are not famous for beautifying any language. Fewer people are aware that German has been subjected to linguistic purges. The most far-reaching was carried out by Dr Goebbels and it naturally meant eliminating foreign words. Now, students of nineteenth-century literature are obliged to thumb the glossaries of paperback editions to understand words that were common currency before the Second World War. These reforms to the German language continue, but largely unheeded. The German language is certainly not without humour, and political events require new words to describe them. When the *Wende* came, people spoke not only of 'Ossis' and 'Wessis', but also of 'Jammerossis' (whingeing Easterners) and 'Besserwessis' (know-all Westerners).[28] Neither translation does the word justice. Helmut Kohl's reconquest of the East was written off as 'Kohl-onization'. In the old DDR, there came a whole vocabulary to describe the new situation: a *Wendehals* (wryneck) was a turncoat, who deserted the SED regime for the temptations offered by the West. Perhaps the best known of these coinages from the time of the *Wende* is *Ostalgie*: nostalgia for the Eastern state.

Before Hitler banned it in 1941, deciding that its origins were Jewish, Germans could fox all those who sought to understand them by writing in their special cursive script, *Kurrent*. In its neatest, most comprehensible form, it is *Sütterlin*, while the formal script on fifteenth- to nineteenth-century proclamations and legal documents was *Kanzleischrift*. People engaged in historical and literary research are well advised to learn it, but it is not easy, and everyone's handwriting has its quirks. Hugh Trevor-Roper, by that time ennobled as Lord Dacre of the North, admitted that he could not read it, and yet he nonetheless authenticated the fake Hitler Diaries, which, oddly enough, were written in *Kurrent*.

* * *

For all its austerity and police spies, the DDR could be fun. Lutz Schramm, who used to orchestrate the punk-friendly youth radio station Parocktikum, was an SED party member.[29] There were plenty of DDR jokes, but it was sometimes risky to tell them. Many will remember the Stasi canteen scene in the film *Das Leben der Anderen*. In another, Honecker loses his watch and calls the Stasi to investigate. The next day, when he finds it under his bed and rings the Stasi to call off the search, they reply that it is already too late: 'We have arrested ten people and those ten people have already confessed.'[30] I have seen examples of dry humour in Berlin bars. In one in the Friedrichstrasse I observed a crowd of drunken British brickies. One of them kept ordering rounds of drinks. Naturally he addressed the publican in English. The publican was always polite, but called the brickie Rudolf. 'Rudolf' would then retreat to his table, beaming with pride that the publican had understood his order. When he had come up half a dozen times, another German man at the bar asked our host why he persisted in calling the Englishman 'Rudolf'. The publican replied, '*Wegen seiner roten Nase*'—because of his red nose.

Germany is generally a friendly place; at least that has been my experience. Maybe I am lucky to be white-skinned, but I generally find Germans courteous. Some even go out of their way to help you. Only last year, on a particularly miserable day in late April, I made the foolish decision to walk from the station into Kempten in the rain; despairing of finding my hotel, I asked a middle-aged man for directions. The man not only walked with me for about half a mile until we came in sight of the place, he covered me with his umbrella along the way. I could feel how much he was longing to ask me where I came from, but I only put him out of his misery at the end. I sometimes feel like the animal in the old joke: 'We don't see many gorillas around here...'

RACE AND RELIGION

The racial unity that formed such a huge part of Hitler's platform was to some extent a myth. Even in 1933, neither the swarthy 'Alemanns' of Swabia nor the stocky Bavarians were recognisably the same tribe as the tall, blue-eyed and blond beasts of the north. Germany had 450,000 Jewish citizens then; there are far, far fewer now, even if their numbers have increased dramatically since the '90s, when many Jews came to Germany from Russia. On the other hand, there are plenty of Turks and Kurds, who began arriving as *Gastarbeiter* or guest workers in the '60s, taking on the menial jobs that West Germans disdained after the postwar *Wirtschaftswunder* or Economic Miracle. Along the way one of them, Kadir Nurman, is said to have invented the döner kebab on his stall opposite the Tiergarten station in Berlin. Berlin is the largest Turkish city outside Turkey. Since 2015, increased refugee numbers following Angela Merkel's generous offer to accommodate them have caused a political stir—her 2017 electoral setback can largely be ascribed to the unpopularity of this policy.

The question of nationality in relation to the Turkish population has also become an important political debate in recent years. Some argue that the majority's retention of Turkish nationality—naturalisation is difficult, and dual citizenship is not permitted—has been an impediment to integration, citing the few German Turks who have been radicalised, like a small minority of Muslims everywhere, and the fact that many of the German Turks' families come from the poorer Turkish regions such as Anatolia where the increasingly authoritarian President Erdogan finds his political heartland. For his supporters, the more liberal values of the '70s and '80s are now strictly taboo. However, not all Turks are backward-looking Erdogan disciples by any means. German Turks now operate in many walks of life; they sit in the provincial Landtags as well as the Bundestag in Berlin. Many are staunchly opposed to President 'ErdoWahn', as the Germans call him, playing on the word *Wahn* (delusion or madness).

In 2016 the satirist Jan Böhmermann brought the 'Turkish question' to the boil when he wrote and performed on air a dirty poem about Erdogan, accusing him of unnatural vices with goats. It might have been naughty, but the Turkish president is a fair target for the jibes of German political commentators, given that he uses the German Anatolians as pawns in his power games with the EU. And in Germany, with its high number of Turkish citizens, Turkey's political campaigns are also carried out across most of the country—although far less in the eastern parts, because the DDR took no *Gastarbeiter*.

* * *

Religious Germans are still required to pay a 'church tax' for the upkeep of the churches, but Christianity is as much in decline in Germany as it is elsewhere in the Western world. Germans may opt out of the tax if they claim no religious adherence. Before Nazism, Germany was a bewildering tessellation of Christian loyalties. In some areas it is still true that one village is Protestant, the next Catholic. Evangelical National Churches were formed in the early nineteenth century on the model of the Anglican Church, and ruled over by bishops. During the Third Reich many of these were infiltrated by narrow-minded 'German Christians', even if a third of the Protestant clergy refused to sanction this Hitlerian theology.

East Germany was mostly Lutheran, and pastors chiefly in Leipzig played a huge role in the dismantling of the republic on 9 November 1989. Although most of the leading Nazis were Catholics, there was a well-orchestrated move to destroy the Church of Rome by fabricating sex scandals, which led to a dogged opposition to Nazism among the faithful, particularly in Bavaria, where it was resented that schools were forced to remove crucifixes from classrooms. Later it was the Catholics who led the campaign to stop Hitler from murdering the mentally ill. That resistance to state authority was encouraged by churchmen from Bishop Galen to Archbishop Frings, and increased the kudos of the Catholic Church both during and immediately after the war. These days the scandals appear to be less in dispute, from Pope Benedict's brother running a Bavarian Dotheboys Hall to the former Bishop of Limburg, Franz-Peter Tebartz-van Elst, seemingly wanting to emulate some Renaissance prelate and surround himself with luxury. The Church now appears to be destroying its reputation all by itself.

The religious map of Germany can be misleading. Kempten, like other former Holy Roman Imperial cities in the south—Lindau, Isny, Kaufbeuren and Memmingen—went over to the Protestants at the time of the Reformation, while the country around them remained Catholic. Kempten, however, possesses a mighty Benedictine abbey and basilica, and after the Reformation the Catholic part of the town was separated from the Protestant by a wall. The Allgäu became Bavarian in 1803, which meant rule from Catholic Munich, and yet progressively more Protestants arrived in the region as the cheese business became more profitable. That meant Swiss people in the mountains and Protestant labourers constructing the new railway lines. Now there are Protestant parishes all over the Allgäu.

A similar split occurs in Württemberg, where Catholicism reigns on the Bodensee—particularly in the old territory of

Hohenzollern-Sigmaringen—while Stuttgart and the region to the north is Evangelical. Württemberg is now tacked onto Baden, which is also Protestant in the north, and Catholic in the south. Both the king of Württemberg and the grand duke of Baden were naturally Protestant too: *cuius regio eius religio*—whose realm, his religion.[31] When I'm wearing my wine hat, I am often astonished by the very Catholic names of the leading vineyards of the Pfalz, such as the wonderful Kirchenstück and Jesuitengarten in Deidesheim. The historian in me also knows that Elector Frederick V was the famous Protestant 'Winter King', James I of England's son-in-law whose election to the Throne of Bohemia in 1618 set off the Thirty Years' War. He not only lost his throne, but was ousted from his Electorate and died a sad joke. After his deposition, the Bavarian Wittelsbachs took over in the Pfalz, and the principality returned to the Catholic fold.

The Mosel appears profoundly Catholic, and many of the wine estates celebrate their previous church ownership, but as the genial Dr Dirk Richter in Müllheim will point out (preferably over a glass of his excellent wine), Brauneberg in the Mittelmosel is Protestant because the village was previously the property of the Pfalz-Zweibrückens, as part of the County of Veldenz. The rest of the valley was chiefly in the pocket of the Catholic Archbishop of Trier. In the seventeenth century, it was decided that villages in the Mosel might have one church only, so when the village church was reconstructed in the late eighteenth, it became a 'simultaneous church', with Catholics worshipping in the nave and Protestants in the choir.

GERMANY AND THE WORLD

Germany's relations with its neighbours—Poles, Czechs, Dutch, Danes, Austrians, Swiss and French—are still coloured by nationalism and the Second World War. Many of the new nation-states that arose after 1918 occupied territory previously at least partly populated by Germans, from Czechoslovakia to Romania and Hungary, from Yugoslavia to Poland. Substantial numbers of German families lived in the Baltic States and Russia as nobles, traders, civil servants or academics. On the Volga they were also farmers. Hitler's demands for restitution, followed by wars of conquest and atrocities in the Second World War, have left a sour taste in many places.

In Hungary and Romania, tourism has rectified much of that. Hungary in particular used to be the favoured destination of many East German tourists, who paid for the development of hotels and boarding houses around Lake Balaton. Most younger Germans accept the post-1945 borders, and are ignorant even of the German names of Polish places like Szczecin or Wrocław that were such important German towns and cities before 1945. Willy Brandt did not formally recognise the Oder-Neisse Line until 1971, however, and while it is unthinkable that Germans should attempt to reconquer their old territories today, Poles and Czechs cling to opt-out clauses in EU treaties to ensure that Germans may not acquire property in former German areas such as East Prussia, Hinter Pomerania, Silesia or the Sudetenland. In some instances, this is a pity: the many crumbling, abandoned German manor houses could be turned into attractive hotels for German *Heimatgruppen*, who set out in buses in pursuit of their roots. Few Poles have an interest in acquiring them. *Heimatgruppen* are big business: their coaches trundle forth as far as the Volga in search of the places where Germans of a previous generation were once at home. A few years back, a UK photo exhibition of crumbling Schlösser in Silesia brought it home to British architecture-lovers how far this situation has led to the ruination of much of Silesia's best architecture.

Some maintain that this new 'Ostpolitik' in today's Federal Republic is not always innocent—that there are German businessmen and women who use their wealth to re-establish hege-mony in long-lost provinces. I am not convinced, but there is an attempt where possible to establish cultural relations with the current administrators of former German territories. The manor house at Kreisau near Wrocław where Hitler's opponents in the Kreisau Circle planned the future Germany is a joint Polish-German venture today; there are Baltic Institutes looking into the historical links that previously animated the area, and they say that German money has mysteriously found its way to Kaliningrad, the former coronation city of Königsberg in Prussia. I was told Germans had paid for the restoration of one of the city's gates. In 1985, Helmut Kohl caused a stir by agreeing to address the Silesian *Landsmannschaft* or expellees' association, which at the time was insisting on the slogan '*Schlesien ist unser*' (Silesia belongs to us). Such people are not generally mentioned in polite society. They are condemned as '*Ewig-gestrigen*' (eternal yesterday's men). Their cause was very largely abandoned by mainstream politicians after Willy Brandt's Ostpolitik. Before then, however, they had their own minister and civil service department, as well as clubs and newspapers. Until 2014, the expellees had a vociferous spokeswoman in Erika Steinbach, a CDU deputy in the Bundestag until January 2017, when she quit the party in protest at Frau Merkel's refugee policy.

Relations are often bad specifically with Germany's German-speaking neighbours. There have been ructions with the Swiss, but much more mud-and-guilt slinging has taken place between Germany and Austria. Yet that relationship is complex: Germans are dismissed with the slur 'Piefkes', and Austrians complain about their overbearing manner and the bargain-basement tour-ists in Burgenland and elsewhere looking for sweet wine and *Gemütlichkeit*—but they also bring money, patronising small hotels and guesthouses. From Passau to Vienna and in particular in the Wachau they clog up the roads like so many porpoises on bicycles. It is true that Austria no longer gets the top-notch German traveller. Germans have been more adventurous holiday-makers since the heyday of the Economic Miracle. They go to Kenya or Thailand, or their own section of Tuscany near Montalcino and Siena; they mop up the red wine in Spain and Portugal and buy up whole villages in Greece. Where possible, Austria has altered its image in an effort to disassociate itself from the actions of the Third Reich, creating a non-German identity that emphasises Austria's different dialects and specifically its *Tracht*, or regional dress. A Styrian winemaker told me that people in Hamburg had laughed at him when he appeared on the Alster dressed in embroidered leather plus-twos. What did he expect?

Similarly, after the war, most Alemannic-speaking Alsatians in France thought it wisest to desist from using their dialect, but there has been a revival in the past few years. Elsewhere, de Gaulle and Adenauer contrived to put the war behind them and construct an enduring relationship as the two most powerful countries on the European continent. In most cases, EU membership has cured the resentment that lingered after the various Nazi occupations. The standard Dutch response to Germans used to be 'Give me back my bloody bicycle', but nowadays I find many Dutch people are not only happy to speak German, but spend time in the country and are great enthusiasts for German wine. Britain's relations with Germany are complex, and probably more affected by commercial rivalry or jealousy than any abiding rancour stemming from world wars. Negative attitudes towards a perceived German economic hegemony were almost certainly an important factor in the 2016 Brexit vote. There are still a few thousand British troops stationed in Germany.

At least at first, the DDR was openly anti-Zionist and Paul Merker of the SED was sentenced to eight years in Hohenschön-hausen for advocating compensation for the Jewish victims of the

Third Reich. The 1961 Eichmann Trial in Jerusalem coincided with the beginning of a trading relationship between West Germany and Israel, and led to demonstrations in the latter. Adenauer had not wanted to hear about Eichmann, and when pressed on the matter by the Israelis said, 'Eichmann is not a German citizen'.[32] It was his short-lived successor Chancellor Ludwig Erhard who initiated the trade, supplying the Israeli Defence Force with tanks. In Israel, and to some extent in the United States, Germany must walk on eggs, although American ex-servicemen remain attached to the places where they were formerly stationed. They have their own itineraries in Germany, and form a regular clientele in locations like the Jazz Bar in Wiesbaden's Kurhaus or Schumann's bar in Munich. They congregate in Rüdesheim in the Rheingau and do the chicken dance, and I am told they are thick on the ground in Heidelberg.

Many Americans from the Midwest also have strong German connections. Quite a few US politicians are relatively 'fresh off the boat'. Hamburgers were not happy to be reminded of the fact that Donald Rumsfeld's people were from their city; as for the other Donald, mentioning his connection to Kallstadt, home to the meaty *Saumagen* (stuffed sow's belly), is a good way to wind up a Pfälzer.[33] A winemaker snapped back at me that there were no Trumps left in the village itself, but he admitted to President Trump having a baker cousin in Freinsheim who has had some success with his Trump-Schnitte cake since 2016. It is topped with the American flag and comes with a picture of the Donald.[34]

PRINCES AND NOBLES

In the East the cult of the proletariat was more a celebration of the *kleiner Mann*; most of the rest had left. In some places, particularly villages, the Schloss was either torn down or used for some other, preferably denigratory, purpose: as a lunatic asylum, a school or a holiday home for the police or the Stasi. In others, the great house that had dominated a town before 1945 was turned into a museum of feudalism; the Stolbergs' great Gothic Revival castle above Wernigerode in the Harz was used to educate young East Germans about the evils of feudalism. The Stolbergs themselves were dispossessed in 1945 and do not appear to have wanted their castle back since.

While the East cultivated the Germany of the proletariat, in the West, economic prosperity meant that the country was dominated by a prosperous middle-class *Bürgertum* or bourgeoisie. The little jobs could be operated by helots from Turkey. Even before the end of the DDR, there were increasing numbers of Vietnamese and Africans performing the menial work. The German nobility was uprooted in the east, either losing their livelihoods across the Elbe or both their homes and estates (if not their lives) across the Oder. In the West, the nobles were compromised by their roles in the Third Reich, above all in the higher ranks of the Wehrmacht and by the failure of 20 July 1944. The DDR paid a mealy-mouthed tribute to the many nobles in Infantry Regiment 9 of Potsdam, which boasted the most Plotters of any regiment, and the street where they had their barracks was renamed in memory of Generalmajor Henning von Tresckow.

There are still plenty of princes about. The present royal duke of Coburg lives in Schloss Callenberg just outside the town. When I met him in 1998 I asked him about the cousins, and how he got on with all the different Saxe-Coburg-Gothas. Starting as distinctly small fry in the realms of royalty, they became the greatest achievers of the nineteenth century, marrying into the reigning families of Britain, Spain and Portugal and becoming kings of Belgium and Bulgaria. They had all been to visit, he told me: kings and pretenders, even the royal children—

Charles and Andrew—but the Queen herself kept her distance. The reason for that was the duke's grandfather, Charles Edward. The ducal line had died out with Ernest II and two British princes had been sent over to continue the dynasty. The first was Alfred, Duke of Edinburgh, Queen Victoria's son, but when his son and sole heir died the British court dispatched Charles Edward, Duke of Albany, one of Victoria's grandsons. He came straight from Eton and was adopted by the Kaiser, becoming more German than the Germans (although his grandson says he never lost the accent). In 1914 he led his regiment into battle against the country of his birth and in 1917 he was the first prince to sever the connection with Britain. The British Saxe-Coburgs responded in kind and renamed themselves Windsor—hence the Kaiser's witty remark that he was looking forward to a performance of *The Merry Wives of Saxe-Coburg-Gotha*.

Charles Edward did not stop there. He fell for a certain Adolf Hitler and was the first of the German princes to invite the brown hordes to his court, right back in 1920. He remained a committed Nazi and the Americans took it out on him in 1945. When they finished with him he was blind, and in an abject state he died in a small cottage outside Coburg in the '50s. The Coburgs are one of many royal families in Germany that graduate from former emperors and kings like the Prussian Hohenzollerns, to mere kings like the Bavarian Wittelsbachs; then there are a few grand dukes and dukes, and the odd royal count. In the old days, these people could marry one another, but their blood became polluted as soon as they wedded someone who was not *standesgemäss* or of royal blood. In the case of a king or royal duke, that could even be a countess or a baroness of ancient lineage—woe betide anyone who chooses the path of the British monarchy and marries morganatically! Since royalty and nobility were abolished in 1919, the process of supplanting royal pretenders has continued whenever one or another has chosen to marry below his or her rank.

Beneath the collection of royal families in Germany, there remain many nobles, old and new. They are recognisable by the particle 'von', or sometimes 'zu'—and sometimes both—in their names, which remained legal in the Weimar constitution. Titles became part of their surnames, so Count Paul von Metternich, became 'Paul Graf von Metternich', and so on. Although the law has declared them an irrelevance, old nobles don't forget. On the day in August 1997 when the Adlon Hotel reopened after a sleep of nearly forty years, I sat with a couple of Eulenburgs and asked them about Prince Philipp zu Eulenburg, the Kaiser's best friend, and the homosexual court scandal that rocked the Empire to its foundations in 1909. They were able to tell me that there had been a recent reconciliation between the branches, and that his descendants were now received by theirs. Bygones had become bygones.

The *Wende* had also had an effect: suddenly, dispossessed nobles were able to claim back property across the Iron Curtain. The same week that I met the Eulenburgs, I lunched with a PR lady from an old Prussian Junker family. Her father had got back the family house that had been situated in the KGB 'fortress' in Potsdam. She was an old stager who had worked for thirteen years in Berlin hotels. She looked down on the Moltkes, Alvenslebens and Hardenbergs, who had all pitched up only after 1989 looking around to see if there was anything for them.

German noble families can be extremely extensive, so that degrees of cousinage are hard to compute. Reference has to be made to the 'Gotha', which will tell you whether the family is 'knightly', 'baronial' or dignified with the title of count or prince. These days, *Familientagungen* are organised as clan gatherings. I once ran into a lot of Plothos in Kyritz, a former princely Wendish family who lived in the Mark Brandenburg before the Germans and were accommodated into the local nobility. The best known Plotho was probably the Baroness Elisabeth von Ardenne, whose marital infidelity and the duel it occasioned is thought to have inspired Theodor Fontane to write his best-known novel, *Effi Briest*. Elisabeth lived until 1952, and several people I met at the conference could describe her in her declining years. When I went to Kyritz in 1996, attitudes to the nobility had changed so much that there was a Plothostrasse again, and the town mayor had organised a reception for them with beer and sausages. Not everyone in Kyritz was so happy about the rehabilitation of the Junkers. The July Plotter Fritz-Dietlof Graf von der Schulenburg had been a onetime resident, and in 1991 they renamed a street in his honour too—some neo-Nazis promptly daubed the sign with paint.

REFUGEES, OR *VERTRIEBENE*

The word *Vertriebene* has a special meaning for Germans. After 1945, when Germany lost over a fifth of its territory, 16.5 million men, women and children had to be accommodated in a much reduced area; *Vertriebene* has more of the sense of 'expellees' than 'refugees'. Nor was this the first time that ethnic Germans had crossed the frontier carrying no more than a suitcase: only twenty-seven years before, Germans from Alsace, northern Schleswig, West Prussia and the Grand Duchy of Posen had all had to fall back on post war borders. On that occasion, at the end of the First World War, Germany had lost a seventh of its surface area.

Along with people concealing their Nazi pasts, postwar Germans had to deal with the ghosts of the lost eastern territories. Officially, no one was meant to mention them, but in reality, people carried over with their belongings the experience of the trek from the lands they had once known. Many lost their fathers too, and made the perilous journey in the company of their mothers alone. Some of the fathers returned later, after long years in the Soviet Union, Yugoslavia, Czechoslovakia or Poland, where they had been set to work repairing the damage caused by their countrymen. Many were reluctant to discuss what had happened in the intervening years.

Between 1945 and 1948 these *Vertriebene* from the east were settled in designated villages and often patronised as 'poor refugees'. Some tried to maintain local traditions and speak dialects that would otherwise be destined to die out. While most retained a stolid Prussian reserve, others grumbled through their political organisations or *Landsmannschaften*. Not all *Vertriebene* are on the right, but many are: a notable exception was the Green former foreign minister Joschka Fischer; another was the Nobel Prize-winning novelist Günter Grass. The heroine of Christa Wolf's *Divided Heaven* (1963), like Wolf herself, is a *Vertriebene*.

In Berlin, the 1920s modernist Deutschlandhaus in Kreuzberg— being redesigned, at the time of writing, as a 'document centre'—used to lodge the *Landsmannschaften* from all the lost regions. They seem once to have had a floor each, but their state subsidies were wound up in 1999, when the theme of 'refugees' was enlarged to take in, among others, the Jews. The fate of German refugees and Germany's ability to accommodate them has been invoked with reference to the Syrians and others who have settled in the country since 2015. Germany's openness to settlers is partly economic policy, dictated by an ageing population, but it is also, like so much else, a deliberate means of atoning for the crimes committed during the Second World War. Tolerance is an article of faith for most young Germans, and they extend it deep into their personal lives.

* * *

The stock Saxons, Rhinelanders, Prussians, Bavarians and Hanseats invoked by most Germans ignore the massive demographic changes wrought in 1945, when Germany was shrunk to fit into the borders dictated at Tehran, Yalta and Potsdam. Those who survived the treks or the cattle-trucks that shunted them from East Prussia or the Sudetenland were settled where local authorities could see a space. Rural Germany can be deceptive as a result. Take, for instance, Franconia, the northernmost province of the Free State of Bavaria. It was originally a collection of principalities part ecclesiastical, part temporal until it was tacked onto the Kingdom of the Wittelsbachs in 1806. It doesn't feel very Bavarian; indeed, half of it is Protestant. There is wine Franconia to the west and beer Franconia to the east. People say the natives are rude and nasty, but my experience has been precisely the opposite; when I used to seek solitude in lovely Bamberg, people always went out of their way to find out where I came from and sometimes even offer me a drink. As the eastern part of Franconia nudges Czechia, many German-speaking Bohemians ended up settling there after the war. The Bamberg Symphony, for example, was entirely created by the former Prague-based conductor Joseph Keilberth from the post-1945 stream of refugees from Czechoslovakia.[35]

A couple of decades ago I stayed in Franconia in Pegnitz's now defunct Pflaums Post Hotel. The atmosphere at Pflaums could only be described as 'camp'. Bayreuth was only ten or fifteen minutes away, and many of the leading lights of opera stayed in its suites designed by Dirk Obliers, where one could enjoy piped Wagner, sprawl on Brobdingnagian beds and relax to huge screens playing videos of *Lohengrin* or *Parsifal*. I was told that Pavarotti had been the first man to sleep in my bed. I was surprised that the springs had survived. At one point, a door of my bedroom mysteriously unlocked and I found myself wandering Alice-like through all the neighbouring suites. Each was individually decorated in the same lavish, operatic style.

When the atmosphere became too much for me I went out to explore the little town, which in its tranquillity contrasted starkly with life at the hotel. There didn't seem to be much in the way of amenities, but I dimly remember a pub. I popped into a church and read the notices outside. At that moment I realised that everything had been written in an unfamiliar dialect: part of Pegnitz had become a refuge for Upper Silesians after the war, and the parish notices were written in Wasserpolnisch. Now, these *Vertriebene* in Pegnitz were trying assiduously to keep their language alive. They were the ones who got away. Nearly half a million Upper Silesians had been isolated in their region after the war, chiefly when they 'opted' for Poland rather than Germany. The Poles liked to see these Catholics as their own people, and many were culturally both Polish and German in a way that few in largely Protestant Lower Silesia were. The reason why so many German-speakers had chosen Polish citizenship was that it was perceived as a means of stopping the nightly rapes and violence to which others wishing to remain German had been subjected. It also meant that they were not expelled from their homes and driven across the Oder-Neisse Line.

Before the 1991 German-Polish treaty of friendship, the remaining Germans in Upper Silesia experienced persecution by the Polish authorities and the German language was as good as banned. In August 1992 I was in the southern Polish town of Opole, formerly Oppeln, and met a woman who offered to pray for my soul if I gave her 10 Marks. The money also paid for a fairly vivid description of what life had been like for Germans in Upper Silesia since the late '40s. She was a widow who lived with her mechanic son in a country village. The German-speaking minority was not supposed to be in Opole, which was for Poles only. Her 88-year-old sister-in-law lived in Hamburg, and the year before she had been to Germany for the first time since the war. She had her eyes on a German pension, which was a little more generous than the 1,200,000 Złs (£50) she was getting every month from the Poles. She had actually come into Opole to have her passport stamped so that she could apply to receive a

German one. Living in Germany would put an end to her having to clean and take in washing for others in order to make ends meet. All in all, her existence was a little reminiscent of what the Nazis had had in mind for the Poles.

Although Poles learned German in order to get better jobs on leaving school, her own children were discouraged from speaking German for fear of being beaten up by the police, and places in higher education, she said, were not open to them. Poland's relations with Germany had been 'normalised' by the Treaty of Friendship the previous year, but improved further when Poland joined the EU in 2004. Young Upper Silesian Germans could now find full- or part-time work in Germany, even when they spoke next to no German. Friends of mine in the Mosel Valley, for example, employed them in their vineyards for the semester lasting from budburst to harvest. The rest of the year they could live on their fat at home.

Some Upper Silesians simply moved to Germany after 1989. The woman I met in Opole referred to it quaintly as '*das Reich*', 'the Empire'. This was an unconscious allusion to Hitler's policy of *Heim ins Reich* (Home in the Reich), which was intended to bring ethnic Germans back into their own racial territory. The Führer had used it selectively, generally to get Germans out of the Soviet sphere of influence before the 1941 invasion of the Soviet Union, or to please Mussolini when he yielded up the South Tyrol and parts of German-speaking Yugoslavia in exchange for support in Austria and the Mediterranean. The West German government echoed this policy when they sought to alleviate the various persecutions that took place after 1945 in Romania, Hungary, Yugoslavia and Poland. Any ethnic Germans arriving in the Western republic were housed and financially compensated. After 1989 the policy had a largely detrimental effect in destroying the last vestiges of ancient German communities: there were some 900,000 Siebenbürger Saxons living in Romanian Transylvania before 1989. There can't be 20,000 now.

In 1990 I made my first journey to Transylvania. We visited one of the beautiful *Kirchenburgen*, fortified churches, between Brasov (Kronstadt) and Sibiu (Hermannstadt). I saw an obvious 'Saxon' girl sweeping a porch and greeted her with '*Grüss Gott!*' She replied with the same without so much as lifting her head from her task. The probability is that, since then, she and her family have left too. A culture that dates back to the Middle Ages has been lost. One shining example bucks the trend: Klaus Iohannis, a former schoolmaster from Sibiu, became president of the republic in 2014—but his parents hadn't stayed in Romania long enough to witness their son's success. They had already emigrated to Germany.

A year before my meeting with the woman in Opole, I had encountered a Prussian near Malbork, the former Marienburg, home to the magnificent red brick castle of the Teutonic Knights. I actually met him on the train crossing the Vistula. We had been watching one another for some time. He was a man in his late sixties, accompanied by a little girl who was playing with his Polish passport. He seemed interested in my book, a history of modern Danzig/Gdansk, which had a large swastika on the cover. When I got up to photograph the castle from the corridor he followed me out and addressed me in German. He asked me where I came from. When I said '*Grossbritannien,*' he told me he had been there as a POW. It took a moment for the penny to drop: 'In the Polish army?' I queried, '... *Aber nein—Sie waren im deutschen Heer!*' (You were in the German army.)

He told me he had been captured in Holstein and that they had sent him to Britain. He had spent four years in the camps there. He must have been in the SS: most of those captured in Schleswig-Holstein were quickly released, not shipped to Britain. They let him go in 1949, but he determined to return to his West Prussian *Heimat*. Most of his family and friends had already been killed or deported, but he kept his head down and worked on the railways. He didn't want to be called Prussian—he was German, he said. Now he was retired and he was going to go to Germany, where he had been informed they would settle him in a nice, comfortable, modern flat.

He informed me that there was a concentration of 'autochthones' in Olsztyn, the former Allenstein, in the Masurian Lakes. The town was anything up to 20 per cent German. I went to Olsztyn the following day, and the very next morning I chanced on its Evangelical church. It was locked, so I had a look round the castle of the Teutonic Knights and then had a good walk, taking in the old garrison church instead. The next time I passed the Evangelical church, the door was open. There was little to suggest a German connection besides a notice in German reminding tourists to dress appropriately in God's house. Then a man came out of the vestry and addressed me in Polish. I replied in German. He answered in kind, and took me into the vestry. He had things to show me: a picture of Martin Luther, and the chandelier—a present from Queen Louise of Prussia dating from 1811. He could think of around 300 Germans remaining in Olsztyn.

The pastor confirmed what the SS man on the train had told me, adding that there were still around 200 families living in isolated farmhouses. They worshipped in his church on Sundays and were buried under the altar so as to avoid being noticed by the Poles. I assume most of these have now followed my ex-POW back to the '*Reich*'. I don't know how many of these pockets still exist. There are certainly some in the former Yugoslavia and the Czech Republic who are betrayed by their German names, but in reality they have probably long since ceased to think of themselves as Germans. In Hungary, there are still concentrations, and German-speaking Danube Swabians make the country's best red wine in Villány, or 'Wieland', as they might call it in unguarded moments.

* * *

Of course, other people have made their homes in Germany in the meantime—not only Turks, Africans and Middle Easterners, but also Jews and Russians. Many Jews came to Germany after Perestroika. They bought up businesses and opened synagogues. In Berlin in the mid-90s they were often to be seen in a kosher restaurant in the Oranienburger Strasse called the Café Oren. Germany has always had a vociferous Jewish Council based in Berlin, ever ready to step in and represent the relatively small number of Jews who live in Germany today. Ignatz Bubis was a prominent president from 1992 to 1999; he was succeeded by Josef Schuster.

Most *Achtunddreissiger*—chiefly Jews who left in or around that watershed year of 1938—are now very old, if not dead. Those who are not were very small at the time of their emigration. Many of their children grew up conscious of their roots, and the German connection is a powerful bond that unites some of them to this day in a love, at least, of German culture. Anyone who has attended the first night of a Wagner opera at Covent Garden will have seen that many London Jews do not subscribe to the contention that the composer's music should be banned.

With each generation, however, the cultural bond is weakened. Children who heard their parents whisper to one another in German learned the language imperfectly. Some of them were harder on the Germans of the Third Reich than their parents had been. I can think of several people born in the '50s or '60s who contacted me after the appearance of my book *After the Reich* who nurtured homicidal thoughts about Germans, and yet who admitted that their parents had told them there were good Germans, as well as bad. This was true of a charming old lady I visited in Finchley. Her mother, father and little brother had been killed in the camps, and she had escaped as a 'Winton Jew' on a *Kindertransport*—yet she wanted to see me in order to encourage me to write a book on German culture in Bohemia.

Her daughter, whom I also knew, felt very strongly about Germans, to the degree that she would not stay in the same room as one.

A few years back, I interviewed Sabine Henschel for *The Times*, former director of London's Goethe-Institut cultural association. When I suggested that the institute should target the children and grandchildren of *Achtunddreissiger*, she looked quite horrified. And yet both my children have learned German at school, and both are keen to maintain the family connection with Austria. When I made my annual pilgrimage to Wiesbaden in the old days, to taste the best German wines of the previous vintage, I was also struck by the strength of the *Achtunddreissiger* connection; on my left was usually San Francisco's assistant DA, whose Jewish parents emigrated from Germany and Austria; then there was Rudi Wiest, the top German wine importer in the US, who was actually born in Germany; and several others of this sort. On the British side, Anthony Rose, Stephen Brook, Michael Schuster and myself all had a strong interest in German culture that may have derived from our Central European roots.

* * *

When the Russians finally quit their bases in 1994, an awful lot of the men and their dependents refused to go home. Some became gangsters—a repeat of 1945, when many 'DPs' (displaced persons) took to crime. Others went native, blending in with the landscape. You used to see some of the artistic ones in the Café Hegel in Berlin-Charlottenburg. Many must surely remain. In forty years, there will also have been a great many half-Russian children born. The towns that appeared most denatured before the Russian departure were the garrison towns; Potsdam was one of these. Once, I strayed over the hill at the back of the Ruinenberg behind Sanssouci towards Bornstedt and found a series of slum-like streets that, it seemed to me at the time, were

100 per cent Russian. I think they must have been married quarters, because there were plenty of women and children about. Even in the centre there was evidence of prostitution. Again, for decades, there had been a ready market.

THE ONES THEY LEFT BEHIND

In the course of 1991 and 1992 I crossed the Oder several times in pursuit of Prussia, as I was working on a book on the subject at the time. My first goal was to get to Kaliningrad (Königsberg), located in the Soviet oblast that covered the top half of the old province of East Prussia. Getting there had involved a complicated duplicity, in which I was assisted by kind Poles to whom I was introduced by my old Bulgarian friend Evgenii Dainov. Principal among these was Paweł Gieorgica from the University of Warsaw. Both Evgenii and Paweł had been involved in the Perestroika movements in their respective countries. Obtaining the necessary papers had proven a long drawn-out business of traipsing between Polish government offices (re-entry visa) and the British and Soviet embassies (this was back in 1991). I very nearly had my application rejected because I did not have $15. Fortunately for me, a Vietnamese girl with a British passport was ready to take £10 from me in exchange for the dollars.

Once the application was lodged, I had to wait a few days for my visa. To kill the time, I decided to go to Gdansk (Danzig) and Malbork, where I met the former SS man on the train, who gave me the idea of going on to Olsztyn after picking up my visa in Warsaw. Apparently, I was going to Kaliningrad as an interested party in a joint venture investing in the oblast, the project of a nice lady in Ostrałenka called Jadwiga Karpińska. We left from Ostrałenka. In Galliny (Gallingen) we stopped to look at a sixteenth-century Prussian manor house that had belonged to a branch of the Eulenburgs before 1945. Jadwiga told us it was for sale, and would make a good hotel for German *Heimatgruppen*—only Germans weren't allowed to buy property in Poland. The old house, 'a profusion of gables arranged around a courtyard with a plain, main *corps de logis*', was near the former Bartenstein. 'A farmer lived in one wing; the rest was ruinous.'[36] We could see Bartenstein's town walls from the road. Shortly afterwards we reached the frontier, where there were ordeals to be gone through orchestrated by both the Poles and the Russians. I was greatly relieved when the Soviet official waved us on: I was finally on my way to Kaliningrad.

The city was a great disappointment: 'A few redbrick buildings, schools and the like, appeared to have survived the onslaught of British bombs and Russian bulldozers. We passed the miserable shell of the Cathedral.[37] The whole central island of the city had been levelled to make a park. Across the water, the old Stock Exchange was intact.'[38] We found a hotel and drank Königstor beer—a dark, amber-coloured fruity brew. The label showed a picture of a Germanic-looking brewery and announced that it was made by the Kaliningrader Brauerei, founded 1910. In the market I met a Swedish journalist who told me that in the suburbs there were streets with German street signs still, and shops with the German names still written above the windows. I saw a few of these later, when we left the city again for Poland.

There was a community of some ten Germans living in the city, who worshipped at the old Kreuzkirche. Their leader had fled to Latvia in 1945, and—like the SS man on the train—drifted back when he thought the coast was clear, in his case in 1970. The next day I saw him escorting a German *Heimatgruppe* and telling the story of his return from Latvia. He looked shabby. In Svetlogorsk, formerly the pretty little coastal resort of Rauschen, Germans had been busy writing the German names underneath the signs in Cyrillic. Such things, I reflected, would not have been possible in Poland then. I climbed down to a beach and watched another *Heimatgruppe* take off their shoes and socks, waggling their toes in the sand before paddling in the Baltic: experiencing, for the first time in decades, the sweet waters of home.

In 1992, I ventured out to Poznan, and down to Wrocław and Opole in Silesia. The soprano Elisabeth Schwarzkopf was born in the Grand Duchy of Posen in 1915, but the province ceased to be German at the end of the war three years later, as a clear majority of the locals were stock Polish. My interest there was in the huge Neo-Romanesque palace that the Kaiser had been constructing at the outbreak of war. It now serves as a 'cultural centre' for the city and is the home of the Poznan Philharmonic. Wrocław, formerly Breslau, turned out to be much more promising. Even the railway station reminded you this was former Prussian territory. The Monopol Hotel where Hitler addressed the Breslauer during the 1937 Gymnastics Festival was next to the Opera House by the younger Langhans, son of the Carl Gotthard Langhans who designed Berlin's Brandenburg Gate— Hitler was between operas in Bayreuth. My great-uncle Josef was working as a repetiteur there when he went off to war in 1914. He was killed the following year.

Wrocław had a buzz to it, one that I didn't find in Opole—but Upper Silesia remained home to anything up to half a million 'native' Germans, whereas the Teutons of Breslau had been thoroughly ejected and replaced by Poles from Lvov (the former Lemberg, now Lviv). In 1992, the Poles were still in denial about the so-called 'Recovered Territories', and no allusion was made in Gdansk, Poznan or Wrocław to the fact that these cities were once German. In Wrocław, I found that the famous Theresianum, the University of Breslau for which Brahms wrote the Academic Festival Overture, had carried over the traditions of the

University of Lvov, and many of the redbrick churches that had once been the stamping ground of German Lutherans were now administered by the successors to priests brought in from Lvov. Some Germans had made brave attempts to retrieve their old property. The late Gottfried von Bismarck told me that one of his aunts was applying for Polish nationality in order to recover the Iron Chancellor's house at Warcino (Varzin). She did not succeed. Otto von Bismarck's daughter-in-law Sybille committed suicide there in 1945; the last person to see her alive was the East Prussian journalist Marion Gräfin Dönhoff, who rode up on her horse on her way to safety across the Oder.

My final trip that year was to Szczecin (Stettin) on the left bank of the Oder. Strictly speaking, the West Pomeranian capital—then Berlin's port—should never have been given to Poland in 1945. The Allies, however, wanted Poland to have control of traffic on the river, and so it came to pass. The usual carpet bombing had ripped out much of the centre, but the Soldier King's two gates were standing—even if the Poles had lopped off the Prussian eagle and replaced it with a Polish one. Frederick William had acquired Stettin from the Swedes, and I saw a good stretch of Prussian barracks buildings on my way to the hotel. What I noticed at once was that there was less obfuscation about the history of the town than I had encountered in Wrocław or Gdansk. The people of Szczecin seemed ready to admit that it had only recently come to Poland. There was a market selling junk, much of it German: old watches and bad amber, SS buckles and a dagger. My eyes alighted on a little porcelain pill-box marked 'Schreiberhau' in Kurrent: a souvenir, presumably, from a pre-war holiday in the Silesian Riesengebirge. 'Packen?' the Polish lady asked in German, 'Fünfundzwanzig Mark.' 'Packen,' I agreed. I still have it.

The best bit of Szczecin is the Hakenterrasse overlooking the Oder. It is lined with big, confident Wilhelmine buildings that replaced a fort and some ancient ruins. There were whole stretches of tenement buildings that had scarcely registered their change from Germany to Poland. It struck me at the time that you could make films about pre-war Germany here more easily than in most parts of Germany itself.

CREDIT AND LOSS

There may have been little or nothing left of Germany in 1945, but some Germans were able to do very nicely out of the chaos, and end up dying in their beds, leaving millions of millions to their heirs. Some made a killing out of the black markets that proliferated among the ruins, bartering cigarettes for goods. Others turned their swords into ploughshares, like Captain Brückner in *Murderers Among Us*, who recycles steel helmets. A similar case was Karl Diehl in Nuremberg. Born in 1907, Diehl joined the family firm at the time of the Wall Street Crash, so he was schooled in economic disasters. His father had created a foundry that had sold products to Krupp and Man. Diehl joined the Party in 1933 and continued to make arms and munitions for both the Reichswehr and the Wehrmacht that succeeded it. As production stepped up during the war, Diehl employed slave labour and prisoners of war in his factories. After 1945 he was banned from business, but he managed to convince the Americans that he was just a fellow traveller looking after his family. Once he had his feet under the desk again, he made a fortune by selling off rusting military hardware as scrap metal. By 1980 his company was one of the most prominent in Bavaria.

Diehl still made the military hardware that was once again in demand when Germany remilitarised in 1955. The new minister of defence, Franz Josef Strauss, was as keen as mustard. The firm made clusterbombs, air-to-air missiles and as many as 644 warheads, not to mention fuses and timers. Diehl not only sold them at home, he had a good customer in the state of Israel, which he visited often in his private aircraft. To clear the air, his eldest son Werner had been sent to Israel to apologise in person for the company's use of concentration camp labour during the war. Not everyone believed that Diehl had done enough to atone for his actions, however. When the city made him an honorary citizen in 1997, there were loud protests. Ten years later Diehl gave Nuremberg a present of €100 million to restore or rebuild buildings damaged or destroyed in the war.[39]

Business slowed down in Germany after the *Wende*, which proved a costly undertaking. Nor could huge profits be made in the East for the time being. Any major ventures were hampered by the question of ownership. The business that did take off was small-scale: a profusion of sausage vans was about the first obvious sign of a new market economy; that and Italian restaurants of a cheap sort, which opened in virtually every corner of the old DDR, together with a smattering of Irish pubs. Once the Treuhand, the privatisation agency, had delivered its findings, however, the West could move in and grab what plums there were.

Some years after reunification, I was taken to the Volkswagen Factory in the Grosser Garten in Dresden, where they made two cars: the ultra-swanky VW Phaeton and the Bentley Flying Spur. It remains my only such visit to date. There was a certain logic in making both cars under the same roof, as I am assured that the Phaeton uses a Bentley engine. The factory was in an all-glass building by Gunter Henn, and was entirely silent. If my memory serves me right, the Phaeton cost around €160,000, so anyone who bought one was treated with respect. You came to the factory to pick it up, and were entertained in great luxury to all good things. I didn't have the nerve to ask whether they plied you with champagne. If they did, I presume they would then stop you from driving your car home and put you up at the city's best hotels: the Taschenberg Palais or the Palais Bülow for the night. In any case, the 'factory' was not all that it seemed: it was essentially an assembly plant for parts made in Zwickau. Bentley production has since returned to Crewe in the UK, and the factory stopped making cars in 2016. The Phaeton was the car that the extreme right-wing Austrian politician Jörg Haider was driving when he was killed on 11 October 2008. The name of the vehicle struck me as significant at the time.

Germany has ridden the storm of reunification, and looks sleek and prosperous again; but German economists will tell you that much is wrong. First and foremost, the country exports too much, far more than it imports. There is a surplus of €261 milliard. This would not be a problem were it not for the fact that other countries can't keep up. In France President Macron announced in 2017 that he needed to adapt the system of remunification, as production costs are higher in France. Germany is criticised for this on all sides. Even Donald Trump has tweeted, 'Bad, very bad.' The system forces other countries to borrow to pay for German goods, risking them falling into debt or even defaulting. Because neighbouring states can't pay for German goods, the Germans are forced to give them away: in 2000, €600 million disappeared in this way.[40] Politicians, it seems, are largely oblivious to the problem, or simply point out that Germany makes wonderful things: cars, washing machines, fridges, not to mention children's toys and all that *artisanat* that survives here and virtually nowhere else.

Another frequently heard complaint is that Germany has taken advantage of the Euro to trounce the opposition and wield a malign might over the rest of Europe. Had the Deutsche Mark still existed, they would not have been able to keep wages so low. German trade unions have remained weak and have not campaigned for higher wages, which would help the overall economic situation in general through the workers' increased purchasing power. Moreover, Germans would take more holidays abroad, thereby redistributing their wealth to other countries.[41] In Britain and Ireland, Germany has not only won out with its cars and dishwashers, but has also triumphed over native supermarkets with its discount stores, Aldi and Lidl—although I suspect that not one Briton in a hundred knows that they are actually German. Perhaps they are taken in by Lidl's cunning ploy of selling their brands in Britain with patriotic names like Waterloo, Trafalgar and Agincourt?[42]

Germany's richest businessmen tend to be shy, retiring people, and possibly for good reason. Like the banker Jürgen Ponto, Aldi's co-founder Theo Albrecht was one of the men who made his first steps in business back in the time of the cigarette economy. He was kidnapped for seventeen days in 1971, although it appears that the motives were entirely pecuniary in this instance and he was not threatened with Ponto's fate of execution (by the Baader-Meinhof/Red Army Faction). His kidnappers demanded and got DM 7 million, about £2.3 million at the time. The 'Pudding King' Rudolf Oetker was also subjected to a non-political kidnapping, even if his Nazi past might have made him a more likely candidate for the Baader-Meinhof groups. This time, the victim was his son Richard, who was brutally tortured until Oetker paid the sum demanded of DM 21 million.[43] Oetker is famous for mass-produced food and cheap fizzy wine, but the company still has a portfolio of good things, from breweries like Radeberger, Dortmunder Actien and Schöfferhefe, to wines like G H Mumm and Schloss Johannisberg, and hotels such as the Bristol in Paris and Antibes' Hôtel du Cap-Eden Roc.

Another victim was the cigarette baron Jan Philipp Reemtsma, who was abducted from his home in Hamburg-Blankensee on 25 March 1996. He was released on payment of DM 30 million after a month spent in a cellar in Garlstedt. When I was recently on a boat off the Côte d'Azur, the luxurious villa owned by one of Harald Quandt's five daughters on Cap d'Antibes was pointed out to me. The Quandt heiresses still possess a fair chunk of the German motor business, and their descent from Magda Goebbels must make them tempting morsels for this sort of crime, both for political and financial motives. Overall, though, such kidnappings seem to be in decline.

THE OUTDOOR LIFE

I have very little interest in sport and have only once in my life watched a game of football—as it happens, in a friend's flat in Berlin's Bayrische Viertel, when I saw the German national team thrash Brazil 7–1 in the 2014 World Cup semi-final. With the various heats going on during my time in the city, I was amazed by the very dignified way in which Germans digested their football, often sitting before large screens outside cafés while they ate their dinner. When the German team scored, there was cheering, but never any riots, even when the opposing team lodged a ball in the net. Sometimes people would take themselves to one side and let off a rocket. Then they would go back to their dinner and watching the match.

The Nazis were keen on football because they said it was sufficiently proletarian to suit their ideology. They held back from embracing it wholeheartedly, however, because they also considered it too 'foreign'. In the end, there were very few German sports to choose from. The best was athletics, and Germany won the 1936 Olympiad by a sizable margin over its chief rival, the United States. Dosed up with steroids, it seems, East Germany packed a huge punch at the Olympic Games between 1968 and 1988. Before then it participated in the Games as part of a united German team. In 1974 East Germany achieved the unthinkable and beat West Germany at football 1–0. Before the war, there was considerable enthusiasm for horse racing in Germany, with famous tracks in most cities. I have heard that there is good racing in Baden-Baden, and there is flat racing in Berlin-Hoppegarten, Munich, Hamburg, Frankfurt am Main, Bremen, Dortmund, Cologne, Krefeld and Mülheim an der Ruhr. I suspect motor-racing has more fans these days. Polo is obviously a minority sport, but I can boast that I have watched it played on the Maifeld in Berlin, the only time I have been inside Werner March's Olympic Stadium. I was told it was the sole custom-built polo pitch in the world; in 1936 the English team beat the Germans here. If they lack for team sports, Germans are certainly greatly taken with the outdoor life, be it cycling, hiking, hunting or skiing. The Hitler Youth gave hiking a bad name, but after the war the *Wandervogel* movement of youth rambler groups was revived, though it failed to keep up with the popularity of the German Scouts.

A fondness for returning to nature might account for the popularity of naturism in Germany. 'FKK' (free body culture) has its fans everywhere in Germany, but one seems to find more public nudity the further east one travels. We have only to think of Expressionist paintings—all that nudity in the dunes.[44] You might be excused for seeing something pagan in it. Near Berlin, for example, there is much naked bathing in lakes like the Scharmützelsee and the deep Stechlinsee of Theodor Fontane fame. It seems that, if you are not vigilant or stray too far, nudists will inevitably emerge from the woods. Even I was roped into it once. I was by far the youngest member of the party. Someone indulgently tossed me a towel as I came out of the water. Berlin friends go to the Hallensee early in the morning and Bavarians enjoy skinny-dipping too; there is a special nudists' reserve in Munich's Englischer Garten. A few years back there was a rumpus over certain naturists' tendency to float down the Isar river for some distance and come back to the park by bus. I don't suppose anyone asked for their tickets.

I am no more a huntsman than I am a football fan, and for that reason I have never stalked wild boar in the depths of Bavaria. A friend long resident in Vienna, who believes in the theory that some parts of Germany are still essentially pagan, has tried to teach me about German hunting lore. Of course, in this I have no real means of comparing, say, to French, Italian or Bulgarian practices, as I have never been hunting in those countries either. Fox hunters in Britain used to do odd things with the mangled corpse of the fox before it was handed over to the hounds. In your own country you do not ask too many questions.

Of course, to my eyes, it did look strange. I watched a film where a doctor was teaching new hunters the laws of the chase, and he explained everything clearly, placing the emphasis—as you might expect—on safety. Naturally, he said, the aim was not to shoot one another. The main beast to be shot was the wild boar, which he referred to as a '*Sau*' in the Bavarian manner, as if the male of the species (*Eber*) did not exist. To begin there was a proper greeting with hunting horns and a few '*Halalis!*'—the equivalent of the British foxhunter's 'tally-ho!' The new hunters stood around, mostly in day-glo jackets, but some wore pseudo-military gear and, as if to punctuate the doctor's speech, there was a lot of *Tuten und Blasen* by men and women with their hunting horns, holding their left hands on their hips. Every mention of '*Waidmannsheil*' (happy hunting) elicited the response '*Waidmannsdank*' (hunter's thanks), and vice versa. Non-hunters could greet hunters, but only if they used the correct formula.

A hat is obligatory, not least because it has a practical purpose: without one, you may not display your trophies. When the dead beasts were brought in they had to be eviscerated—the dogs profiting from some of the more perishable organs—and then laid on their right-hand sides. This, I learnt, is to prevent the *Erddämon*, the demon of the Earth, from possessing the animal. The leader of the hunt then proceeds with the awarding of the laurels. In this case, they were pine fronds, also used in Prussia to cover graves—which is almost certainly a pagan custom too. The *Schützenkönig(in)*, King or Queen of the Hunt, gets a sprig to place in his or her hat. Another is then laid on the head of the dead animal. Then there is more *Tuten und Blasen*, and a few more *halalis*. At the end of the hunt, of course, there is eating and drinking—and possibly a bit more of the latter than the former. The *nomenklatura* of the DDR liked hunting too, but they were keen to evolve a more 'socialist' and not entirely convincing version of the ritual.

I don't know if prostitution can be classed as a sport, though for its customers it must be at least a leisure activity. In Germany I suspect it is more often found indoors than out, in licensed brothels. The most famous brothels in Germany were the Eros Centre on the Reeperbahn in Hamburg and the Pasha in Cologne. The Eros Centre has since closed. The numbers of prostitutes operating seems to be vague, for all the obvious reasons. The figure falls somewhere between 50,000 and 200,000. There were believed to be 5,000 prostitutes in Berlin in 1995 and half of these were non-German. Many of them operated from seedy bars along the Lietzenberger Strasse in Wilmersdorf. After 1989 it was said that away-day Polish ladies undercut the prices of the licensed brothels. The border was only 60 kilometres to the east, and they took up their stations on the Kurfürstendamm, particularly on the stretch between Uhlandstrasse and Meinekestrasse.

DICHTER UND DENKER

The old Germany was perceived as the land of 'poets and thinkers'—although people said the Third Reich was more the country of '*Henker und Richter*': executioners and hanging judges. Traditionally Germans were proud of their education, both in their *Gymnasiums* or grammar schools and in prestigious universities like Heidelberg, Göttingen or Bonn. Many of Hitler's attitudes were anything but stock German: he despised the *Herr Doktors* and, despite the toadying of intellectuals like Martin Heidegger, he had scant regard for the universities, many of which he reduced in size or closed down altogether. The nobility also figured high up on his hit list, and he opposed the aristocratic *Mensur* or duelling clubs and *Burschenschaften* fraternities, banishing them in 1935. After 1945, educationalists like Robert Birley reopened the universities in the British Zone and Germany slid back to something like its former self; anything Hitler disliked couldn't be all bad, after all; so the duelling clubs were resurrected as well.

It was different in the East, where there were also prestigious universities like Jena, Leipzig, Halle and Berlin. When the capital's centre fell under Soviet control, some students fled from the old Friedrich-Wilhelms University in the Linden to found the Free University in the American Sector. The Friedrich-Wilhelms University dropped its royal Prussian name to become the Humboldt University, but the rest stagnated. Their resources were a fraction of the funds available to universities in the West. With the destruction of the old German universities east of the Oder-Neisse Line, such as Königsberg and Breslau, their traditions were adopted by universities in West Germany such as Marburg in Hesse, which became famously conservative and a haven for duellers.

Twenty years later, students claimed the atmosphere in the universities was 'suffocating.' Educational reform was one of the chief goals of 1968. Many Nazis had also slipped back into the faculties, including those who had worked on racial theory. There was a degree of anger with the academic establishment that stretched as far as condoning the Baader-Meinhofs. Since the '70s, the universities have adapted, while trying to maintain a semblance of excellence. German schools have also been reformed: the *Humanistischen*, based on the teaching of Greek and Latin, remain at the top of the pyramid, although access is no longer as limited as it was in the past. The hierarchical divisions at secondary level into *Gymnasium* (grammar school), *Hauptschule* (closer to a secondary modern) and *Realschule* (in between) are less noticeable now than they once were, and the *Gesamtschule* puts them all in the same box, so that children may aspire to move up a class. The *Abitur* leaving certificate has been simplified to open up the universities to greater numbers, challenging the supremacy of German higher education for the first time. Many of the most famous private schools have disappeared, but Schloss Salem flourishes, and is favoured by nobles. It is the father of Gordonstoun school in Scotland, which was created by Salem's Jewish first headmaster, Kurt Hahn, when he fled in 1933. Prince Philip came with him, hence the royal connection.

* * *

West Germany was an open society. Children were not indoctrinated by the state. In some cases they might have been corrupted by their parents, in others possibly by the churches. In the DDR, the Free German Youth (FDJ) slipped into the boots of the Hitler Youth. The regime, much like its predecessor, set store by controlling youth. The *Jugendweihe*, or youth initiation, was in lieu of confirmation, and involved a rite that, once fulfilled, declared the 14-year-old applicant a professed socialist.[45] Like the Hitler Youth, the FDJ was not always compulsory, but it was a ticket to mobility and helped young people go to university or otherwise prosper under the regime. About a quarter or more of all East German children were members, wearing their tell-tale neckerchiefs. Also like the Hitler Youth, they were occasionally despatched for political acts, such as the destruction of any lingering artworks with negative connotations: some villages, for example, had wanted to retain their statues of Frederick the Great, but the FDJ was sent in with orders to destroy them. Chancellor Angela Merkel is often attacked for not only being in the FDJ but for also remaining in its administration until her thirties. Yet, in a family such as hers, which inhabited the doctrinal periphery of the regime—West Germans, father a pastor, mother a West-German-trained teacher—it was important for little Angela to show her commitment to the regime if she was to succeed in her chosen academic field. Totalitarian societies are a mystery to people who have had the privilege of growing up in freedom.

The junior version of the FDJ was the Young Pioneers. Just as in Nazi times, impressive holiday camps were arranged for young people, where the cocktail of indoctrination was not so onerous as to spoil the fun of being in the mountains or at the beach. Sport was of huge importance, and anyone who excelled at it had a chance to make their way courtesy of the state. One of the greatest disappointments for people all over the Eastern Bloc when the *Wende* came was the loss of the privileges gained through their sporting prowess. Behind the Iron Curtain, different countries had different sporting specialities—in Bulgaria it was wrestling. When the wire came down, East German youth could enjoy the pleasures offered by the West instead: unalloyed access to pop music, McDonald's and Western television. With time, some former East Germans began to question what they had actually gained from reunification.

Of course, West German youth was not always sweetness and light. Working in the Staatsbibliothek (the 'Stabi') in Berlin for many years, I was able to observe the bad behaviour of German students. One habit which proved frustrating was the reserving of seats for their friends. British Germanophobes would be reassured to hear that they performed an action reminiscent of the famous 'towel-on-the-beach' beloved of the tabloid press. One student would arrive early at the library and get to the front of the queue. Once he reached the section that he and his fellows favoured, he would scatter books from the open shelves at all the places where he wanted his friends to sit. They would then roll in at their leisure over the course of the morning. The Stabi features in Wim Wenders' film *Wings of Desire*. It looks dated now, as so much has changed, but when I saw the film in Berlin I was amused to see my favourite seat, the one to which I always had to run like a hare to secure, and the library filled with angels rather than its more habitual trolls. Towards the end of the film, viewers see a pop concert in the bar in the Esplanade that has since become the Kaisersaal.

* * *

My brushes with academic life in Germany have been mostly confined to libraries and archives. I cut my teeth on the old Geheimes Staatsarchiv in Berlin-Dahlem, where I laid the foundations of my *Prussia* book. My first tussle with the Humboldt University occurred in 2005, when I attended the ICCEES conference on 'Europe Our Common Home.' Darra Goldstein, professor of Russian at Williams College in the US, had organised a conference on the history of food, and I read a paper on the contributions made by the Nazis and the Communists. It was my first time through the hallowed doors of the university. After the Allied bombing and the Russian campaign, I don't suppose there had been much left of the palace of Frederick the Great's brother, Prince Henry, which had been converted into Berlin's first university in 1810. The foyer had been rebuilt in a '50s idiom with a lot of gaudy marble. The lecture room assigned to our deliberations was at the end of a long, gloomy corridor right at the back of the building, and a complete slum. My second conference was organised in the summer of 2014 as part of 'Beyond Enemy Lines', a joint venture between King's College London and the Humboldt itself. Maybe the participation of the host institution was responsible for the rather nicer room we received, which looked out over the *cour d'honneur*.

About one German in a hundred is called 'Herr or Frau Doktor'. Traditional German tertiary education was shaken up by the Bologna Declaration of 1999, which led to Germany adopting an Anglo-Saxon model of BAs, MAs and credits. The old, long-winded process of *Diplom*, *Staatsexamen* and *Doktor* has been eroded, even if it still exists in some subjects—notably law, medicine and theology. Doctorates are really a German system that has conquered the world, probably via the United States. Oxford did not award any before the twentieth century, and in my time many tutorial fellows were still plain Mr or Mrs. This has completely changed now, when it would be almost impossible to get a university job without one. German lawyers might take their doctorates while they are doing the German equivalent of pupillage or articles. A physician could do his before the final qualifying exam. That being said, it is pretty well unthinkable that a physician or surgeon should be without one, and be addressed as 'Herr' or 'Frau': *das geht nicht an*—all doctors are doctors! I had a young friend in Berlin doing a medical doctorate. It involved a few cancerous cells, which he inspected from time to time, and about which he would eventually write a report.

Germans intending to teach at university level have to submit a second thesis, their *Habilitation*. In theory this will make them 'Doktor, Doktor'. With so many doctors in the German broth, there has been a recent spate of challenges to doctors among the great and good: Defence Minister Frau Doktor Ursula von der Leyen—a medical doctor—was accused of plagiarism. Her thesis was checked and her name cleared. Politics' golden boy Karl-Theodor zu Guttenberg, then minister of defence himself, was not so lucky. He too was accused of cutting and pasting, and had to resign in 2011. He has since quit politics altogether. The world looked on stupefied. You could not imagine anyone challenging John Prescott's O Levels; in any case, he probably would have admitted with pride that he didn't have any.

* * *

Most reputable journalists would have doctorates, which might account for the higher tone of German dailies. As the German press had become the voice of Joseph Goebbels by 1945, the Allies collapsed it, and carefully supervised the newspapers that came out of their separate occupation zones. The British were ultimately responsible for *Die Welt*, modelled on *The Times*, the mass-circulation tabloid *Bild*, modelled on the *Daily Mirror*, and the other papers that originated in Hamburg, which were at the core of the Springer Group. Also from Hamburg were the upmarket weekly *Die Zeit* and the various magazines like *Stern* and *Der Spiegel*. The latter was created by an Englishman, John Seymour Chaloner, who based it on *Time*. Other Britons owed their careers to brushes with the occupation press at the time, such as the broadcaster Cliff Michelmore, who worked for British Forces Network radio in Hamburg. The Reformation historian A.G. Dickens edited the local newspaper in Lübeck. It is perhaps ironic that the British took such trouble to rid German newspapers of propaganda after 1945. Today the German press could teach British newspapers a thing or two about avoiding propaganda.

The Americans had two bases: Frankfurt and Munich. The *Frankfurter Zeitung* was the German paper allowed its liberty for longest under the Third Reich, and the *Frankfurter Allgemeine Zeitung* (FAZ) historically nods to it. In Munich, the *Süddeutsche Zeitung* was founded just after the war. Most of these occupation-licensed papers were first edited by German-speaking Jews. In the Soviet Zone, the Russians created the *Berliner Zeitung*. The first paper to wrest itself free from Allied tutelage altogether was Erik Reger's *Der Tagesspiegel*. *Die Tageszeitung* (TAZ) is a useful far-left-wing cooperative newspaper based in Berlin that goes against the grain. Not only are the German papers solid and reliable; the remarkable truth about Germany is that you can even read informative stories in the local press. Even in smallish towns like Bamberg you can get the national and international news from a local paper; the same will be true of Memmingen or Kempten, which, although almost certainly produced in the same stable, are effectively tailored to their local readerships, while sharing national and international reporting with other papers by the same company.

In East Germany, news was chiefly disseminated by *Neues Deutschland*, a notorious propaganda sheet that was the mouthpiece of the ruling SED. It still exists, although its kudos is much diminished today. Just before they were ejected from their premises in the Französische Strasse, I had a privileged tour of the old Aufbau Verlag. Aufbau was the regime's publisher *en titre*, producing the books of favoured authors as well as very nicely bound (and cheap) versions of the German classics. The building, a former bank, was going to be returned to its original Jewish owner. The lift still contrived to smell of brown coal in 1995, and there was a club room where the old socialist publishers were waited on at table.

MODERNISM BECOMES ORTHODOXY

An ambivalent attitude to the past has affected the arts too. In this, postwar Germany was well tutored by the Nazis themselves, who were hardly tolerant of anything that resisted orthodoxy—although much that the Nazis promoted was traditional academic painting and sculpture of the early years of the twentieth century, rather than 'Nazi' art, of which there was comparatively little. After 1945, the Allies decided nothing was to remain of the traditional Germany, be it art, music or literature.

This remained mainstream thinking after the establishment of the two republics in 1949 and to some extent it is the same today. Figurative art was taboo, new music was Darmstadt, and Darmstadt exceeded all expectations by becoming a place of pilgrimage, attracting talents like Pierre Boulez to its electronic music. When Bayreuth was eventually resurrected, it was without the Master's sets, costumes and stage directions—the music said one thing, the production quite another; and yet, until comparatively recently, men and women attended performances in evening dress at dozens of provincial opera houses, as Germans always had done, filled with quasi-religious respect for music. Productions stuck strictly to the text and the audience listened in reverential silence: the day of *Regie*, where directors take liberty with the text, had not yet dawned.

In 1945, vast tracts of Germany had been destroyed, and only a fraction of residences were still inhabitable, yet one of the first moves made by the Allies—with the US leading the way—was to announce that more buildings had to come down, particularly if the structure exhibited militarist tendencies. Exceptions were made in cases where the building was useful to the Allies—the Olympic Stadium and Tempelhof Airport remained, for example, as did the Nazi buildings on the Fehrbelliner Platz and Göring's Air Ministry in Berlin. The Soviets were less fanatical about tearing down buildings. That was left to the SED once they had their own republic. At that point, the party blew up the Berlin and Potsdam palaces, the Garrison Church and Bismarck's birthplace in the Altmark. The latter was condemned for 'militarism', but one other Bismarck Schloss survived.

The Red Army raped the women and drank the wine, taking trophies where they could and bearing them back to Moscow and all points east. Artworks were no exception. In May 1945, the surviving sculpture from Hitler's Chancellery was appropriated, but in the end the Red Army decided against shipping it back to the USSR, depositing it on the barracks sports field at Ebersfelde on the River Oder. Shortly before the East German regime keeled over in 1989, men appeared with fistfuls of cash and the sculpture was taken away. That was the last anyone saw of the Reich Chancellery sculptures until the middle of May 2015, when they were unearthed at a storage facility in Bad Dürkheim in the Pfalz. When the news broke, it was assumed that they were just fixtures from the Garden front: two massive horses by Josef Thorak, a large relief by Arno Breker and a couple of nudes by Fritz Klimsch, but since the police first found the horde and made a series of arrests, two more Breker works have been mentioned, and there were reports that the police had recovered one or both of perhaps the most famous Nazi sculptures of all: *Die Wehrmacht* and *Die Partei*, the two male nudes by Breker that flanked the entrance to the Chancellery. Apparently some of Göring's treasures have pitched up too: sculpture from Carinhall, his country house, which was blown up at the Russian approach.

It is remarkable that anything survived. Much of the art created in the twelve-year history of the Third Reich was destroyed by bombs; other works were lost in the chaos of defeat; thousands were possibly burned, particularly in the US Zone, as a result of the Joint Chiefs of Staff Directive (JCS) 1067, which targeted the trappings of Nazism and militarism; while another 8,722 works were collected up by Captain Gordon W. Gilkey and shipped to the Pentagon as trophies. The vast majority of the latter have now been returned to Germany. Some of this official art of the Third Reich was found lying around when the Allies invaded, and a little has survived, buried deep in the cellars of museums throughout the land. The pictures returned by the Pentagon were taken to the Bavarian Army Museum in Ingolstadt where, it seems, they are kept in storage away from prying eyes.

Although there are a few private museums dedicated to artists who flourished during the Third Reich, such as Breker, there is still no official tolerance of Nazi art. The result is that there is no marketplace or guide prices for works of this sort. Collectors— and they do exist—prefer to remain anonymous, lest their motives be questioned. 'Dirty' pictures encourage shady dealers supplied by crooks. It has been suggested the men involved in the Chancellery heist were big batters in Germany's underworld. That they were able to hang onto the goods for a quarter of a century—and the works in question aren't exactly miniatures—is a testament to the continued embarrassment surrounding the Nazi regime. The art world would rather turn its back on the whole period.

Some Nazi works are displayed at the German Historical Museum in Berlin, but they are presented as historical artefacts, not art. As several national newspapers and Culture Minister Monika Grütters have said, what Germany needs now is a museum in which a collection of artworks could be displayed by Party members (of which there were in fact very few), fellow travellers (of which there were many more), war artists, portrait painters, unpolitical painters, artists forbidden to paint (including the universally admired but convinced Nazi Emil Nolde), and those branded 'decadent' by the Third Reich, who are more likely to find favour with art lovers today. Some contemporary artists—Breker, Franz Eichhorst, Albert Birkle, the etcher A.P. Weber—were excellent, and if the quality of the official works only rarely touches the sublime, this might simply prove the point that it is hard to make great art in a time of tyranny.

The discovery of the works not only revises our picture of what survived the bombing, but it also informs us of a shadowy world of Nazi art aficionados that might have been exposed long ago, had the German authorities exhibited a more grown-up attitude to the art of the period.[46] Even the well-meaning 'Gegen Kunst' exhibition at Munich's Pinakothek der Moderne, which ran in the second half of 2015, fell into the same trap of showing Third

Reich paintings and sculptures extracted from their own cellars and displaying them alongside selected modernist works—a technique painfully reminiscent of the 'Decadent Art' exhibition staged by the Nazis themselves in the same city in 1937. There were no denigrating captions as such, but the artworks were 'described' in texts that hung alongside. Germans therefore knew what they should like, and precisely what they should admire. To make the message clear, the gallery asked visitors to say which pictures they liked best. Naturally, the German public preferred the modern works. They would have been most reluctant to favour something that was branded 'Nazi'. In some ways, German official views of their art under the Dictatorship have scarcely changed since 1974, when Berthold Hinz wrote that the art of the period was 'either in private hands or hidden in sealed vaults.'[47]

Together with architecture, sculpture—particularly monumental sculpture like the pieces from the Chancellery—was more vulnerable to wanton or political acts of destruction and retribution than paintings, which makes the discovery of the Brekers, Thoraks and Klimsches all the more significant. Small paintings were liable to be stolen, as they could be easily taken off their stretchers, rolled up and hidden. It is quite possible that any number of fairly well-known Third Reich paintings are still concealed from view in Russian vaults, or suburban attic rooms in Montana or Wyoming. Who can tell what the future might bring to light?[48] Many people have suggested that the Allies—the American military in particular—destroyed large numbers of paintings in the more radical opening phase of the Occupation. Cora Goldstein, for example, contends that the Office of the Military Government, United States (OMGUS) 'obliterated the visual culture of the Third Reich', selecting the elements of 'Germanness appropriate to the new democratic Germany'. This purge was carried out in the interests of removing Nazi propaganda by the MFA&A, the famous 'Monuments Men', on the basis of JCS 1067.[49]

According to Gilkey, the top art man brought in by the US Army to assess the pictures, thousands of Third Reich artefacts were destroyed. He may, however, be referring to the pictures he himself decided against shipping back to the Pentagon, which were largely limited to war art.[50] Other sources refer to widespread looting, particularly by well-organised gangs of Russian displaced persons. The American authorities 'smashed countless statues' and 'burned thousands of paintings', although some were spared by theft. Many of Breker's works perished in a 'fit of vandalism'.[51] Christian Fuhrmeister of Munich's Zentralinstitut für Kunstgeschichte disputes this. He does not believe that the American military authorities indulged in more than sporadic acts of vandalism, such as mutilating Hubert Lanzinger's portrait of Adolf Hitler in armour.[52]

From what we know, over 80 per cent of the Munich-based sculptor Bernhard Bleeker's works were stolen or destroyed. Klimsch's studio was partly destroyed and the Americans plundered those of his works they found in Salzburg. Bernhard Graf von Plettenberg's sculptures for the Nibelungen Bridge in Linz were shattered and thrown into the Danube. The 3.5-metre *Mother and Child* was destroyed and his other works stolen. Otto Schliessler, Milly Steger and Gustav Seitz's studios were wrecked; as for Thorak, they smashed his Frederick the Great series as well as the Märzfeld groups, while GIs used his *Bekrönung* for target practice. Some pieces were mutilated, others were despatched to the US.[53]

* * *

Whether or not the works themselves were destroyed, the American military government's culture boffins made sure that the only art that prospered under the occupation was opposed to everything the Nazis stood for. The authorities used their own means to make sure that no one who was keen to adhere to the old idiom was allowed to work or exhibit, in much the same way as the Nazis themselves had controlled artistic output. Artists required permits in order to paint, and most Germans in 1945 or 1946 were more concerned about where the next meal was coming from than the fate of their masterpieces.[54] It was relatively easy to convince them to adjust. To name but two prominent Third Reich artists, both Werner Peiner and Arno Breker's styles changed radically after 1945. The chance of receiving a CARE parcel might even reaffirm your belief in 'non-objective' art.[55] Just as in the Third Reich, subject matter was circumscribed after 1945: painters could not depict genocide, Jews, the world wars or the Allied occupation. They were not encouraged to base their art on the world they saw around them.[56]

The Information Control Division was a 'non-violent version of the RKK', the body that oversaw the arts in Nazi times.[57] For many artists, this was otiose, as they had turned their backs on the more literal, pictorial art approved by the Nazis from day one. Others have attested to a positive flowering of the arts amid the ruins, a sort of 'compensation for the denial of materialism'.[58] Cora Goldstein says that some German artists threatened OMGUS with migrating to the Soviet Zone, where the Communist writer Johannes R. Becher was promoting artistic liberty, but this window was only open for a brief period. Once the Cold War began, it was slammed shut and Becher discredited. Imported art gurus such as William Constable of the Boston Museum of Fine Arts recommended a diet of non-German paintings for German artists, 'to correct the violently nationalist emphasis'. OMGUS, for its part, exhibited African, Asian and Pre-Columbian art,[59] and Germans snaffled it up with a huge appetite for culture in the immediate aftermath of the Third Reich. Contemporary American painting was also on the menu, and American art scholars were shipped in to lecture the Germans. *Amerika Häuser* came into their own as galleries for

American art and as places where Germans might be reacquainted with modernism. They could also 'advertise American achievements abroad and counter Soviet propaganda'.[60] JCS 1779, however, which eventually replaced the Morgenthau Plan-inspired JCS 1067, decided against the 'Americanisation' of Germany, opting for a gentler, more pragmatic approach.

The sight of modern art was supposed to civilise Hitler's former subjects, and American paintings were despatched to Germany to this end.[61] Between 1945 and 1949, there were 1,100 exhibitions in Germany; and in 1946 alone, over seventy in Berlin.[62] In the Soviet Zone, so-called 'degenerate art' was thought to be the medicine required. In August 1946, works by Barlach, Dix, Beckmann, Kirchner, Klee, Kokoschka, Käthe Kollwitz and Schmidt-Rottluff were exhibited together in Dresden.[63] In the West, Hellmut Lehmann-Haupt acted as a consultant to both the 'Monuments Men' and OMGUS, and encouraged the resurrection of non-Nazi German painters. Some, though by no means all, of those artists who had prospered under the old regime were handled roughly. Göring's favourite, Werner Peiner, was arrested by the British in August 1945 and not released until the middle of January 1946. His property was seized and he was incarcerated with 8,000 former Nazi *Prominenten* in Recklinghausen.[64] Wilhelm Petersen was interrogated for nine months in Neuengamme. Such brutality was rare, however. In general, the British were soft. They seized Goebbels's friend, for example, the rabid Nazi poster-painter Mjölnir, but released him upon payment of a small fine. The denazification judges deemed that 'political propaganda' was not a criminal offence.[65] OMGUS did not share this view—Philipp Rupprecht, the antisemitic cartoonist of *Der Stürmer*, was given six years' hard labour.

The 'Michelangelo of the Third Reich', Breker was probably the most spoiled artist of the period, and his oeuvre suffered accordingly. It was initially believed that everything the Russians found at Breker's studio in Wriezen was destroyed along with the neoclassical manor house.[66] He did not mention the works left in France at the end of the war that were auctioned off.[67] Breker's reliefs on the Nordstern-Gebäude and his fountain on the Rundeplatz were naturally shattered by bombs.[68] His studio in the Grunewald was also seized, and there are dramatic photographs of his sculptures lying in piles under a blanket of snow.[69] It is not clear, however, whether the works were eventually salvaged. Breker himself did not suffer particularly as a result of his service to the Third Reich. He re-established his clientele and was receiving official commissions from the Republic by the '60s.

In some cases, artists took care to disguise the Nazi element in the art they produced during the postwar period. Adolf Wissel's painting of a young girl in her BDM uniform was exhibited at Munich's Grosse Deutsche Kunstausstellung. After the war, it was returned to the painter with a request to paint over the offending dress.[70] The tapestries made for the German Foreign Office from Werner Peiner's cartoons were moved in 1944 to Schleswig-Holstein, where they were confiscated by the British and handed over to the Oberfinanzdirektion in 1948 or 1949. The latter offered to return them to the Foreign Office, but the diplomats were not interested. They are now to be found in the Conference Hall of the Northern Command of the Bundeswehr in Kiel.[71] Some things have survived in odd places. In the old Prussian House of Lords, Göring's fief by dint of his office as first minister of Prussia, Peiner had decorated the main hall with murals. These, I am told, were covered in plaster after the war. According to Christian Fuhrmeister, a similar fate befell Wilhelm Dohme's graffiti in Braunschweig Cathedral.[72] A lick of paint covered the Sistine Chapel of the Third Reich, Franz Eichhorst's murals in the Rathaus Schöneberg, but so far I cannot tell whether the changes were made more permanent in the years that followed. There is every chance that the murals are recoverable.

THE GERMAN PEOPLE

THE DENAZIFICATION OF ART

The American military government carried out a process of 'architectural denazification' from the start,[73] and a draconian purge was unleashed against the surviving oeuvre of Nazi architects. Although the issue remained undiscussed at Potsdam, when the Allies were meant to talk about the elimination of Nazi propaganda, on 22 June 1945 Munich City Council was ordered to remove all Nazi insignia from the city's buildings. OMGUS was created on 1 October 1945 and rapidly put through the Control Council Directive 30 issued on 13 May 1946. This was based on decisions taken at Yalta, where, on 11 February 1945, the Big Three had pronounced: 'we are determined to ... remove all Nazi and military influence from the cultural life of the German people.'[74] The Directive called for 'the removal of all Nazi-militarist influences from public office and from the cultural and economic life of the German people.'[75] Memorials and museums were in the line of fire, as the measure was designed to stifle the German military spirit.

The Americans were still on the lookout for visible signs of Nazi fascism such as eagles and swastikas. US Army Law 52 lumped traditional German art in with Nazi art and military art. All museums were closed on 24 July 1946 if they were deemed to perpetuate militarism or Nazism.[76] The order went out to the MFA&A and the Bavarian Office for the Preservation of Monuments that Nazi buildings had to be 'completely destroyed and liquidated by 1 January 1947', unless they were an 'object of essential public utility or great architectural value'.[77] Law 52 also made provision for the seizure of all property formerly belonging to the Nazi Party, the Reich or its states, or to any persons declared by OMGUS to belong to a prohibited organisation. It 'drew no distinction between the classic works of traditional masters and the martial designs composed by German war artists.'[78]

OMGUS' Title 18 covered the status of immovable works of art: churches, palaces, museums and libraries, as well as cultural objects and movable goods, archives, documents and books. The Monuments Men had a lot on their plates, and restitution was only a minute part of it. 'All collections of works of art relating or dedicated to the perpetuation of German militarism or Nazism will be closed permanently and taken into custody.' JCS 1067 had called for collection pending a decision, whereas Law 52 specifically stated that the works in question would be removed to the Pentagon—they were hell-bent on trophies.[79]

The Allies left nothing to chance. Control Council Order no. 4 ordered the confiscation of literature and material of a Nazi or militarist nature. This could be argued to include paintings. On 28 April 1946 came a directive to the commander-in-chief of the US forces of occupation, which was sent to Truman and transmitted to Eisenhower on 15 May: 'All archives, monuments and museums of Nazi inception, which are devoted to the perpetuation of German militarism, will be taken under your control and their properties held pending decision as to their disposition by the Control Council.'[80] The outgoing US secretary of war, Henry Stimson, created an Historical Properties Section within the Office of the Army Headquarters Commandant, charged with the collection of items for the Pentagon. Former chief of staff George Marshall made clear on 11 June that this encompassed paintings, photographs, maps and trophies. The document was then revised on 12 September to stipulate that the pictures and items taken were to be of 'actual or potential historical interest.' A fresh amendment added on 7 November that the booty should be sent directly to the Pentagon.[81]

Bavaria quickly appointed its own culture boffins after the war. A Dr Stenzel was placed in charge of denazification in the arts. His boss, Dieter Sattler, wanted to see an end to the mistakes of the Third Reich, but no 'art dictatorship, ancient or modern':[82]

in practical terms, that meant removing the *Hoheitszeichen* from public buildings—eagles and swastikas. Changes were made, for instance, to the Neo-Baroque House of German Physicians. The swastikas were struck off, but the eagles were left—some voices had been raised against the idea of taking off the eagles and OMGUS allowed for an element of flexibility.[83] There was no objection to the demolition of the surviving parts of the Wittelsbacher Palais, which had served as Gestapo HQ during the Third Reich, together with the Palais Törring and the Lotzbeck Palais, which had also functioned as Nazi buildings.[84]

The biggest rearguard action was fought over the Nazi temples commemorating the 'martyrs' of the failed 1923 Beer Hall Putsch, constructed on the Munich Königsplatz to Paul Troost's designs in 1935. Advised by John Nicholas Brown, Eisenhower ordered their demolition in late July 1945.[85] The Bavarian government, however, called for the retention of the temples and for the building of a monument to the victims of Dachau. In the summer of 1945, the martyrs' coffins were dug up and taken away. Cardinal Faulhaber proposed saving the temples by turning them into churches.[86] Despite the outcry, they were destroyed on 9 and 16 January 1947. The foundations have been retained because it proved impossible to destroy the 4-metre-deep air raid shelters beneath them.

Other Nazi buildings on the Königsplatz remained, however, because the Americans deemed they were 'objects of public utility'. These included the Führerbau and the Verwaltungsbau, though the earlier Braunes Haus in the former Palais Barlow had been gutted by bombs and was indeed demolished. Their *Hoheitszeichen* were nonetheless removed.[87] The Haus der Deutschen Kunst was virtually unscathed. The dramatist Carl Zuckmayer recalled seeing it as an American officers' mess during a student demonstration that threatened to get ugly in the summer of 1948. The Munichois had called it the 'Greek Station'.[88] The US military government co-opted it, and Americans played indoor baseball tournaments in the Hall of Honour.[89] Just as the East Germans were later to do at Hermann Giesler's Haus Elefant in Weimar, attempts were made to soften the Nazi lines: in the late '50s, a row of maples was planted to obscure the Third Reich facade.[90]

The other Allies also exempted intact Nazi buildings from destruction. The British maintained the Nazi buildings in their zone and Berlin sector, including the headquarters of the Arbeitsfront on Berlin's Fehrbelliner Platz, as well as the former Finanzamt in Charlottenburg. The eagle is still in situ in the last instance, but the swastika it once held in its claw has gone. Even in Soviet Mitte, part of Goebbels's ProMi was retained and is now the Federal Republic's Ministry of Transport. The largest reminder of Nazi times is Göring's immense Air Ministry.

GORDON GILKEY AND HIS TROPHIES

The Americans had got the bit between their teeth and begun looking for art under every bush. Two hundred masterpieces from the Kaiser Friedrich (now Bode) Museum in Berlin had been located in the Kaiseroda Salt Mines on 6 April 1945 and the pictures were taken in forty crates to Washington on the *SS James Parker* on 20 October.[91] The appropriation of this valuable national collection caused protest, but Senator Fulbright tried to prevent the entire haul from being returned before there was a recognised government in Germany.[92] The US military commander in Germany, Lucius Clay, was also in favour of retaining the paintings in the States until a gallery was ready for them in Germany, adding that 'the American public was entitled to see these art objects'. That Truman overruled him was in part due to Captain Walter Farmer, the author of the Wiesbaden manifesto, which protested against 'trophying' and encouraged prominent

Americans to do the same. The English-born, Oxford-educated art historian Captain Edith Standen was one of the signatories. The return of the horde was sanctioned in March 1948,[93] and the first consignment was shipped back to Germany on 17 May that year.

It is ironic that Gordon Gilkey's brief—to remove a large number of artworks produced during the Third Reich—may have performed a good turn for historians of the period, in that he inadvertently created a collection of Nazi war art. A print-maker and art teacher, Gilkey had joined the US Air Force in 1944, but did not see action. He was attached to the Office of the Historical Division of US Forces European Theater in Frankfurt on 9 May 1946. Large numbers of art repositories had been located, and their contents were transferred to the collection points at Wiesbaden, Offenbach, Munich and Marburg. Marburg was shut down on 15 June 1946.[94] At its height, the depot at Wiesbaden housed 700,000 objects, guarded by Edith Standen.[95] The works were all by Germans; none of them was looted from elsewhere in Europe.[96] The Pentagon was chiefly interested in military art. The quality of the pictures themselves seems to have been a minor consideration. Of these more martial collections, the Luftgaukommando VI collection was tracked down to Schloss Ringberg, near the Tegernsee, the home of the Bavarian prince regent.

Hitler's larger war paintings had been taken from Munich in 1944 to preserve them from the bombing and relocated to Bad Aussee, but they had been too big to go into the salt mines as planned. They were 'concealed in salt bins in the salt-refining plant where I found them', wrote Gilkey in his report.[97] He found similar treasures in a second-floor dance room above a pub in Sankt Agatha, Austria. In Frauenau, Bavaria, Gilkey located both Hauptmann Luitpold Adam and his collection of Army High Command paintings. They had been brought there by train; although it had been strafed, the pictures had emerged unharmed. The larger canvases had gone on to Schloss Oberfrauenau, the home of Hyppolyt Freiherr Poschinger von Frauenau. The watercolours and drawings were stored in a hut on the border, where they had been hidden by Adam, his wife and a 9-year-old boy.[98] There had been a battle between rival units of the SS around the hut and subsequently mice had damaged the paintings, but most of those retrieved by Gilkey remained in good condition.

Gilkey suffered from a few misapprehensions: he believed that the exhibitions at the Haus der Deutschen Kunst had been only open to Party members and that everything he found there was thereby fair game, but not even Wolf Willrich was a member of the Party, let alone Eichhorst, and the idea may have been aired simply to justify the US Army's policy of appropriation. He found what he was looking for in the basement. There were large rolled-up canvases from the 1944 show, but Gilkey was told that they were not 'war art'—but some martial pictures had been stashed behind the nudes and 'pastoral landscapes', and he also located some collections belonging to Hitler, Himmler, Bormann and other *Bonzen* in the Führerbau and further Nazi buildings. These may well have been dutiful acquisitions made with a view to distributing them to local museums and Party offices. Himmler's collection—which was more important—was found in the Befreiungshalle in Kelheim. Gilkey said that he unearthed works from the Chancellery itself, and others by artists who 'did not want their works left out of our distinguished collection'.[99]

In seven months, Gilkey put together a collection of 8,722 works by 379 German artists.[100] Some of the Third Reich artists were quite obscure, and many of the better ones left out altogether. OMGUS described this as 'legitimate booty' and there were plans to house the collection in a National Military

Museum,[101] just as the Soviets had originally planned to put their collections in a spanking new museum in Moscow. Gilkey organised a taster in the guise of an exhibition of 103 pictures at the Städel Gallery in Frankfurt, which launched on 6 December 1946 and was open to Allied army personnel only. It was held in the gallery's three serviceable rooms, the others having been destroyed in the bombing. It was very cold, as the rooms were unheated. When the show closed the pictures were returned to HQ.[102] Gilkey referred to German art as a 'tool to spread the manure of Nazism and Nazi-directed German militarism.' He believed in his role. Had the pictures been left in Germany, he said, they would have rekindled old passions. They needed to be delivered to the Pentagon.[103]

According to his own testimony, Gilkey laboured intensely, 'ignoring Sundays and holidays and working in an unheated damp room, with no ventilation or outside light, I became a recluse.' He put in between fourteen and fifteen hours a day, seven days a week, from 16 December 1946 to 20 March 1947. All the pictures were identified, to protect the American government from late claims and German demands.[104] Gilkey maintained that he had been scrupulously fair. He had talked to war artists and examined their works over a ten-year period. He had looked at studio paintings of the First World War as well as paintings and drawings by artists in the field in the Second. Roman Feldmeyer, for example, had painted pictures of Fromelles, where Hitler served, and Hitler duly bought his entire production. Gilkey was naturally interested in Feldmeyer's work. He immersed himself in the work of Otto Engelhardt-Kyffhäuser and Otto Bloss as well. They painted heroic feats. Gilkey believed that Germans had been corrupted by the things they had seen around them: 'These helped to build up a warlike spirit among the German people and were a manifestation of the feelings of the time.'[105] Gilkey's report also attempts to tell the story of the different German war artists and of the propaganda companies attached to the Wehrmacht and the SS.

Gilkey made another spectacular find of 1,000 paintings in Torgau in the Soviet Zone, guarded by a Lieutenant-Colonel von Fromberg. The Americans had moved out of Saxony in order to comply with the divisions established at Yalta, so it is not clear why these canvases fell under their jurisdiction. Gilkey also seized the collection of Luftgaukommando VI in Potsdam, again in the Soviet Zone, and watched over by one Walter Wellenstein. Possibly the Soviet authorities had granted him permission to fish in their pond? It hardly seems likely. Perhaps they had already taken any pictures that appealed to them. Gilkey was unable to find the Waffen SS paintings from the Kurt Eggers Group, which had been based at Zimmerstrasse 92. They were still missing at the time he filed his report. He was plain wrong to characterise Hitler, who had little time for modern painters, as a man who only liked 'monumental realism'; the Führer's taste in Bavarian nineteenth-century painters was more inclined towards cute genre paintings of toping monks. Signing off his report on 25 April 1947, Gilkey reiterated, 'If [the war art] had been left in Germany, it would have been a potential threat to the world through its future reinstallation and German mis-use.'[106] It may have been, however, that the tide was already turning: on 14 February 1946, Charles Fahy of OMGUS's legal division had made 'the seizure or damage or destruction of ... monuments, works of art, subject to legal proceedings', citing Article 56 of the Hague Convention. The wild times had been short; now international law was being re-established.[107]

WEATHER WITCH

Among the many things that remain vague about the postwar period, there remains a mystery concerning a particular exhibition of German paintings in New York. It seems that some art aficionado may have sent back things besides the work of German war artists. According to the weekly magazine *Der Spiegel* of 15 September 1949, some official Third Reich pictures were being shown. The article implies that they were all by Sepp Hilz, one of the most respected painters of the Third Reich, chiefly famous for his peasant scenes and nudes. The article, entitled 'Three Hundredweight of Weather-Witch', reported: 'Two million visitors in New York saw pictures that had formerly hung in the House of Art in Munich when it was still "brown". Who brought them across the ocean is a mystery to officials from the US Collecting Point.'[108] It is not clear exactly which pictures are meant, but the article specifically mentioned Sepp Hilz's *Die Wetterhexe*, which was certainly not a bit of war artistry, but rather depicted some mythical hocus-pocus.

To make matters more complicated, this very same painting was recently unearthed from a Czech monastery where it had lain since 1945 or thereabouts. There is no plausible explanation for it having been shipped back from the US to Communist Czechoslovakia. The story of the weather witch's reappearance on the Continent broke on 28 February 2012, when *The Daily Mail* reported on an amateur art historian called Jiri Kuchar, who had tracked down seven canvasses from a lot of sixteen, all of which had been shown at the German Art Exhibitions in Munich in 1942 and 1943 and then purchased by Hitler, to award to provincial art galleries after Goebbels's men had denuded the collections of most of their modern art. The paintings were discarded by the Americans in Czechoslovakia after the war. Hitler bought *Die Wetterhexe* for 35,000 RM in 1942. It is the hardest of the Kuchar paintings to make out in photographs published at the time; for some reason, there is no proper photograph of it. The composition, however, was well known in the last months of the war, as a postcard of it was published. After a five-year search, Kuchar had located this missing collection of Hitler's in a Premonstratensian monastery in Doksany, north of Prague. He had already found seven in Zákupy Castle, one at the Military History Institute and one in the Law Faculty of the Charles University in Prague. These were all that remained of an original lot of seventy pictures, thirty statues, a writing table and some gifts stored in Vyšší Brod Monastery. When the monks got their abbey back after the war, they took a dim view of the paintings, which went their separate ways. Perhaps *Der Spiegel* received false information about the Hilz painting, but the story is nonetheless confusing.

RESTITUTION

On 2 September 1949, OMGUS was dissolved and replaced by the office of the US High Commissioner for Germany. It was formally abolished on 5 December 1949. Perhaps the Americans took stock of Gilkey's assertion that the pictures would have a deleterious effect on those who saw them, for the projected museum was never built, and the Gilkey collection soon became an embarrassment to the US government. On 4 October 1950, it was decided that 1,600 of the artworks removed to America had no military relevance at all, and that they were to be returned to their painters. It was also stated that 1,560 pictures had been 'erroneously seized'.[109] Bonn refused to accept the Nazi pictures at first, but eventually 1,659 paintings were returned and stored in the Führerbau in Munich.[110] In 1955, the Sudetenländer Olaf Jordan petitioned the US government for the return of thirty paintings, all his other works from the period having been destroyed by the Czechs. A similar petition was presented for Claus Bergen's maritime paintings, but it required a Congressional bill before they could be released and returned to Germany.[111]

Even after Ronald Reagan approved the return of 5,850 pictures from the Gilkey collection in 1982, there were problems at the receiving end, caused by German embarrassment about the art of the Nazi period. When the pictures were returned from the United States they were instantly buried in the vaults of the Bavarian Army Museum in Ingolstadt, and only those with genuine academic credentials were allowed to see them.[112] They have since been transferred to the Museum of German History in Berlin, but they remain in storage and are only shown when they fit into the theme of an exhibition. At the time of writing, about 450 works remain in the United States. In theory, at least, they are hardcore Nazi war art; in practice, however, that is not always the case. Together with four of Hitler's friend and photographer Hoffmann's own collection of the Führer's paintings, they include a typical SA picture by Elk Eber, three military Eichhorsts, four Engelbert-Kyffhäusers, three Fritz Erlers, two Feldmeyers of Fromelles, one Gehardinger, two Olaf Jordans and two Franz Gerwins; three Conrad Hommel portraits including a Hitler and a Himmler; three SA scenes by Hermann Otto Hoyer, including the celebrated *In the Beginning Was The Word*; the famously slashed Lanzinger picture of Hitler in armour; four Lipuses; as many as fifteen pictures by Wilhelm Otto Pitthan, including portraits of Bormann and Rosenberg; six woodcuts by Georg Sluyterman, and four by Eduard Thöny; Vietze's portraits of Frank and Heydrich; and four Willrichs. There are portraits of Hindenburg, Bismarck and Ludendorff too, and quite a few pictures painted before the onset of war, as well as a few that even date from before the Third Reich.[113]

Since the war, Jewish or part-Jewish art collectors have played their different roles in enriching Germany's collections again. One of these was Heinz Berggruen, who, despite the way he was treated during the Third Reich, was convinced to return to the Berlin of his birth—together with 113 canvases that would form the nucleus of the Berggruen Museum in the affluent borough of Charlottenburg. In 2000 he sold 165 works to the museum, including eighty-five Picassos, for around a quarter of their market value. For Berggruen, it was a 'gesture of reconciliation', after the Nazis had impoverished German collections of modern art. He even convinced his fellow Berliner Helmut Newton to donate his photographic collection to the city. He was given a flat above the museum, and one of his chief pleasures was to show people round.[114]

But you win some, and you lose some. Although it was widely supposed that the collection of decadent art housed in Cornelius Gurlitt's Munich flat did not rightfully belong to him, it did, and it ended up going to the Swiss in Basel. It was the most spectacular discovery of lost art treasures of the young century. On 3 November 2012, the German magazine *Focus* splashed the story that 1,406 valuable canvasses had been found lodged behind fruit juice cartons and food tins in the northern borough of Schwabing. A litany of famous names was pronounced: Picasso, Matisse, Chagall, and the Germans Nolde, Franz Marc, Beckmann and Liebermann. Most of the art, it seemed, was modern, but there were old masters too, such as Dürer and Canaletto.

The gestation of the story was remarkably long: on 22 September 2010, the septuagenarian Cornelius Gurlitt was stopped on a train travelling from Switzerland, on suspicion of carrying an illegal sum in cash. Further investigation revealed him to be a life-long tax evader. The following spring, inspectors raided his flat and found the pictures. They had been assembled by Cornelius's father, Hildebrand Gurlitt (1895–1956), who had led the Zwickauer Museum until 1930 and specialised in the avant-garde. Hildebrand's father had been in the business too, and a nephew, Wolfgang, ran the family gallery in Berlin.

Naturally, neither Hildebrand's less-than-pure Aryan ancestry nor his fondness for modern art had endeared him to the Nazis, but he had found his feet. In 1937, a group of 'experts' assembled by Propaganda Minister Joseph Goebbels dropped in on various state-owned galleries throughout the Reich and confiscated works deemed to be 'decadent'. There are believed to have been as many as 20,000 of these, including works left behind by Jews forced to emigrate or worse. About 650 of them were put on show during the art week that accompanied the Great German Art Exhibition in Munich in July 1937. The show toured other cities before being inspected by Hitler in January 1938. He decided that the whole collection should be destroyed.

Goebbels was more pragmatic, and thought that some money could be made from this 'manure'. He might have been on the side of the angels: he had been a collector of Nolde and Barlach himself before 1933. A team of salesmen was assembled: two Gurlitts, Kurt Buchholz, Bernhard Böhmer and Ferdinand Möller, who were compensated with a 20 per cent commission. The collection proved hard to sell, however—when the project ground to a halt in June 1941, there were still 5,000 works left. These disappeared without trace before the end of the war. Gurlitt had other work. Through his friend Hermann Voss in Dresden, he was supplied with credit to acquire pictures for the Führer's planned museum in Linz. The Dürer and the Canaletto in the horde found at his flat might have been bought for that purpose. He also attended auctions at the Hôtel Drouot in Paris and acquired both Impressionists and part of Paul Rosenberg's famous collection. These pictures were not for Hitler, however, who had no time for Impressionists.

After its discovery, Gurlitt's collection was examined by Rosenberg's son, Alexandre, and found to contain many pieces of art that had once hung in his home; but it is to be assumed the sale was legal. Hildebrand Gurlitt cruised through the denazification process after the war: a Jewish grandmother helped, as did the admission that he had given Jews money—that is, he had sold them Hitler's rejects, or had bought their paintings at risible prices. As for his own stock, he said it had gone up in smoke in the Allied bombing of Dresden. Of course, he was wrong not to own up at the end of the war, but at that time the Russians had been in the process of shipping a horde of 800,000 stolen paintings back to Moscow, and, as we've seen, the Western Allies were not so scrupulous either. Most soldiers were looking for souvenirs, and some small acts of plunder were considered normal, if not justifiable.

NO TIES WITH THE PAST

A country out of love with its past is prone to acts of iconoclasm. At a Bielenberg family wedding in County Carlow in 1997, where many of the guests were German, a middle-aged East Berliner asked me to help him tie his tie, as he had never learned how to do it. An interesting discussion ensued. He felt that all monuments to Germany's past needed to be destroyed to remove the stain of the Third Reich. I asked—tongue in cheek—if we should destroy the German language too, as that was equally stained. He reflected for a while before answering that yes, that would also be a good idea. The destruction of monuments that were not created under the 'right' conditions could be advanced in highly educated circles. A friend was not, I think, joking when she told me that she approved the destruction of the Pyramids in Egypt because 'they were built by slaves and women were not equal to men.' Apparently, in this proponents of political correctness and ISIS share some common ground.

The sociologist Urs Müller-Plantenberg once told me that the removal of ties had been one of the great achievements of 1968. Karl Heinz Bohrer tells a story about this in the latest volume of his autobiography *Jetzt* (Now): some time in the early '70s, the philosopher Jürgen Habermas and his assistant came to a small New Year's Eve celebration at Bohrer's flat in Frankfurt. Two couples were already there, dressed in dinner jackets with starched shirts and bow ties. Habermas was obviously dressed in a shirt and tie, but he had brought an assistant, who was got up in jeans and jumper. Bohrer's guests were, a lawyer and a man doing his *Habilitation* in the philosophy of law. Habermas's assistant shouted at them, 'You penguins, you bloody arseholes, you exploiters! What do you think you look like!' The women were castigated as whores. When the assistant tried to rip off one of the offending ties, the legal philosopher punched him hard enough to send him reeling from the room. The concerned legal philosopher's wife found him crying, clinging to a lamppost in the street below—by now sobered up and too ashamed to return to the party.[115]

WIEDERGUTMACHEN

Wiedergutmachen is another way of saying 'making it alright again'. Since the *Wende* some of the Eastern buildings that were so insufferable to the SED have gone back up. In other cases there are still plans to rebuild them. In Dresden, the DDR had already painstakingly rebuilt the Zwinger palace, the Catholic court church and the Opera, and made a start on the Royal Palace. Since the *Wende* other marvels have been performed; the Protestant Frauenkirche has finally been rebuilt from the salvaged and numbered old stones, and reconsecrated. The Green Vault treasury has been opened to the public, along with the Crown Prince's residence in the Palais Taschenberg. As a culture boffin in Dresden memorably informed me, 'We are the only city in Germany that can boast of a greater number of historic buildings every year.' The area around the old market square, now supposedly reconstructed to look as it once did, now has a Disney-fied, touristy atmosphere—possibly not helped by the identical brand names found in the centre of every city in the world.

In Berlin, the Royal Schloss is due to be completed in 2019. The only piece of the vast complex to survive the barbaric demolition of 1950 was the window from which Karl Liebknecht announced the socialist republic on 9 November 1918, although much of the sculpture had been taken away and stored before the demolition men went in. When I was last in Berlin in 2014, I found it fascinating watching the new building taking form. From the far side of the Spree you could still see the base of the colossal statue of William I erected by his grandson, which replaced a range of ancient buildings called the Schlossfreiheit. The new brooms in 1945 showed no sympathy for the Begas statue, and swept it all away in the fight against militarism. I admired the little bit of Schinkel's Bauakademie, which had gone up as a foretaste of things to come. On the steps of St Hedwig's, I met a man from Leipzig who was speaking at the same conference. Unlike me, he deplored the construction of all these expensive 'fakes'.

I had been in Berlin briefly the year before to give a lecture on Frederick the Great at Schloss Charlottenburg. I went to a tasting in the Potsdamer Platz and saw how the area around the Stabi had become a lake surrounded by beaches, but didn't have time to go to the Linden and see what progress had been made on the Schloss. The DDR restoration of the Linden had been less scholarly than some. In one or two cases, the buildings that went up were mere pastiches, but at the eastern end, at least, you had a feeling of the Linden's grandeur at its zenith. Since the *Wende*, the old military governor's palace has been rebuilt from scratch as the headquarters of the Bertelsmann publishing empire.

In its destructive zeal, the SED had knocked down what remained of the Bauakademie in 1962 to build its foreign office. In

April 1996, I saw that the latter had been pulled down to expose the same architect's perpendicular gothic Friedrichswerdersche Kirche, with a view to possibly rebuilding the Bauakademie; one corner had been re-erected. This operation was not entirely successful, as I noted at the time: 'The church has a big bottom.'[116] Perhaps the oddest spectacle I witnessed in 1996 was watching the workers crating up the Kaisersaal of the old Esplanade hotel and shipping it across the road in preparation for the Potsdamer Platz development. In the process, they destroyed the Neo-Baroque decoration at the back of the remaining piece of the hotel. More than ten years later, no more bits of the Bauakademie have reappeared. Fortunately the reliefs had been put into storage, like almost all the exterior stonework from the palace in Potsdam. I recall walking round the site at Potsdam in 2013 and watching, to my delight, lorries pitching up laden with baroque curlicues and volutes. A year later, I attended Mass in the Hedwigskirche—which serves as the city's Catholic cathedral, and was also gutted during the war—and saw that there were plans to rid it of some of the more jarring features introduced at the time of its reconstruction.

One of the most prominently restored buildings has been the Reichstag. It was partly restored and redesigned by the British celebrity architect Norman Foster, who supposedly modelled the new dome on a table lamp. I have been round it a couple of times, once as a guest of the VDP wine association, and on another occasion when I attended an A.T. Kearney CEOs' conference as a Berlin expert. On both occasions I had the chance to look at the preserved graffiti from the time the Russians captured the building, but the staff are quick to tell you that the more obscene elements have been washed away. It was also on the A.T. Kearney trip that I had dinner in the Frank Gehry-designed DZ Bank building on the Pariser Platz. The exterior subscribes to the usual bland style of the new square, but on the inside there is an enormous fish, or rather a Leviathan, which is used for conferences.

The guest of honour at the dinner was the former West German president Richard von Weizsäcker; there was a small queue to shake his hand at the close. A.T. Kearney put us all up at the Adlon. For me, at least, the reconstruction of the Adlon Hotel was a special case. This was not a faithful reconstruction by any means, and many chances were lost when an unconvincing pastiche went up on the site of the old building, most of which had been consumed by a mysterious fire soon after the Soviet Army occupied the city. Some bits had survived, however: it is astonishing to think the dining room was only demolished in 1984. I had a little suite overlooking the Holocaust Memorial, which was just beginning to be built at that time. Much later, I would watch my 11-year-old son gallivanting around the stones, occasionally disappearing and re-emerging. I was not certain that I was entirely convinced, but he and many other children were having a good time. Now I hear from the same source that children are no longer allowed to jump on top of the stones. To some extent, the same impracticality of design is also found at Daniel Liebeskind's Jewish Museum, where I was shown around by a young woman who had clearly drunk deeply from the architect's theories, including the huge projection of his own ego. The design itself was nonetheless impressive, particularly when it came to the notions of oppression, dead ends, or brutal fate; but once the spaces filled up with exhibits, it was no longer quite so stark or shocking. Indeed, using the space as a museum was bound to nullify the whole concept.

Potsdam lost much of its charm with the bombing of 14 April 1945. More went in the Cold War period as a result of the SED's determination to obliterate the Prussian past: the Royal Palace, the Garrison Church, the Heilig Geist Church (demolished in 1974),[117] and other significant ruins. In their stead had come

Plattenbauten—vast canvasses for spraypaint vandals. The post-*Wende* restoration began with the canals, buried since 1945, and continued with the Royal Palace, which returned as the new local parliament building, or Landtag. Large amounts of the money required were provided by the computer millionaire Hasso Plattner, who has since financed the rebuilding of the nearby Palais Barberini—bombed flat on 14 April 1945. The site was briefly occupied by a corrugated iron shed that served as a theatre.

Now, visitors to Potsdam who arrive from the east see the place as it was. When I was last there, plans were afoot to pull down the concrete building behind the Palace and reconstruct the Garrison Church to the south, a veritable temple to Prussianism. The greatest eyesore left in Potsdam today is the high-rise hotel originally built as an Interhotel and most recently managed by the French Mercure chain. Plattner also offered money to have it removed. To a lesser extent, the television host Günther Jauch—another Potsdam resident—has also helped finance the restoration of the city's lost or dilapidated monuments. Hanover's Herrenhausen Palace, formerly home to the Hanoverian dynasty who became kings of Great Britain, was also rebuilt to celebrate the tercentenary of the kings' translation to London.

ARTS EAST OF THE ELBE

In April 1996, I took a bus from Berlin to Gera with a group of up-and-coming British painters who were exhibiting there. Naturally they were all considered avant-garde, and the newly liberated East Germans in the Thuringian city lapped it up. There was a calf's head from Damien Hirst and a medical cabinet filled with tampons and ill-spelled letters about abortion by Tracey Emin. I forget the author of an arrangement of chamber pots and a blanket—possibly I was distracted by a black-and-white photograph of a woman with her legs apart performing fellatio. I am sure the other works were equally distinguished. The locals loved anything that flew in the face of tradition; the British were clearly onto a winner, and German millionaires would stop at nothing to obtain the latest shock-horror pictures from Britain. Having put up with socialist realist works throughout the DDR years, now the people of Gera had their chance to appreciate something truly contemporary. The West, too, wants its spaces dedicated to the truly modern. In October 2002, I was allowed to look over the new Pinakothek der Moderne in Munich a few days before it was opened by the CSU leader Edmund Stoiber. It was a refreshingly relaxed occasion: 'A Braque lay on the floor, a Picasso had been tossed against a wall. A few Marcs and Kandinskys were already hung, as were the modern heroes, Beuys and Baselitz.'[118]

The East had had vaguely different objectives—not only to fight the memory of Nazism, but also in opposition to the imperialism of the West. Painters in the Soviet Zone and then the DDR were no freer than they had been under the Third Reich. They were to avoid formalism—no art for art's sake; instead, arts had to embrace social realism, and each picture was to be a statement about society—socialist society. Another banned area was abstraction. Where American art fanatics in particular had encouraged abstract expressionism, the East German authorities were as opposed to it as Hitler had been. East German art had to pay permanent lip service to the Soviet Union's role in liberating the country from Nazism. The true appreciation of Bach, they were told, was only possible after the destruction of German fascism by the armies of the Soviet Socialist Union.[119] *Kulturbarbarei* was summed up by jazz, Western dance music, abstract painting, crepe soles, blue jeans, stripy socks and chewing gum.

The saddest story of culture in the early history of the DDR was that of Johannes R. Becher. He had been a fine expressionist poet before the war, had taken refuge with the other *Moskowiten* in Moscow's Hotel Lux, and had returned in 1945 to serve as the DDR's chief cultural spokesman. Many of the leading lights of German literature had emigrated during the Reich; most returned, and quite a few of them to the East, where Becher offered them a safe haven. Only a handful of hardened Marxists like Brecht stayed on the far side of the Elbe for long after Becher fell from grace. It was a tragic decline.

LITERATURE IN THE WEST

In the West, the schmalzy, nationalist literature of the Third Reich gave way to a new school of realism. Gruppe 47 heralded the rebirth of literature among the younger generation, and Heinrich Böll described the new Germany in its formative years in his short stories and novels. With time, it seems, realism was opposed by magical realism, while many German writers have been challenged by the past, and the need to answer the obvious questions about 'why'. That other great postwar voice and fellow Nobel laureate, Günter Grass, put the Nazi period and the post-war years under the microscope in *The Tin Drum* (1959) and in *Crabwalk* (2002). The latter examines three generations of the same family who react against one another: the grandmother was a Nazi, her son is an *Achtundsechziger*—one of the student revolutionaries—and one grandson is a neo-Nazi. It all rang true. I had read an interview with a skinhead in *Die Zeit*, pictured giving a Nazi salute. When the interviewer asked why he did that, he replied, 'Because it provokes my mother.'[121]

By the '60s, German literature was roughly cleft between the materialists and the fantasists. The right-thinking left wing of the first generation to come of age after the war clung to Marxism, rejecting magical realism as bourgeois pap. Karl Heinz Bohrer, who has held the two most important jobs in German literary life—literary editor of the *Frankfurter Allgemeine Zeitung* and editor of the monthly *Merkur*—had left school in the early '50s as a devotee of French surrealist literature. In the '60s, he witnessed the rediscovery of Walter Benjamin, the Jewish critic who committed suicide fleeing the Nazis in 1940. German literature found an unusual arbiter in the form of Marcel Reich-Ranicki, a Polish Jew brought up in Berlin and expelled across the border in 1938. Once the Germans invaded Poland less than a year later, Reich-Ranicki went into hiding, while his family was fed into the jaws of the Final Solution. His television programme, 'Das Literarische Quartett', and his stinging criticisms were enough to provoke terror in the breasts of both budding and established novelists. When Martin Walser wrote *Tod eines Kritikers* (Death of a Critic*)* in 2002, about a writer murdering a Jewish critic, it provoked outrage: there are some things you simply cannot do in Germany, and that was one of them. Reich-Ranicki himself contented himself with giving the book a suitably bad review.

German literature is like German everything else: obsessed with Germany's past. Writing is a form of atonement. W.G. or 'Max' Sebald had the distinction of being a German writer who was, for a time at least, better known in Britain than in Germany. His long, stream-of-consciousness novel *Austerlitz* (2001) deals with a former *Kindertransport* child who is trying to piece together his past and understand his mother's death in Theresienstadt. Hans Magnus Enzensberger's biography of General Kurt von Hammerstein-Equord, *Hammerstein oder der Eigensinn*, takes another approach. It dwells on an intriguing moment when the German army could have eliminated Hitler before it was too late, and on the chief of the General Staff who allowed his sons to participate in the plot to kill him. Kurt von Hammerstein died in 1943, but approved their actions. His son Ludwig I later met and interviewed at his home in Dahlem. On

20 July 1944 he had been in the Bendlerblock with Stauffenberg. He managed to escape because he knew the building intimately—his father had had a flat there. My tea with Ludwig Hammerstein was one of the most moving experiences I have had in Germany.

CINEMA

After the war, German cinema came quickly back to life on both sides of the wire—even if, at first, some of the better films were made by the state studio in the Soviet Zone. The studios had survived intact in the Potsdam district of Babelsberg. The West German equivalent developed in Munich. One film made at Babelsberg was the 1946 *The Murderers Are Among Us*, which went straight to the heart of the matter. The film was directed by Wolfgang Staudte. What makes it so unusual now was that the themes that would be shunned in the '50s are all there: Auschwitz, the killing of civilians, unrepentant Nazis hiding from justice, and the fate of refugees. The film was made at Babelsberg after permission was granted by the Soviet cultural supremo, Colonel Alexander Dymschitz. The other Allies refused to help. It premiered on 15 October 1946 at the State Opera House (Titania Palast) in Berlin, the same day as the death sentences handed down at Nuremberg were carried out.

After a brief intermission, the Babelsberg studios passed into the hands of the SED. That did not bring good films to an end by any means. Take *Somewhere in Berlin*, a 'Trümmerfilm' shot in the ruins that focused on the city's children, who see the shattered urban landscape as a huge adventure playground. It featured Fritz Rasp as the classic German villain; he had been the 'Thin Man' in Fritz Lang's silent film *Metropolis*. Also released in 1946, *Ehe im Schatten* (Marriage in the Shadows) was inspired by the tragic suicide during the Third Reich of the actor Joachim Gottschalk and his Jewish wife.[122] *Man of Straw* (1951), also directed by Staudte, was an adaption of Heinrich Mann's book. Its ending was a little bit marred by ideology, but it was mostly faithful. The film version of *Divided Heaven* spouted a more propagandist line than was clear from the original book. The DDR state studio also produced pure propaganda, generally concentrated on the heroes of the new socialist Germany, such as the biopic *Ernst Thälmann* of 1954.

The Original Sin (1948), made in Bavaria by Helmut Käutner, was a little satire sharply critical of the cultural policies of the Allies, and the United States in particular. Something of the same message is implicit in *Hallo Fräulein* (1949), in which Maria must choose between the jazz-playing American Tom or the classical musician Walter—she goes for the latter. Wolfgang Borchert's 1947 play about returning soldiers, *The Man Outside*, was filmed as *Love '47* by Wolfgang Liebeneiner, one of the most successful directors of the Third Reich, who had speedily turned his coat. Borchert himself died that same year, at the age of twenty-six. Two years later, Veit Harlan was put on trial in Hamburg for abetting the Third Reich through his antisemitic propaganda film *Jud Süss* (Süss the Jew) of 1940. When Harlan was acquitted, the British demanded a new trial, but he was freed once again. In his defence, he cited the British film version of *Oliver Twist* (1948), in which Alec Guinness gave a true-to-Dickens interpretation of the Jew Fagin.

Hitler remained a controversial theme on both sides of the fence, and not one to be tackled lightly. In many ways, the Austro-German film *The Last Ten Days*, directed by Georg Wilhelm Pabst in 1955, said it all; there are many echoes of it in Oliver Hirschbiegel's *Downfall* (2004), a film decried for 'humanising' Hitler. Since then, the Führer has returned by popular demand: *Look Who's Back*, based on the novel of the same name, was a 2015 comedy about Hitler returning from the dead in modern Berlin. *Schtonk* (1992) was an earlier comedy that focused on the farce of the fake Hitler Diaries, with thinly disguised characterisations of Konrad Kujau (who faked the diaries) and Gerd Heidemann, who sold them to *Stern* for over DM 9 million. Heidemann was involved with Göring's daughter Edda at the time, but in the film the lover is Göring's niece. The banalities in the bogus diaries were apparently a revelation: Hitler was 'a bloke like you and me'.

Many German actors were rapidly denazified and soon reappeared on celluloid. One of these was the great comic performer Heinz Rührmann, who played the title role in Helmut Käutner's screen adaptation of Carl Zuckmayer's famous play *The Captain of Köpenick* in 1956. Bernhard Wicki's *Die Brücke* (The Bridge) of 1959 proved a breakthrough as far as representations of senseless Second World War valour were concerned. *Das Boot* (1981) was perhaps the first German war film to be universally admired outside Germany. Many of the war films in both Germanys focused on Stalingrad, preceding Joseph Vilsmaier's moving account of the battle (1993). Many West German films ranged from pap to soft porn until a new generation of filmmakers emerged in the '70s, but in 1966 Alexander Kluge's *Yesterday Girl* achieved classic status for dealing with the trials of Anita (played by Kluge's sister Alexandra), a young Jewish girl and former concentration camp inmate come to the West from the DDR, who becomes mired in a life of larceny. The state prosecutor Fritz Bauer makes a brief appearance as himself, calling for more lenient sentences for petty crime.

The new brooms were Fassbinder, Schlöndorff, Herzog, Wenders and Syberberg. *The Lost Honour of Katharina Blum* was Schlöndorff's adaptation of a Böll novel in 1975, but his most famous film was probably *The Tin Drum*, based on Grass's long, semi-autobiographical novel. Rainer Werner Fassbinder had a startling career before his early death, beginning with the film *The Bitter Tears of Petra von Kant* in 1972 and encompassing other literary adaptations such as *Effi Briest* (1974) and the ambitious, fifteen-hour-long televised version of the Döblin novel *Berlin Alexanderplatz* (1980). Werner Herzog often put the actor Klaus Kinski to the test in his films, beginning with *Aguirre, Wrath of God* in 1972. His performance was particularly pungent in *Fitzcarraldo* ten years later. Accounts written at the time bear witness to the demands made of actors and actresses by Herzog, and the rate of attrition among the cast acting in the Amazon Jungle. The 'Heimatfilm' or 'homeland' genre achieved its *nec plus ultra* with Edgar Reitz's *Heimat* in 1984, which eventually ran to thirty-two episodes covering much of the history of the twentieth century. In 1988 Gerhard Polt took the Bavarian *Spiesser* or vulgarian on holiday with *Man Spricht Deutsch* and *Go Trabi Go*. The latter was a post-*Wende* road movie, narrating the fortunes of a Goethe-loving Ossi schoolmaster and his family in Italy in 1991.

Rewatching Wenders's *Wings of Desire* after twenty-five years, I was naturally struck by the enormous changes that have taken place in the city since 1987. The film represented the Berlin I first encountered. Now, the vanished Potsdamer and Leipziger Plätze are back again, although the film's old man Homer would not recognise them. The city no longer turns its back on the East. For an historian, a film or a photograph is a document in which the past has been freeze-framed; but still, I recognised the delightful magical realism of it all, and assumed the writer Peter Handke was paying a debt to the novelist who had founded the German magical realist school as an antidote to the banality of existence: E.T.A. Hoffmann, also a sometime Berliner.

MUSIC

Music suffered in a similar way: the romantic tradition represented by Hans Pfitzner or Franz Schmidt was no longer possible—it was 'compromised' by Nazism. There were exceptions: Karajan, who joined the Party not once but twice, somehow contrived to become the face of German music; Carl Orff, with his popular *Carmina Burana*, similarly survived despite his association with Hitler. I saw a wonderful open-air performance of *Carmina Burana* once, on the steps between the Severikirche and the cathedral in Erfurt. Others, who were far less opportunistic, like Wilhelm Furtwängler, found their paths blocked. Furtwängler was publically scourged; other German and Austrian conductors who rode the storm, from Hans Knappertsbusch to Clemens Krauss, got off with a warning. Some Jews returned, including Otto Klemperer, who had been the *enfant terrible* of Weimar; and others, like the American Leonard Bernstein made a career in Germany—but nowhere in Germany were there the lamentable scenes that greeted Jewish conductors in Vienna. According to a friend who played with the orchestra, Lorin Maazel resigned his chief conductorship of the Vienna Philharmonic when one of the players shouted '*Saujud!*' ('filthy Jew') at him behind his back.

The classic case was Wagner and what to do about his music. Hitler had been an enthusiastic Wagnerian and had not only been close to the composer's English-born daughter-in-law, Winifred, but had entertained the whole family. Bayreuth had been a family business, and with time the Wagners got it back. The granddaughters had some accounting to do: Friedelind went to Switzerland and the United States, where she agitated against her mother; Verena had married Bodo Lafferentz, who was a Nazi intellectual. The boys, Wieland and Wolfgang, both had questions to answer as well, but managed to slither round them. When the coast was clear, they set about fumigating the Master's productions. Wieland produced stripped-down designs and mothballed the sets and directions that had been part of Wagner's idea of a *Gesamtkunstwerk*, or total art. Wieland has been accused of being the father of *Regieoper*, which, like *Regietheater*, tears up any stage directions bequeathed by the composer or dramatist and allows the director to make of it what he or she wills. It not only shines a green light on sex, violence and historical revisionism, but at worst it openly mocks the work being performed. Germany is the home of *Regie*, but has now succeeded in exporting it worldwide.

Germany still remains the land of music. With its huge numbers of provincial opera houses and concert halls, there is a respect for music that you find almost nowhere else. Woe betide the person who breathes at the wrong moment during a performance on the Green Hill in Bayreuth. When I was a boy, I had an eccentric older friend who used to tell me what it was like going to provincial opera houses in Germany. The men all wore black tie, and there was outrage when he turned up in sandals. This is a survival of the attitude that brought Berliners to the roofless Philharmonie in February 1945, while bombs fell all around them, in order to listen to Brahms. The architect Will Dambusch, who lived through the time, told me about going to *The Threepenny Opera* at the Hebbel Theatre in 1945 or 1946. The audience was all in tails or some lesser form of evening dress, with *Waffenröcke* or greatcoats thrown over their clothes to keep out the cold. The Philharmonic's concerts at the time were performed at the Titania Palast, which had contrived to survive the war.

One of the luminaries of Berlin music today is the Argentinian-born conductor and pianist Daniel Barenboim, music director of the Berlin State Opera since 1992. He managed to play a snippet of Wagner at a concert in Israel in July 2000, but has not succeeded in reversing the unspoken ban despite his valiant efforts to do so. He created the West-Eastern Divan Orchestra in 1999 with the late Edward Said. The aim was to bring together musicians from the Arab world to perform with Israelis. Barenboim is a contender for the Nobel Peace Prize if ever there was one. For unexplained reasons, he has never been on the shortlist.

I know as little about popular music as I do about sport. In the early years of the DDR, the regime chased its tail trying to define 'proper' popular music in a socialist state. Jazz was out, and rock 'n' roll later suffered the same fate,[123] written off as American imperialism in the '50s. This review of Elvis Presley published in *Junge Welt* gives a fair idea of what the SED thought:

> his 'singing' was like his face: dim, monotonous and brutal. The chap was completely unmusical, croaking like a crow suffering from whooping cough and hoping to make up for the weakness of his voice by wildly swinging his hips about in imitation of Marilyn Monroe ... he jumped this way and that like a first-rate lunatic, shaking his pelvis, as if someone had fed him neat hydrochloric acid, and as a result he roared like a wounded stag, but not as melodiously.[124]

What was permitted in the postwar era was 'dance and light music', severely regulated by the appropriate body, the Verband Deutscher Komponisten und Musikwissenschaftler, created in 1951.

In the '60s, the Beatles in particular challenged popular music in East Germany, with groups like Die Sputniks, Die Rockys (in Erfurt) and Die Lunics trying to capture some of the Liverpool sound. Die Butlers sailed too close to the sun and earned themselves a severe ticking-off from First Secretary Ulbricht after a concert in Leipzig in October 1965. Not only were they banned, but forty-four out of forty-nine other groups had their licenses revoked. In 1968, the DDR saw its first hippies. Things got easier in the '70s when 'consumer socialism' was introduced under Honecker, and the group Die Puhdys enjoyed some success. There were a few mild protest groups performing punk in the DDR: Feeling B, Sandow, the singer Flake, and the amusingly named Pankow.[125] Sometimes a mild dissidence was implied. Right at the end of the regime's existence, there were huge concerts in Berlin-Weissensee, with 85,000 turning up to hear Joe Cocker in June 1988, and 160,000 for Bruce Springsteen.

I have never been to a pop concert in the West, but I am a fan of the Ruhri Max Raabe, born Matthias Otto in Lünen, who has been successful at bringing back a certain Berlin cabaret style from the Weimar years.[126] He trained as a baritone in the '80s before deciding the opera was not for him. He has a deadpan manner, a razor-sharp delivery and an incredible vocal range. He can be very funny both as a presenter and in his own compositions, such as 'Kein Schwein ruft mich an' (No Bastard Ever Calls). I first saw him on stage at the Ronacher in Vienna in 1995, and then again in 1997 at the Wintergarten in Berlin, the stage he has made his own. The Wintergarten is a successful recreation of the popular venue that was in the Friedrichstrasse before the war.

PART III

ON THE ROAD

THE THREE GERMANYS

My friend Urs Müller-Plantenberg has made his own map of Germany, which he divides up into 'Schnapps Germany' in the north-east, 'Wine Germany' in the west, and 'Beer Germany' in the north and in Bavaria and Saxony. The former Prussian lands mostly fall within 'Schnapps Germany'. After the war, American soldiers were told to sniff out 'Junkers', who were perceived as militarists, by finding out whether they had a potato schnapps distillery on their estates.[1] The map is not always up-to-date, nor is it always an easy one to follow: Beer Saxony will include the small wine region around Dresden, Meissen and Radebeul; Thuringia is also in 'Beer Germany', despite another tiny wine region on the Saale; 'Wine Germany' produces significant beers such as Kölsch from Cologne and Bitburg from Rheinland-Pfalz, and Germany's best schnapps is actually made in Baden-Württemberg, which is at the very heart of 'Wine Germany'. You might be tempted to believe that religion also follows the same rules—that 'Wine Germany' is Catholic and that Beer-and-Schnapps Germany is Protestant—but this isn't so. Northern Baden is Protestant where it touches the Pfalz, and so is the top half of Württemberg; Bavaria is both Catholic and a byword for beer.

Of the three Germanys, Schnapps Germany is perhaps the least well known to outsiders. This is partly because so much of it disappeared with the lands across the Oder river in 1945. Apart from the delicious fruit schnapps made in south Germany, which serves to get rid of surplus fruit, most schnapps production originated as a way of dealing with surplus potatoes and corn—that meant Pomerania and all points north. The gardener Dörr in Fontane's novel *Trials and Tribulations* of 1888 says that a Berliner needs only three things: 'Berlin white beer, Gilka and leeks.' Gilka's Kaiser-Kümmel still exists, although I doubt it is as beloved now as it was in the late nineteenth century. Kümmel used to be popular with the British Army, whose officers generally called it 'Kimmel' and preferred Wolfschmidt, or 'Wolfie', over Gilka—but that might have been a simple question of availability. At least the British drank German schnapps. The other Allies influenced German tastes, and it is still true today that if you ask for a whisky in Germany you will get Bourbon.

Despite Germany's decades in the dog-house, Beer Germany, on the other hand, has always maintained world renown. It must still be true that the pilsner style is the most popular, and therefore one that came from Bohemia in the nineteenth century. Beer Germany has two, possibly three, heartlands: Catholic Bavaria and the industrial Ruhr, with the third being southern Saxony where it borders on the Czech Republic. As a rule of thumb, Ruhr beers are more bitter than those of Bavaria, which are sweeter. Northern German brews are not popular in the south, and vice versa. Since 1989, more and more breweries have been rolled into the big conglomerates owned by Dr Oetker and others. The swillers grumble and say that things are not what they were. The result has been the creation of increasing numbers of brew pubs. Even in the south, more and more craft brewers are replacing the big brewers in Germany's pubs and inns.

Before the First World War, wine was one of the principal reasons why tourists visited Germany: to see the stunning landscapes of the Rhine and the Mosel, gasp at the Lorelei rock and spout Heine, then sample its wines. Germany's top growths sold for prices comparable with the best of Bordeaux. German wine fell from grace as international tastes shifted from white to red and from sweet to dry. Few people could find the time to sit down with some ancient Auslese and savour the wine without food. In the '80s, the Charta movement pushed to make all German wines dry, with the exception of a few nobly sweet wines when climatic conditions made such things possible. Thirty years later, sweet German wines are indeed the exception, and the *Grosses Gewächs* category has been introduced by the VDP, the organisation representing the top estates. This is based on the Burgundian *climat*, which leads on '*terroir*', rather than the system of '*Prädikat*', which defines wines by levels of sweetness. A timely worldwide Riesling craze has led to a revival of interest in German wine, its dryness making it easier to place in the context of a world market.

German food is another neglected field. At its worst, it is a sort of breakfast served with minor variations three times a day and confusingly called *Brot*. The bread is very often the best part of it, as Germany has a fair claim to making the best in the world. It comes served with slivers of Emmental and Tilsit cheese (the latter once made in East Prussia), perhaps also some soft, curd-like cheese, and slices of different sausages, sometimes accompanied by yoghurt and fruit and some sort of undressed salad—Germans dress salad with cream. At breakfast a boiled egg seems to be pretty well de rigueur—it is extremely hard to fight it off—and at lunchtime they might throw in a bowl of soup. I will cross the road for a good bowl of potato or pumpkin soup, but this is not exactly gastronomy. A popular dinner will include *Pellkartoffeln* (potatoes boiled in their skins), which are served with fresh *Quark*, or curd cheese.

At its best, German food follows the seasons. In the case of asparagus, the season runs from 1 May to 25 June, but Germans love it so much and await it so eagerly that you are sometimes able to procure it earlier; I chanced on some in Kempten last year on 25 April. You pay highly for the privilege of eating it before the season kicks off; even after 1 May *Solospargel*—thick white spears—can be pretty expensive. Traditionally asparagus is white in Germany; there are iconoclasts who will try to serve it green, but the reaction will be similar to comments made about jazzing up a Beethoven Quartet or setting *Der Rosenkavalier* in a New Orleans brothel. Good asparagus grows in sandy soil, which means that many parts of Germany claim to having the best: in Baden it is Munzingen, in the Rhineland Schwetzingen, in Brandenburg Beelitz; Schwabach in Bavaria, Bamberg in Franconia, Kutzleben in Thuringia, and Lauenburg in Schleswig-Holstein. As for other seasonal foods, there is chamois and plaice in May—naturally the latter is celebrated more on the northern coast—strawberries and *Matjes* herrings in June, chanterelles in July, ceps in August, game in September, geese in November and, naturally, more geese at Christmas. Christmas is also the time of *Weihnachtsgebäck*, Stollen and other sweetmeats. On New Year's Eve a pink marzipan pig, generally from Lübeck, is placed on one's pillow, for '*Das Schwein bringt Glück*'—the pig will bring you luck.

The slices of Emmental and Tilsit on the breakfast table should not put you off German cheese any more than the ubiquitous 'blue brie' of the Cambozola type. There are excellent cheeses in Germany, chiefly in the Black Forest and the Allgäu in the south and Schleswig-Holstein in the north, where many East Prussians who used to make Tilsit in their *Heimat* put down roots after 1945. The best of German cheese, as in Austria, tends to be Gruyère-style *Bergkäse*. Transhumance is still practised: the beasts are driven up the mountains in the spring and brought down again in September. During a trip to Kempten in 2016, I went up to the *Sennerei* or Alpine creamery at nearby Diepolz and bought some 2-year-old *Bergkäse*. My host wanted to show me a resplendent view of the mountains, but there was a thick mist and visibility was limited to about 100 metres. I might not have known there were any mountains at all, had she not told me.

Modern German cooking can be surprisingly good, and it is not for nothing that the country has more Michelin stars than any other besides France. It is usually the case that the most interesting restaurants are in the towns and cities where the greatest wealth is concentrated: Munich, Hamburg, Düsseldorf and, more recently, Berlin. The region most famed for good things is the Black Forest, and there is a profusion of hotel-restaurants there with reputations that extend throughout Germany.

SCHNAPPS GERMANY

Schnapps Germany counted for rather more in the past than it does now. Before 1945 it would have stretched not only as far as Mecklenburg to the west, but across the Oder to the east, taking in the wheat and potato fields of Pomerania and West and East Prussia. The classic Junker estate would have contained a still, where the least presentable potatoes were quickly transformed into rough spirits. Grünberg in northern Silesia was one of Germany's least reputable wine regions, and a byword for nastiness before the war. I am told that most of what was produced there in the twentieth century was sparkling, because they had trouble ripening the grapes. In recent times, the Poles have revived wine production in Zielona Góra, as Grünberg is now known. The fairest thing you could say about the Polish wines I have tasted from there is that they are 'encouraging'.

There is still a very obvious consumption of schnapps, even if many Germans in the north-east are now more committed to beer. The kiosks on U-Bahn stations in Berlin certainly used to offer a plethora of small bottles of Korn and Doppelkorn. You don't see so much Gilka these days, but Schinkenhäger, Jägermeister, Doornkaat and Nordhäuser Doppelkorn abound; not to mention some of the specialities from across the Oder that are now made in Germany, such as Bärenjäger,[1] Bärenfang (made by Teucke & Koening in Steinhagen, Pomerania and flavoured with honey), or Danziger Goldwasser, with its little flecks of gold leaf. In the mid-90s, at least, quite early in the morning you would not only see Berliners buy these miniatures, but drink them too, accounting for the red faces of many Berliners on the U- and S-Bahn. Tipsy Berliners of both sexes wearing brightly coloured synthetic shell-suits remind me of the paintings the *Wahlberliner* or adopted Berliner Heinrich Zille made in the early years of the twentieth century. This is particularly true of the more working-class districts, such as Wedding and Neukölln. Once you begin to identify them, these characters depicted by Zille are identifiable everywhere, chiefly in pubs and on the U-Bahn. In summer, they repair to the beach at Wannsee, where they were also spotted by Zille in the '20s. There, too, you find them in pubs, drinking beer with schnapps chasers.

CAPITAL

On 20 June 1991, Berlin became capital of Germany again after more than forty years in limbo. I had a busy day—a meeting with the head of the Prussian cultural foundation, and dinner with Clarita von Trott. No one seemed to believe that the Republic would up sticks and move back to the old Prussian base. It was only when I asked a taxi-driver the following morning and then bought a paper that I learned the truth: Berlin had won out by a small majority. Until this development, Germany was a collection of powerful provinces still bearing the stamp of their former occupiers. The Allies had promoted their own hubs in Hamburg, Munich, Düsseldorf, Frankfurt and Cologne. The new Western capital, Bonn, was a famously small town, while West Berlin was chiefly celebrated for its alternative culture.

By the '80s, however, West Berlin had a dated, provincial feel about it, as if it were still living in the afterglow of 1968. There was no glamour. Many Berliners had left the city during the Cold War, and younger people had often settled there from the countryside to avoid national service—residents of West Berlin were exempt. A better-heeled element began to arrive after 1989, particularly once the Bundestag and the civil service came up from Bonn. Some old Berlin hands shun the new Berlin and abide by the survivals from the pre-1989 time. In September 2013, for example, when the Deutsch-Britische Gesellschaft took me to dinner after my lecture in Schloss Charlottenburg, they opted for Don Camillo in the Schlossstrasse, an old-fashioned Italian that had been there since 1979, in preference to the many flashier places that have sprung up since.

Coming to Berlin in the late '80s, I was struck by the time warp in the Western half of the city. There were plenty of jolly little *Kneipen*, small pubs like the Dicke Wirtin in Charlottenburg where people played '60s music and where the publicans had long hair and beards. Restaurants were Turkish, Greek or Italian, cheerful places, but the food was pretty well interchangeable. South of the Kurfürstendamm, off the Uhlandstrasse, you found a few better things, but little that was out of the ordinary. Until the *Wende*, the top place was Rockendorf's out in the French Sector, which opened in 1981, and eventually moved to the Passauer Strasse.[2] Siegfried Rockendorf died in tragic circumstances in 2000. There was also the Austrocentric Bamberger Reiter, and Alt Luxemburg, a one-star Michelin restaurant housed in an incongruous concrete *Plattenbau* near the Kurfürstendamm. The next big event was when Johannes King opened Grand Slam in the old Rot-Weiss tennis club, and the Brandenburger Hof started serving East-West fusion food in an old *Mietshaus* not far from the Gedächtniskirche. A new generation came in the course of the '90s: Vau, Margaux and the Louis Adlon restaurant in the eponymous hotel. It has been a long time since I have been able to afford this sort of meal, so I haven't a clue where you would go now.

Before 1990, the restaurant map of Berlin changed very little from year to year. Traditionalists probably preferred the Paris Bar in Charlottenburg, which was Berlin's take on a Parisian brasserie. There were few survivals from earlier times, unless you included a scant handful of charming old places out in the woods such as the Wirtshaus Moorlake by the Pfaueninsel, or the Kurpfalz-Weinstuben with its dark panelling off the Kurfürstendamm, which opened in the early years of the Third Reich. When stylish restaurants began to appear again in Berlin Mitte in the mid-90s, the menus invariably included Austrian flourishes like Vau. Another was the latest incarnation of Lutter & Wegner, which had migrated to Charlottenburg after 1945, but came back to roost somewhere near the old site. In fact, it settled in the building that had been the home of the wine house's most famous customer: the judge, composer and above all writer E.T.A. Hoffmann. The most successful of the new generation of Berlin restaurants was Borchardt in the Französische Strasse.[3] Again this was an historic Berlin restaurant, half of which had survived the wartime bombing. In its new form, however, it chose to be rather more like a brasserie.

For anyone who knows Vienna, Berlin's coffee houses are hardly worth the consideration. The coffee is often thin and disappointing, and these establishments lack the character of their Austrian equivalent. Some were vaguely carried over from before the war, such as Mohring or Kranzler in the West. There was an attempt to revive the Bauer in the East. The old Romanisches, the only Berlin café to have a truly Bohemian reputation after the Café des Westens closed during the First World War, was never rebuilt after its destruction in November 1943. Its site is now covered by the ghastly Europa-Center. The attraction of these places was an all-day breakfast where one could truly stuff one's face, with two sorts of ham, cheese, quark, an egg, jam and rolls. More baroque versions of breakfast were also available. Of course coffee has improved across the board, and if you want an espresso, you can get one more or less anywhere that has a machine. Some people swear by the café in the Literaturhaus off the Kurfürstendamm or the Einstein near the Potsdamer Strasse. Berlin's great gastronomic institution remains the top floor of the KaDeWe (Kaufhaus des Westens) on the Wittenbergplatz. This is not only one of the best places to buy wine, tea, coffee and other groceries, but also any form of meat, fish, fruit or vegetables. There are a whole series of places to eat anything from *Krustenbraten* to oysters.

Sausages are the favourite snack food in Germany. In Berlin and the Ruhr they have a perverse love of Currywurst—essentially a quite ordinary sausage covered with ketchup and curry powder. In my opinion you can do better. Before the *Wende*, the two halves of the city were defined by soup. In the eastern half they ate *Soljanka*—a sort of poor man's borscht, spicy and invigorating. The western equivalent was *Erbsensuppe mit Wurst*, a favourite snack from the age of all-night balls, which had made the fame of Aschinger in pre-Nazi times. When I was working at the Stabi in the '90s, you could still get this on the Potsdamer Strasse, from the butcher's shop up by the U-Bahn station. Berlin butchers often had an attached *Imbiss*, which was a little like a Viennese *Würstelstand*. The alternative was a mobile *Schnellimbiss* or snack bar, where sausages, other foods and—of course—tins of beer could be obtained. I was impressed to be regaled with a chic 'Berlin' menu when the Adlon reopened, not that Berlin food was ever chic: potato salad, little veal meatballs (*Bouletten*), pork knuckle in aspic (!), a *poussin*—that was stretching things—and some *Rote Grütze*, or 'red grains', a sort of German summer pudding, with a *Baumkuchen* crust. In the DDR toasties were quite the thing: '*mit Käse überbacken.*' I had a *Domtoast* in Magdeburg, 'a collection of sweet peppers and tuna buried under a winding sheet of processed cheese.'[4] Many seemed to involve pineapples. I never had the nerve to try the purported Hawaiian version.

Having spent no more than a few days in the city for several years, I had failed to register the arrival of the Hauptbahnhof when it came and installed itself in 2006 on the site of the old Lehrter Bahnhof by the Spree—opposite the Charité. I got out into a strange townscape thinking I had reached the Friedrichstrasse. In 2014 I stayed in a hotel close to the defunct Bärenschenke, and was able to take stock of how much this stretch of Berlin Mitte had changed. Around the Oranienburger Tor there were huge numbers of trendy bars and restaurants. After much hesitation, I found what I was looking for on the Torstrasse: a proper old *Kneipe* with Gothic script and bogus beams and a long menu of regional German food. My host, who also looked as if he had been drawn by Zille, had to be chivvied away from the television he was studying closely, and I think there were no more than four of us dining that evening. Still, I had good beer, good schnapps and good *Rindsrouladen*.

From a purely gastronomic point of view, there is a danger that, with so much rebuilding and in-filling, the beastly chains will muscle in and Berlin, like everywhere else in the world, will be packed with branded restaurants, cafés and 'concepts'—how do you eat a concept? When Berlin was just an island in a hostile Soviet ocean, the multiples gave it as wide a berth as did all but the hardiest tourists. There were few posh restaurants, and fewer comfortable hotels. You could eat local, wholesome food in the Berliner *Kneipe*, and the city is still good for small food shops; some *Kneipen* are excellent. When I stayed in the Bayerisches Viertel with my family, there were three or four good bakers within easy walking distance offering the *Streuselkuchen* and marzipan *Plunderschleife* my children liked for breakfast. There was a huge array of different breads, with a 50–50 wheat-rye loaf that we ate until they ran out and we took the rye-dominated

Schwarzwälder instead. From the local shop I discovered an excellent initiative to encourage Berlin beekeepers. You could buy packages of three 10cl pots of very strong-flavoured local honey. I stocked up on Brandenburg linden honey for home before I left.

Berlin foods went down well, like the *Bouletten* we had at the Stadtklause in Kreuzberg. This marvellous old pub, quite close to the ruins of the old Anhalt Station, was quite a discovery. From its proximity to the offices of *Der Tagesspiegel* and *Die Zeit*, I should say it was frequented by hacks. It had a collection of pictures of the station from better days. One nice thing about much of the old western part of the city is that nothing changes quickly. Walking through another of my old stamping grounds in Wilmersdorf, I noted that a fair number of the places I used to go twenty years earlier were still operating, including a Swabian restaurant called Besenwirtschaft where I used to eat *Spätzle*.

One great Berlin institution has only recently bitten the dust, and that is Zum Nussbaum on the Bundesplatz. My friend Urs used to go there once a year in January to eat roast venison and celebrate his escape from East Prussia in 1945, when he was a boy of eight. His family managed to get the last train from Marienwerder before the Red Army cut off the Germans. Many who missed it were killed outright; others were starved to death. The rest were only banished to the west months and years later. I must have last eaten at Zum Nussbaum less than a month before it closed down. The food was much as I remembered it. There was wild boar, *Sülze* (aspics), *Kartoffelpuffer* (potato cakes), *Pfannkuchen mit Speck* (bacon pancakes), *Königsberger Klopse* (Königsberg meatballs) and other stock north-east German 'delicacies'. There was a pretty front garden under the nut tree that gave the restaurant its name, but inside were two dark-stained, panelled Ur-German rooms with antique posters and photographs and the old-fashioned *Theke* or bar.

Another such place in Berlin is Diener, a *Kunstlerkneipe* or artists' pub just off the Savignyplatz. I went in 2014 to look at the pleasantly authentic scruffy interior, full of photographs of bohemian worthies. The waitress was in a bad mood and the customers were simply lining their stomachs in preparation for the Germany-Brazil match, crowned with such a sensational victory a few hours later. The menu, however, was just right: there was *Griebenschmalz* (dripping) and toasted rye bread, *Leberkäse* (meatloaf) and *Kartoffelpuffer* with various toppings, *Matjes* herrings and *Königsberger Klopse*.

SOUTH-WEST BERLIN

In 2002 I spent a week in California's Sonoma Valley at a guest-house run by a German called Klaus. Klaus told us that his father had been chief of police in Heidelberg. Homosexuality was illegal then, and out of consideration for his father he had moved to Berlin, where the atmosphere was more tolerant. From Berlin it was an easy shift to California and he'd been there ever since. Berlin has always had a 'diverse' side. Two hundred years ago, homosexual men used to meet in the Kastanienwäldchen on the Linden and in parts of the Tiergarten. There is a well-frequented Schwules Museum or Gay Museum in the Lützowstrasse nearby, not to mention the annual Love Parade. Klaus Wowereit was the city's most famously gay mayor.

In 2013 I was put up in a hotel in the Motzstrasse, which is the heart of gay Berlin. There are bars, clubs, restaurants and a multitude of antique shops. The bar next door to my hotel was largely empty during the day, except for one old boy who seemed to be permanently asleep at a table outside. The local youths would cycle past shouting '*Wach auf!*' (Wake up!) at him. After my lecture, one of Berlin's most important cultural figures asked me if I didn't find the Motzstrasse 'too gay'. I replied, quite truthfully, that it didn't bother me in the slightest. In the past I had borrowed a friend's sister's flat there. There was nothing particularly new about the raunchiness of this part of Berlin. That it might have been difficult on the other side of the Wall is sometimes denied—there were no official meeting places for gay people in the DDR. Public lavatories were as good as it got.

Not far away is the Bayerisches Viertel, where I had also stayed on occasion. Berlin took off in around 1900 and there is a lot of good *Jugendstil*, or Art Nouveau, in the *Mietshäuser* blocks of flats. This part of Schöneberg was comparatively lightly bombed. In its most extended form, the *Mietshaus* becomes a *Mietskaserne* or barracks block. The traditional Berlin *Mietskasernen* are a phenomenon, particularly in Wedding, or one or two streets in Friedenau, where they stretch back for anything up to ten court-yards. The richer people inhabited the facade facing the street, and the inhabitants got poorer the further back they lived. The door had to be big enough to allow the passage of a fire engine.

West Berlin retained its plush areas, even after 1945. I suppose that Russian oligarchs have bought the villas on the Schwanen-werder Peninsula in Nikolassee now, but there are plenty of big villas in Zehlendorf, Dahlem or Wannsee. There is Grunewald, for example, which was written about so eloquently by Nicolaus Sombart. I stayed in one of the last remaining villas, which had been taken over by the Hotel Vier Jahreszeiten, and the designer Karl Lagerfeld had assumed responsibility for everything that was good, right down to the bathroom towels—though he had not designed the various very grand rooms of c. 1900, of course. Lagerfeld has often said that he is a great fan of Prussian history and Frederick the Great. I was given a tour: the villa had been owned by the von Pannwitz family, and I was told all sorts of stories about the Kaiser and how he had had a von Pannwitz as a mistress. I got the chance to see Lagerfeld's suite too. He had a copy of Menzel's *Tafelrunde* hanging on the wall. The painting was famously lost when the Humboldthain Flak Tower caught fire in 1945. It depicted Frederick the Great having dinner with Voltaire at Sanssouci.

EAST BERLIN

I had my first view of East Berlin only a year or so before the Wall came down. An English soldier asked me if I had anything to do with the services. I said no, and he let me pass. I changed my DM 25 into 25 Ostmarks. I looked at the Linden and the site of the old Schloss, and wandered about the streets filled with *Plattenbauten*: the featureless residential blocks that had been the priority of the DDR planners. I trudged around for hours before I found a bar called the Bärenschenke in the upper reaches of the Friedrichstrasse and ordered a beer.[5] It was not long before a man sat down beside me for a chat. I bought him a drink and he told me that his name was Egbert and that he worked around the corner as a porter at the Charité Hospital. I did not have to be back in the West before midnight, so I let Egbert take me on a tour. He wanted to show me 'his' Berlin; he very obligingly took me to Bert Brecht's grave and then to the Charité, where he fetched me various books from an office to which he possessed a key. The hospital had once been the pride of Prussia: known as 'the Pepinière', it was the leading training institution for military surgeons. In the DDR era it specialised in spare parts for sportsmen and women. To prove its importance, there was a brand new skyscraper ward positioned in a bend in the Spree, with views over West Berlin. When I left, Egbert asked me for my address. He was going to send me cuttings from the East German papers to counter the propaganda I received in the West. I had several small packets of cuttings before November 1989. After then, I never heard from Egbert again.

Nearly thirty years later and we hear of *Ostalgie*, most famously expressed in the comedy *Goodbye Lenin*—but many of those who had ambitions to lead a Western life had in fact made it to the West; for those with means, there was always the possibility of being bought out by relatives. Nevertheless, even some Western historians now cling to the idea that East Berlin was not a bad place after all.[6] For those who saw it at first hand, however, it was hard to rid yourself of certain impressions. The first was drabness: everything was grey. Although the Linden was eventually restored after a fashion, and Polish restorers were brought in to work their magic particularly in Potsdam, for almost everywhere else the townscape was filled with concrete slabs. In many places the wartime scars had not been patched up, so that in parts of Berlin Mitte there remained throughout the DDR period unrepaired buildings covered in pockmarks inflicted by Soviet machine guns during the final battle for Berlin. Several of these buildings, on and off the Oranienburger Strasse, survived for years after the *Wende*. One or two are still there in the early twenty-first century. One that I photographed in 1991 had been taken over by anarchists; they had turned a Trabi parked outside into a flowerpot and were growing plants in the engine. The other lasting impression of East Berlin was the smell—of Russian tobacco and brown coal, which lay around in great slagheaps next to public buildings.

Ostalgie also recalls the many jokes about life in the DDR. One concerned a propaganda TV programme called *Der schwarze Kanal* (The Black Channel), presented by a man with the unusually aristocratic name of Karl-Eduard von Schnitzler—he was commonly referred to as 'Karl-Eduard von Schn...', because that was the moment when viewers reached for the television to switch it off.[7] Schnitzler's programme was designed to pour scorn on the West. He was later tracked down by Anna Funder, who found him in a drab house on the outskirts of Potsdam. By then he had plenty of time on his hands.[8] On 28 March 1995, I noted an article in *Der Tagesspiegel* in Berlin that someone had revived the Mokka-Milch-Eis Bar, one of the most chic places in the old East. There was even a pop song about it. There were jokes about what this brand of *Ostalgie* would bring: a sign perhaps? Warning that 'You will not be served here!' Or Eastern Bloc-style queues?

The East German writer Karsten Krampitz has recently sought to define just what sort of people formed the bedrock of the old DDR. He cites Günter Gaus, the former permanent representative of the Western republic in East Germany, who called them the '*Staatsvolk der kleinen Leute*' or nation of little people. They were the ones who had been left behind—or rather, those left after extracting those who had the means to escape, and those who had been killed by the Nazis, driven into exile, or dispossessed by the policies of the Communist Party or the SED after the war. Until the Wall went up, masses of people left the DDR, including many academics, because they saw no future for their children; in senior schools and universities, workers' children were given preference. The 'little people' left behind might have had their virtues, and their vices; and their lives might even have been less blighted than others, in that they had less to struggle for. There was no capitalist-style competitive spirit—even if the zealous Stakhanovs were given some small incentives to toil harder and sweat more, they were allowed to amble along gently, provided they didn't look to the right or the left or otherwise rock the boat.[9]

The DDR had its own kitsch—its own version of what in Austria is called *Meidlinger Barock*, as displayed in the restored Kronprinzenpalais on the Linden. In the park at Treptow was the imposing Zenner restaurant, in the shadow of the Soviet War Memorial on the River Spree, which opened its doors in 1955. The idiom was neoclassical-fascist. It appears to have been intended as slightly Bohemian with a bit of 'oompah' thrown in.

I walked by one day looking for relics of the once-famous fishing village of Stralau; the band struck up 'The Continental' and I couldn't resist sitting down for a drink in the beer garden. They seemed to be hosting a convention of artists, as everyone was sketching their neighbours. I never made it to Clärchens Ballhaus, but it was an old-fashioned place to dance in a proper, proletarian way. After the *Wende*, West Germans mounted expeditions to try it out.

In Berlin you belong to a *Kiez*, which is a Wendisch word for a neighbourhood; your village or, as a cockney might say, your 'manor'. Before the *Wende*, some East Berliners were very firmly wedded to their manor, in the way that Angela Merkel appears to be to this day. The five-star Grand Hotel in the Friedrichstrasse in Berlin Mitte was the flagship of the government-owned Interhotel chain and not ten minutes' walk from the Brandenburg Gate. In the two or three years that it was a DDR hotel, it was frequented by the *nomenklatura*. Immediately afterwards it was the Treuhand, the agency working on who owned what. The top Silhouette restaurant was famous for charging hard currency for things that you never saw in the DDR—strawberries, for example, or wines of Meissen. There were other themed places in the hotel, a bit like the famous pre-war Haus Vaterland, where you could do a world gastronomic tour without leaving the building. At the Grand the choice was limited to Germany: a Thuringian restaurant, where Ostmarks were accepted for goose, red cabbage and local dumplings; or a Spreewald restaurant, where you ate trout, and a revived Café Bauer, once the cynosure of the Friedrichstrasse, which looked like a cross between a pub and a Wild West saloon.

I recall being shown round by a woman in early middle age shortly after the Wall fell. She was business-like in the manner of German in-house PRs, but there wasn't much charm in her approach. When I made a little joke about the West, she snapped: 'I have never been to the Bundesrepublik, and I shall never go!' I have not seen her since, so I cannot say whether she has relented, but there were certainly plenty of people who were happy with their lot in the DDR; many of them had never known anywhere else. Just as under the regime that preceded it, if you liked being part of a community and were not tempted towards individualism, you could tick along quite nicely. If you were good at sport, you might even be spoiled, and given spare-part surgery in the Charité Hospital in Berlin. If you were a Party member, part of the *nomenklatura*, you could aspire to a villa in Pankow or a dacha on a reserve in some favoured lakeside corner of East Germany, and you could eat rare delicacies paid for in hard currency.

TRAVELS IN THE MARK BRANDENBURG

In April 1991 I began to travel around the recovered territories of eastern Germany. Potsdam was an inauspicious sight. The first thing you saw was the Interhotel, spoiling what little good impression was made by the restoration of the Nikolaikirche and the Town Hall. I found that the hotel was a 'big, rude, ugly and wholly unjustifiable skyscraper.'[10] More than a quarter of a century later, it is still there, and every attempt to knock it down seems to have foundered. In the latest news I heard, the fate of the council's plans to acquire and demolish the building were in the hands of the courts. An opposition was fighting a last-ditch battle to stop the demolition of this skyscraper and numerous other DDR buildings, and prevent the rebuilding of the spire of the Garrison Church, pleading that it had been the scene of Hitler's Potsdam Day of 21 March 1933, and that this tainted the building sufficiently to make any desire to refurbish it unhealthy. Potsdam didn't need another church, and then there was all that stuff about militarism.[11] I think there was a bit of *Ostalgie* there too—*nostalgie de la boue*.

Tourism had provided Potsdam with revenues well before the *Wende*—hence the need for an Interhotel. Hard by Potsdam's own Brandenburg Gate were a brace of eighteenth-century buildings that had been turned into restaurants, one specialised in fish. From there it was a relatively short walk to Sanssouci and the other palaces in the park. There was a market on Saturdays; I once saw a whole ox being carved up and served with potato salad at 5 DMs a portion. I was in Potsdam during Easter 1996, staying in a twee little suite at the Cecilienhof, the Norman Shaw-inspired palace of the Hohenzollern crown prince. I tried out the *Schnellimbiss* opposite the Friedenskirche that sold everything equine: Bockwurst, Bratwurst, *Bouletten*—all pure horse. Frederick the Great, I felt, would not have been amused.[12] Of course, I should have tried the food in the palace. In those days, at least, you were offered an expensive choice of the menus consumed by Churchill, Roosevelt and Stalin at the 1945 Conference. I noted that they 'looked pretty silly', so I don't think that Stalin's choice can have offered much caviar or vodka.

* * *

It was in the Cecilienhof that I met a former US military intelligence officer—officially a 'protocol officer'—called Tom Blake. He had been part of the Military Liaison Mission that gathered intelligence on Soviet military strength. After doing the very risky work of presenting young staff officers with the layout of the Soviet Union's nuclear arsenal in Brandenburg, he had acquired a post-Cold War job that involved selling off Soviet installations for parks, hotels and golf clubs.[13] The sites were owned by the EAI Corporation of Abingdon, Maryland. Together with R&D Tech, they also undertook to neutralise the sites: ridding them of nuclear and chemical weaponry. They had 1,429 hectares in the

'*Neue Länder*', of which 425 were in Brandenburg. Blake asked me if I would like to tour some of the sites with him. He even promised a good restaurant at Kloster Zinna.

On 8 April 1996, Blake picked me up from Wannsee Station. He scarcely drew breath all day. He pointed out the KGB barracks in the Berliner Vorstadt after we had crossed the Glienicke Bridge, now known as the Bridge of Spies following several exchanges of captured agents. He used to cross the bridge in the old days armed with four different IDs. Under the Four-Power Agreement, the Allies had the right to monitor one another, but naturally obstructions were put in place. On manoeuvres, for example, the tank in front of your car would break down and the mechanics would dismantle the tracks, while the tank behind would conveniently do the same. Blake told me of the death of the Mission's Major Arthur Nicholson in 1985, who was shot and killed photographing a Soviet tank park in Ludwigslust. His shooting was the last cause of serious inter-Allied friction before the *Wende*.

We passed the town of Treuenbrietzen, where the Wehrmacht and the Red Army clashed in April 1945. Blake showed me a communications tower: 'The boys couldn't wait to take that out.' We arrived at the first Soviet camp shortly afterwards. There were some shabby huts where the soldiers had slept fifteen to a room. He showed me a training ground, where instructions took the form of pictograms, and we looked into the tank barns: the Russians had left with everything they could carry. Nuclear weapons were kept in 1930s buildings locked with just four skeleton keys. He explained that the Soviet soldiers spoke many different languages, and comparatively few could read Russian. The pictograms were meant to be universally comprehensible. At the core of the camp were solid redbrick Prussian buildings erected after 1866 when units were withdrawn from a base at Tegel, where Berlin's inner-city airport is still to be found; the troops were transferred to new, custom-built barracks in the Mark. Blake told me of his great moment of triumph, when he convinced George Bush Senior to come to the Cecilienhof for two days in July 1995. 'He was prospecting for Citibank, and told reporters that if he were young again he would invest in these old camps.'[14]

Blake had a few rough words to say about the old DDR officials, whom he charged with sitting around waiting for their pensions or backhanders. Two were singled out for praise, however: Bernd Rüdiger, Bürgermeister of Jüterbog, and Frank Letz, who occupied the same position in Kloster Zinna. Rüdiger had been turning the old barracks compounds into housing. After 1991, there were some quite astonishing *Köpenickiaden* or heists carried out in the *Neue Länder*: Soviet troops would leave their barracks and hold up car showrooms, taking all the cars and shipping them back to Moscow. A smaller fiddle was to sell their tax-free cigarettes to the Vietnamese, who were seen flogging them round the streets of Berlin. Officially, the soldiers were not allowed off the premises, and there were just 120 telephone lines. After 1991 telephones were installed outside the camp gates. That was where the women gathered at night. The only way the Germans could get rid of the soldiers was to pay the Russian government to take them home.

We went to Forst Zinna. This was the former Adolf-Hitler-Lager, an SS camp. Later it became an NKVD school, and the old German buildings had been decorated with pictograms commemorating the crushing of the uprisings of 1956 and 1968. They looked like Roy Lichtenstein without the 'Zap! Pow!' The mess contained more pictograms, this time instructing kitchen details on how to peel potatoes. Blake said that Goebbels had visited, and showed me a ramp he believed had been constructed so that the propaganda minister could disguise his limp. We went to the old Prussian artillery ranges at Jüterbog, walking over to the hard ground where the cannons had been tested. Two villages had been cleared from the site when the artillery moved there. This was where Big Bertha of First World War fame had first been tried out, Blake told me.

He spoke about the breaching of the Wall in 1989: US intelligence had known this was going to happen from May. Two ambassadors had retired from the State Department to buy up property in preparation. We had lunch in the Alte Försterei in Kloster Zinna and looked at the remains of the *Backsteingotik* abbey. Frederick the Great had rebuilt the rest of the town in 1764 at the end of the Seven Years' War, during which it had been wasted by passing armies. The contented townsfolk had put up a statue of Frederick as a tribute. After 1945, there were moves to destroy the statue, but the locals wouldn't hear of it. Then, one night in 1949, a detachment of Free German Youth children arrived under cover of darkness and smashed it. The unhappy people of Kloster Zinna took away the fragments. In 1994, feeling the danger had passed, they put it back together again.

* * *

Kloster Zinna is in the Mark Brandenburg, a picturesque former province with many lakes that is documented in the volumes of Theodor Fontane's *Wanderungen*. Borussomaniacs comb it from top to bottom, chiefly for memories of Frederick the Great and Frederick William, the Great Elector, who trounced the Swedes there at the Battle of Fehrbellin in 1675. In the early '90s, getting to the Mark from Berlin was a nightmare involving a good deal of *Pendelverkehr* (there was still just one line for trains going in both directions), starting from Ostkreuz in East Berlin. My bad experiences of wanting to get to Rheinsberg or Neuruppin at the time were legion: a trip to the latter—no more than 100 kilometres—took about three hours. As an aristocratic Prussian friend drawled at the time, Ossi working habits were positively Mediterranean. He might have been right: I watched incredulous from the train window as our locomotive waited to use the single track and the entire crew sloped off to fetch ices. They then sat down on a bench in full view of the train and ate them. One needed to be determined to make such trips, else one might easily have been reduced to despair. Notwithstanding, it was worth getting to these places, because the rural idyll had somehow been maintained despite forty years of socialism. Neuruppin was actually Fontane's birthplace, and his father's chemist's shop was well preserved.

One day I set out for Magdeburg from the Zoo Station in Berlin. As we stopped somewhere in the east, two men got on wearing those military caps made famous first by Bismarck and Lenin, and later by Jeremy Corbyn. They spoke in hushed tones about bananas and oranges, and how their availability had still failed to sell them the idea of the Federal Republic. Magdeburg was a huge disappointment: apart from the cathedral with its magnificent Barlach war memorial, and a few small fragments, virtually nothing had survived the terrible air raid of 16 January 1945. Parts had been rebuilt in an idiom similar to the Soviet-style parade streets of East Berlin. In 1991, the names of the failing businesses gave them away: the Prag restaurant had gone bust and the Moskwa did not look long for this world. One shop sold wine from Saale-Unstrut, part of the scant handful of viticultural regions in the DDR, and so rare that most citizens would never have set eyes on it. I was almost in despair until I found Savarin in the Breiter Strasse, a proper restaurant with— for me at least—an auspicious name selling fresh white asparagus,[15] I presume from nearby Beelitz.

Despite the cultivated images of smoking chimneys, the DDR had a surprising number of seemingly untouched rural areas. In fact, a startlingly large percentage of the population continued to live in the villages, after land reform had gradually snapped up the soil for the state. One such region that remained attractively rural was the old Prussian Altmark, to the north of Brandenburg and Magdeburg. The Altmark is full of odd little gastronomic peculiarities. Salzwedel is the birthplace of *Baumkuchen*: the dough is dropped onto a turning spit, and as a result forms in rings like a tree. There was even wine from Werder offered in a restaurant near Havelberg. The waiter agreed with me that it was an *Apostelwein*—requiring a dozen men to make you drink it. The farmhouses in the region were comparatively unspoilt. Unlike Lower Austria, for example, the villagers were too poor to ruin their half-timbered houses with glass doors and double glazing. When I toured it in 1996, the large town of Stendal was dirty and closed but towns, or rather 'cities', like Havelberg, Jerichow and Tangermünde were still a delight, particularly the first, with its Romanesque cathedral.

Most if not all of the churches were locked. I assume that one was not encouraged to enter them in the DDR years. Tangermünde is the setting for Theodor Fontane's *Grete Minde*, a powerful evocation of the historical events surrounding the great fire of 1617. All the local villages are popular with storks in season. I had been to Halberstadt several years earlier. As was so often the case when I first visited these German towns and cities, I was greeted by destruction, here wrought by the USAAF on 8 April 1945. Then, if you didn't lose heart, there was the big cluster of magpie buildings in the centre. In 1991, many of them were being done up, and the wattle and daub had been removed from between the wooden crucks. After a while I realised that Halberstadt had the potential to become an attractive city again, as I found more and more gems. I peered through the letterbox of one dilapidated old house to find that the back had been blasted off. Some wag came down the street and shouted at me, '*Niemand ist zu Hause!*'[16] (No one's home.)

I continued to Wernigerode in the Harz Mountains, where disputed ownership had closed many of the businesses in what had previously been one of East Germany's tourist spots. The town was full of half-timbered buildings; up at the top of the crag was the huge castle of the Stolbergs. One story had had a happy ending: the Siegemunde family who had opened their *Konditorei* in 1936, only to have it impounded by the SED in 1951, had just got it back, and were once again making the best cakes in town. I crossed the Harz to Nordhausen on a narrow-gauge train. Most of the passengers got out at the Brocken—at 856 metres, the highest mountain in the Harz; then came the villages of Elend and Sorge,[17] which claimed a few more. Not many continued to Nordhausen, and with good reason. The 'city' was chiefly famous for schnapps—the famous Doppelkorn. Otherwise, it was infamous for the murderous concentration camp at Dora, and the little town was more wrecked than virtually any I'd seen. The only substantial building that showed any signs of having escaped this Armageddon was the railway station, although there were a few clusters of half-timbered buildings givng a tantalising idea of what it must once have been like.

I carried on to the comparatively well-preserved Prussian university town of Halle but, finding no room at the inn, then travelled the short distance to Leipzig to find a bed. I thought the place looked nice, but Halle features largely in Christa Wolf's *Divided Heaven* as a city of smokestacks and polluted water: 'this cursed water that stank of chemicals for as long as they could remember—and tasted bitter'. The novel hardly recommends it, and the jibes are echoed in the film adaptation. According to Wolf the River Saale also stank, and was covered in white foam. The chemical works had poisoned the fish; children hesitated before swimming in it. The direction of the wind was also discernable from the smell: chemicals, malt coffee or brown coal.

Wittenberg was another tourist destination within the DDR that must have caused some embarrassment to the regime, particularly during the time when they were coming down hard on the Evangelical Church. I visited on a day trip from Berlin and inspected both church and Schloss, as well as, of course, the Lutherhaus and *Schlosskapelle*, where an American woman made me pose for a picture 'looking like a Protestant'. There was a *Schlosskeller* with a bogus medieval vault. Little had been done to salvage what was left of Frankfurt an der Oder. The medieval Rathaus had been patched up, but the church, dating from the same time, remained roofless after the *Wende*. There were some good but ruinous buildings down by the river that now formed the border with Poland.

Brandenburg survived better than most Prussian cities, with its Romanesque cathedral on an island in the Havel, and the remains of the famous Ritterakademie. In the cloister there is a tablet inscribed with the names of dead pupils from the two world wars: it contains all the most sonorous names of the old Prussian nobility. A von Hagen had been executed after 20 July 1944, and two others had died in Sachsenhausen. The building of settlements on an island like this was typical of the Slavic Wends, who inhabited these sites before the Germans.

MECKLENBURG

The Prussian style extends up through the Uckermark to the last remaining slice of German Pomerania, east of Greifswald. On the way you pass great expanses of water and redbrick walled towns and churches in Prenzlau, Pasewalk and Anklam. In 1991, the only obvious place to stay in Greifswald was a trade union guesthouse, another relic of the DDR. The town was not yet geared up for tourism. To the west was the region of Mecklenburg, with its 600 or so lakes and their DDR holiday colonies. One year I stayed in a cabin in Neu Canow owned by the sociologist Klaus Meschkat. If you were a good citizen of the DDR, you were able to rent or purchase a little holiday home—three small rooms, close to one of the lakes. One day we went to Himmelpfort, a ruined Cistercian abbey close to Fürstenberg and Ravensbrück, where a monument had been put up to the *Frauenlager*. I was with one of Adam von Trott's daughters at the time. She knew perfectly well that it was not just a women's camp. Her father had been there, along with many other men of the 20 July Plot.

There were delightful villages nearby, like Schneidemühl, with its Hilly Billy Saloon bar. Further towards Hamburg is Schwerin, the former *Residenz* of the grand duke of Mecklenburg, with its fairytale castle in the middle of the lake, and the Weinhaus Wöhler, a proper, old wine pub preserved by virtue of the fact that the Wilhelmine interiors had been put into storage in the '80s. I was taken there by a young woman who felt that her life had been blighted by the *Wende*: 'She thought her teachers had lied to her before 1989.' There was also the Weinhaus Uhle, an institution of similar antiquity. With its *séparés* and painted ceilings, this was the poshest place in town before 1989. The first time I stayed in Schwerin, I was at the Reichshof, which had a reassuring smell of brown coal and cat. The translation of Ostmarks into Deutsche Marks meant that hotels across the old Iron Curtain were always unjustifiably expensive, no matter how crummy or primitive.

Schwerin is also the *Residenzstadt* of reactionary Mecklenburg. Bismarck once quipped that, if the great flood were to come again, it would arrive in Mecklenburg, 100 years late. In the early '90s, I visited the artist Hartwig Hamer and his journalist brother Detlef there. They confirmed that it was possible to lead a decent life if you were prepared to compromise a little. You knew whom you could trust, and when to mind your Ps and Qs. This was called 'Vitamin B', the 'B' standing for *Beziehungen*, or connections.[18] Such things were second nature to people whose fathers and grandfathers had lived through the Third Reich. The Hamers' chief concern appeared to have been the amount of meat they could buy. If you got on with your butcher, they said, it was quite possible to eat well. This was revealed in the course of a lunch at which the table seemed to have been spread with half a hog.

Near Schwerin, I explored some *Widerstand* or resistance sites. The Schlösser associated with the 20 July Plotters were mostly empty. As yet they had failed to attract buyers. During the war, Tisa von der Schulenburg, sister of the conspirator Fritz-Dietlof, had lived in the Schloss at Tressow; under the old regime the place had been used by the local administration. One great tower dominated the lake and its teahouse, where Schulenburg conferred with Stauffenberg at Easter 1944. The locals had smashed all the windows. The Schulenburgs' own house was at Trebbow. The regime had built a lunatic asylum behind it, so potential buyers had to reckon with that, too. More refreshing were the Baltic resorts that inspired some many German painters, both Impressionist and Expressionist.

My little trip round coastal Mecklenburg stopped first at Bad Doberan; I was shown round its magnificent *Backsteingotik* Cistercian abbey by a Dr Haider, who spent his holidays visiting Europe's other 1,400 gothic abbeys. There are also lovely neoclassical parts of the spa. The next port of call was Rostock, which was smashed with a single punch in 1942 when the RAF carried out a training exercise in carpet bombing; mercifully, the Marienkirche and Heiligkreuz Damenstift contrived to survive.

Wustrow became a fashionable resort at the end of the nineteenth century. The cultivation of the sandy Baltic coastline continued into Nazi times, of course, and resulted in the building of Prora, the enormous German Butlins prototype on the island of Rügen. The DDR carried on from the Nazis, and since 1989 there has been an effort to bring a little panache to these old Baltic resorts. Hiddensee was associated with artists, where Ahrenshoop, with its typically Platt name, was open to mass tourism at the time of the Nazi leisure bodies *Kraft durch Freude*

(Strength Through Joy) and the German Labour Front. The DDR continued the tradition—one of the Nazis' least objectionable stocks in trade—of giving the workers a holiday, even if it meant building great slab blocks smack on the coast. Many of these have now been demolished, but when I visited in 2002 there was still plenty of evidence of Zille-style mass tourism in Zingst. Ahrenshoop, I was told by the Bürgermeister, had been a nudist camp since 1941; the special beach had been designated as such by the otherwise notably prudish Nazis.

BEER GERMANY

When Germans think of Catholics, they think first and foremost of Bavaria. Bavarians speak in dialects and have rustic airs—and yet Munich people are seen as quite sophisticated, and there is a bit of 'society' there: men and women with 'vons' to their name, and sometimes the odd *Freiherr* (baron) or *Graf* (count) striding into the Café Luitpold with a self-assured air, greeting all and sundry with a firm handshake or a brace of smackers. The old ruling house of Wittelsbach never seems that far off; everybody seems to know one, have drunk with one, or gone skiing with another. There is a little cult of the 'Mad King' Ludwig II (rather like that of the Empress Sissy in Vienna), with shops selling Ludwig artefacts and ties. Until recently there was even a man who dressed permanently as Ludwig and waltzed around with a Yorkshire terrier. Even when they haven't these trappings of gentility, which were supposedly abolished in 1919,[1] there are the *Schickimickis*, who represent a more leisured class—the children of those who made a packet during the Economic Miracle, who like to drink prosecco and say *bussi-bussi* whenever they give one another resounding kisses on both cheeks.

Schwabing, up by the university, used to be the trendy part of the city—but that mantle is now lost. Glittering Munich society now clusters around the Gärtnerplatz, if it hasn't gone elsewhere once again. Munich's cafés are not a patch on Vienna's. Dukatz has a certain style, but Luitpold, which tends to be the gathering place of posh Munichois, is slightly stuffy and fuddy-duddy. Käfer in the formerly Nazi suburb of Bogenhausen is mostly a luxury grocer, but upstairs there are the curious *séparés* in different styles populated by older *Schickimickis*. In the ancient Stadtschreiberei restaurant, named for the building's former function as office of the *Stadtschreiber* (town clerk), one finds old-fashioned women in hats.

Munich also has its sinister side as 'Capital of the Movement'. Somewhere I have a book that identifies all the surviving and non-surviving buildings with Nazi associations. A few of the most pungent have been knocked down. The Burgerbräukeller beer hall where Hitler launched his 1923 Putsch was demolished fairly recently and replaced by the inner-city Hilton. The late Christian Social Union (CSU) politician Franz Josef Strauss made a big thing of how much his butcher father abhorred Nazism, and him too; yet he was born at 49 Schellingstrasse in Schwabing, next door to the Hoffmann photographic studio where Hitler's court photographer plied his trade and where Eva Braun received her first pay packet. At number 62 was the Osteria Bavaria, Hitler's favourite restaurant, which by some miracle was one of two buildings on the street to survive the bombing, preserving its evocative landscape paintings from c. 1910. The Osteria Italiana, as it is now, is popular with CSU politicians and is a favourite of the former party leader Edmund Stoiber. It was not for nothing that young Franz Josef saw Hitler several times, and even went to observe the Putsch as an 8-year-old armed with an improvised knobkerrie club.

The excuse for Vater Strauss's hatred of his 'neighbour' was that he was a Bavarian People's Party man. The BVP was regionalist, monarchist and Catholic; Nazism rejected all three. It was put to sleep with the other parties in 1933. When Hitler fell, its rump was incorporated into the CSU, which became the Bavarian brother to the national CDU. What is Bavarian stays in the 'Free State'. The CSU was founded by the remarkable Catholic lawyer Josef 'Ochsensepp' Müller after the war.[2] Müller had run between the German resistance and the Vatican, and only narrowly escaped with his life from Flossenbürg concentration camp. His dissident friends, Dietrich Bonhoeffer, Hans Oster and Wilhelm Canaris, were all strung up on the same day: 9 April 1945. Ochsensepp didn't like Adenauer much, and it was seen as politic to keep the Bavarian conservatives separated from the rest.

For most people Bavaria means beer and sausages: the Oktoberfest and images of fat men in Lederhosen singing *Eins, zwei, g'suffa!* at Munich's Hofbräuhaus—except that, these days, the Hofbräuhaus is filled with American tourists, and the stout women I recall carrying a dozen litre Steins on their fists have largely been replaced by men. I remember the ladies well from a disastrous few weeks I spent in Munich in 1975, trying desperately—and to no avail—to find a job. At Spöckmeier in the nearby Viktualienmarkt, customers toss their beer back with a brace of *Weisswurst*, sweet mustard and a soft *Bretzel*. The ritual involved is considerable: the sausage must be eaten before twelve noon, and you must use your fingers; the meat is sucked from the skin and the latter discarded. The *Weisswurst* is made from varying quantities of minced veal and pork—in the Grossmarkthalle, they are pure veal—and flavoured with dried parsley and lemon zest; it must have been run into the intestine of a Chinese pig. German pigs, they say, are too coarse. In January 2004, I went to Munich to cover what was sold to me as a crisis: it was variously reported that the *Schickimickis* had taken over and that no one was drinking beer or eating *Weisswurst* any more. I went to the huge Neo-Gothic town hall to see the then mayor, Christian Ude, who talked about new lifestyles and people not wanting to get fat. There was not much solace for the sausage there.

* * *

Originally a dark brown lager, Bavarian beer has become lighter and brighter in the past fifty years. Once again, much changed under the influence of Bohemian pilsner, which took Germany by storm after it began to arrive by train from the 1850s. Pilsner turned out to be the engine of history as far as German beer was concerned. These days, Bavarian beer is characteristically sweet. Beer is big business in Munich—Richard Strauss was able to enjoy his gilded youth because his mother was from the Pschorr brewing family. When I interviewed Mayor Ude, he signed a bottle of beer for me, brewed with his own fair hands. I still possess it, undrunk and standing proudly on a shelf in my library; it was his calling card, after all. While I enjoy many of the best Munich brews, such as Spaten and Franziskaner, my favourite wheat beer comes from the Bavarian state farm at Weihenstephan near Freising. I used to love the one by Maisel's in Franconian Bayreuth, which was copper-coloured and smelled of pineapples. I once interviewed the owner and regretted that I had let him talk in German, as he spoke only the broadest Upper Franconian. Later I learned that he could in fact manage fluent English, as he had been apprenticed at a brewery in the very German town of San Antonio, Texas. He confirmed that Franconian beer was dark, and that the *Hefeweizen* wheat beer— delicious as it is—was a recent creation; until recently, anyone looking at cloudy beer would have decided it was faulty.

On one occasion in Bayreuth, I stayed at the famous Goldener Anker, where all the Wagnerians pitch their tents for the music festival in his honour. It was a most un-German hotel, in that it is still higgly-piggly and filled with prints and pictures, and some of the rooms didn't have en suite bathrooms. The festival was in full swing when I arrived, but I had no tickets. Mere mortals don't easily acquire them—you are advised to join a Wagner society with an annual allocation, and wait your turn. I went out that night. The Jagdhof was filled with people in evening dress talking about *The Flying Dutchman*. The Goldener Löwe was full of musicians relaxing after the performance. Back at the hotel, they were talking in the lounge about the Master's grandson, Wolfgang Wagner. At breakfast *The Dutchman* surfaced again, while others were looking forward to the first instalment of the *Ring Cycle* that night. The American on my left had been coming to Bayreuth since shortly after the war. I had to make do with some sort of *son-et-lumière* in town, at the Margravine's lovely rococo opera house. I still have never been to the festival.

Germany's beer belt extends south to Kempten in the Allgäu region of Swabia. When I was there quite recently, I was informed that, amidst more and more 'craft beers', the influence of the big Munich brewers was waning. When my work was done I went for a walk to see the imperial abbots' palatial residence and the wonderful early Baroque basilica next door. Once my feet began to ache, I felt I deserved a beer and stopped at the cavernous Stiftsbrauerei for a *Hefeweizen*. I felt I had made a good choice; seeing large plates of good-looking food being ferried out of the kitchens towards customers—Germans eat meals at all times of day—I resolved to go there again, should I ever have cause to revisit Kempten.

Berlin, incidentally, also has its beers. The traditional beer was brewed in Bernau bei Berlin or Werder. It too was reddish-brown. The Berliner Molle was a compromise—essentially a pilsner with a more strikingly hoppy taste. A quarter of a century ago, I was given a tour of Schultheiss's redbrick Gothic Tivoli Brewery in Berlin-Kreuzberg. I was struck by the fact that they had built a chapel for the workers. The brewery closed down soon after, and the buildings were converted into flats as part of the new Viktoria residential quarter. After 1989 the big Berliner Kindl brewery mopped up the Potsdamer Rex in Potsdam. The most noteworthy thing about its beer was the ubiquitous picture of Frederick the Great on bottles, mats and glasses. Some Berliners drink a thin, acid beer called Berliner Weisse. Syrup is poured into the glass to take the edge off it. For most, once is enough. There used to be a Weissbier *Stube* in the Berlin Museum where you could sample it in the green or red versions. The Museum has gone now; so, necessarily, has the *Stube*. Not for nothing did most Berliners and indeed Saxons succumb to the pilsner wave.

The last time I was in Potsdam, I had a lovely organic wheat beer from the Braumanufaktur brew pub, which was now selling its wares all over town—craft beers are taking over here too. A lot of East German beers bit the dust after the *Wende*. I don't know whether that was true of Greifenbräu, which I enjoyed on my excursion to Greifswald. The only restaurant I could find in town in those days had been set up in the university auditorium. They did terrible things to trout. The beer was compensation.

* * *

The other centre of beer production is the industrial Ruhr, in the north-east. Here the beer is generally hoppy and bitter. Dortmund would be the heart of the brewing business, but brands that have made a name for themselves would include Krombacher, DAB, Veltins, Warsteiner, König and Diebels. In Düsseldorf, the speciality is Alt—a top-fermented dark beer similar to an English ale. Catholic Bavarians can't drink beer from the Ruhr and Ruhris can't abide the sweet beer of Bavaria. They prefer something such as a Jever in Frisia or a Bitburger in Rheinland-Pfalz.

Saxony, of course, borders on Bohemia. One of the best Saxon beers is Wernesgrüner, from a small town an hour or two south of Leipzig. In the DDR era I was told it was almost entirely exported for hard currency, and not available to hoi polloi. The sociologist Klaus Meschkat said that he couldn't drink Bavarian beer, and disliked West Berlin beers as well. He was an East Berliner and stuck to his guns. When he couldn't get Wernesgrüner, he drank Radeberger from near Dresden. There is, of course, a small Saxon wine region that exploits the steep slopes of the Elbe around Dresden, Meissen and Radebeul. Most of Saxony's wine comes from the cooperative, a fairly slick operation based in Schloss Wackerbarth. The most interesting grower in Saxony is Klaus Zimmerling, whose small *domaine* includes the former royal vineyard in Pillnitz. A visit is recommended, not least because the *domaine* is enlivened by the sculptures produced by Klaus's wife, Małgorzata Chodakowska. He has a high proportion of Riesling for a Saxon, although Weissburgunder (Pinot blanc) probably has a better track record. In Zadel near Meissen is Georg Prinz zur Lippe's much larger estate at Schloss Proschwitz, which makes some very good reds in particular. The prince is married to a television moderator, and it is a particularly friendly operation all round. There are regular jazz concerts in the Schloss.

KÖLSCH

My first ever visit to the country was to Beer Germany; specifically, to Cologne, home to both a beer and a dialect called Kölsch. There was some trouble at home; I was facing O Levels in the summer and was not expected to excel at German. Gil, a business partner of my mother, suggested I stay a week with his father in Cologne. I knew next to nothing about it, but Gil's father was the brother of the later Nobel-winning novelist Heinrich Böll. Looking at the pictures now, I realise he was either Alfred or Alois. All I remember was that he was bedridden and furiously anti-Nazi. The other brother—Alois or Alfred—

was the headmaster of a *Gymnasium*. He introduced me to Underberg at tea, and I can still feel the burning sensation in the pit of my stomach today—though I have had recourse to it many times since, after indigestible meals east of the Rhine.

I met Heinrich Böll just once, with his son René. They must have come to tea or dinner. He had a house on the west coast of Ireland and had written a book about it, his *Irish Journal*. The Troubles in Northern Ireland were at their height, and most of the table thought the British were wrong and the IRA right. René said something about 'fascism against fascism' that I seconded. I don't think Heinrich and I really hit it off, but then I was fifteen and very shy. At the weekend Gil and his Welsh wife took me to drink Kölsch, which slipped down very nicely. I liked the way they popped another beer mat under the glass when I finished it. The glasses seemed quite small. Then the room began to lurch, and me with it.

Cologne was still being rebuilt in 1970. During the day I would walk into the centre from the British-built suburb where my host lived. I would take a sketch book and draw pictures of the many ancient churches that were still being patched up after the Thousand-Bomber Raid of summer 1942. Particularly striking was the Rathaus. You couldn't see much as it was all under wraps, but I was told it was going to take decades yet before they could restore all the medieval and Renaissance statuary. I went to the Cathedral many times, and walked round the edges of the Roman and medieval city, visited the Wallraf-Richartz Museum—in short, did anything I could to get out of the house and avoid talking to anyone.

WEIMAR

I once had a project to write a book about Weimar as a metaphor for the intellectual history of Germany. Much of the place had been destroyed in the war, and the DDR intended to demolish the remainder to create a proper socialist tribute to Weimar's famous residents: Goethe, Schiller and Herder. The SED never got round to enacting the project. The town, with its National Theatre—famous for the drafting of the 1919 Weimar Constitution—continued to be used as a cultural reward for East German Stakhanovs who were awarded a night or two and a clutch of tickets to the uplifting dramas performed there. In the closing moments of 1993, I booked myself a room at the Elephant Hotel. I explored the town, listened to Max Raabe singing 'Kein Schwein ruft mich an' in the Theater Café, ate roast goose at the famous Weisser Schwan next to Goethe's place on the Frauenplan, and was struck by the presence on the wine list of vintages from the tiny region of Saale-Unstrut, originating in the cooperative at Freyburg. Access to these had been one of the privileges accorded to SED members in the past. Things have perked up a bit since then. Tastings in Wiesbaden and London have revealed the talents of Bernard Pawis, who makes very good Riesling and Weissburgunder. Georg Prinz zur Lippe has also revived winemaking in the vicinity of Weimar itself.

Since I was all alone at the festive dinner on New Year's Eve, the hotel management introduced me to an American woman who had the room next door to mine, with the balcony over-looking the Market Square. She said it had been Hitler's room and let me in to stand where the Führer had delivered his por-tentous speeches.[3] It proved a good spot to watch the fireworks go up to welcome in 1994. I went to the Schillerhaus the next day, and noted with pride that my cousin August Zirner had recently played Posa in Schiller's *Don Carlos* at the National Theatre. I was also intrigued that Frederick the Great and his father—and indeed Hindenburg—had not been the only corpses taken for a ride in 1945: Goethe and Schiller were also unearthed, and hidden in Jena. Only when it appeared that they would not be abused were they returned to Weimar.

Then I came across a few cuttings relating to Hitler's visits to Weimar. These made me curious, and I followed up when I got back to London. The first thing I gleaned was that Hitler had not stayed in my neighbour's small room, but in his own extensive flat at the back of the building, where he had installed a Cranach from the Grand Ducal collection. As the ancient hotel building was in a parlous state by 1935, Hitler took the decision to have it pulled down and replaced by a proper 'modern' hotel designed by Hermann Giesler, whose brother Paul was Gauleiter in Munich. Giesler wrote his memoirs after the war. He was supposed to have had almost perfect recall. He records conversations with Hitler that reveal that very many features of the new hotel were arranged, if not designed, by the Führer himself. The new hotel opened in 1938. One day I sniffed over Hitler's former Gauforum up by the railway station, built with labour culled from Buchenwald concentration camp on Ettersberg hill. I was told that many died digging the foundations. Several years later, I went round the modern art museum there with the eccentric clergyman and former university lecturer James Bentley. On examination, one exhibit proved to be a turd in a tin. Many others were 'untitled'. James and I made up some names for them. I suppose it had been irresistible putting this sort of work in a museum on the site of Hitler's forum.

On another occasion, I explored Weimar as part of an extended tour of Thuringia that took in Jena and Ilmenau, where, according to the authorised version, Angela Merkel was asked to spy for the Stasi and said no. Like the nearby university city of Jena, Ilmenau is associated with Goethe, whose poem *Wandrers Nachtlied* was written there: '*Über allen Gipfeln/Ist Ruh*'.[4] Erfurt is the capital of Thuringia and is actually a rather wonderful city, with its bridge and cathedral, eighty churches and medieval citadel on the Petersberg hill. Founded from Mainz, its early fortunes were made from sales of woad (*Isatis tinctoria*), which grows locally. The colour was extracted with urine, and free beer was supplied so that the men could provide the woad producers with all they needed. Liberation from Mainz came via the Reformation, as Erfurt went over to Luther.

SAXONS

My first brush with Leipzig occurred even before the Wall came down. I was rather impressed by the railway station, which seemed to have been inspired by Piranesi, in scale at least. Many years later I got a chance to visit the Monument to the Battle of the Nations, which must rank as one of the most Piranesi-esque buildings anywhere in the world. Even twenty years ago, there was talk of pulling it down because it was associated with militarism: it was built in 1913, to commemorate the Allied victory over Napoleon a century before. Leipzig was wrecked by the bombing, but some large tracts were preserved, including a lot of early-twentieth-century commercial buildings with good details and carving. We stayed in some luxury on the penthouse floor of the state-owned Mercure Hotel and ate in the vast Ratskeller at a communal table with three clean-cut, possible Stasi men and an Ethiopian engineering student.

Once the possible Stasi men had asked us a great many questions about where we had come from and how long we were staying, they left us to talk to the student, who had already been in Leipzig for five-and-a-half years. The waitress took a dim view of this black man. There wasn't much racial tolerance in the DDR, but if the political complexion of the client state was right, their students could study there. The Ethiopian diner ordered his beers two at a time, much to the horror of the Stasi men (*'Hat er zweimal Bier bestellt?!'*), then asked my companion whether he was married. When the reply was negative, he said:

'What do you do about your biological needs?' 'Same as you, old man,' was my friend's reply.[5] The Stasi scowled, but the Ethiopian laughed. It transpired he was terrified of his Ethiopian party boss, who was sitting at another table surrounded by local ladies. When he had ceased worrying about his political leader, he moved on to concerns about his last bus home, which he had already missed.

The next day was taken up with a little pilgrimage tour of Bach's city: the Thomaskirche and Bach's tomb, a glass of Muscatel wine in the Bachstübl opposite, and back to the church to hear a cantata rehearsed by the choir. I once visited at the time of the great fair, which had brought wealth and prestige to the city in the Middle Ages. The Handel Festival had driven me from Halle, now the Leipzig Fair threatened to do the same in Leipzig. Fortunately, I found a room in one of those gloomy dosshouses opposite the station.

On my third revisit to the Thomaskirche, I was with the late James Bentley, who had written a book about Albert Schweitzer among the several dozen he produced on virtually every subject under the sun. He had briefly been chaplain at Eton, and later at Sussex University, where he also taught Central European history. He no longer wore a dog-collar and spoke in an idiom that might have made a sailor blush. Our tour guide was very suspicious of Bentley, not least because I referred to him as '*Unser Beichtvater*' (our father confessor): 'Why do you call him *Beichtvater*? He is not a priest. Where is his collar?!' I looked at James. It was true that he had precious few priestly airs, and he might not have been wearing anything easily construed as a shirt. For my part, I had just published a full-length biography of Frederick the Great which led me to challenge the guide's DDR interpretation of the king's life and role in Bach's *Musical Offering*: 'Friedrich the Second,' she pronounced, 'for he was not "great"—he played the king's theme [*thema regium*] on his flute, and challenged Bach to make a three-part fugue from it.'

'Pianoforte,' I countered.

'Flute!' she snapped.

'Pianoforte!' said I. She was not used to being corrected and began to gasp in anger, but James, seeing her mood, took her gently by the hand and led her over to the organ, which he had every reason to know had been designed by Schweitzer. He proceeded to explain its salient features. I saw her muttering impotently, her hand still trapped in his. It can't have been an easy day for her.

It would be difficult to imagine how bleak Dresden was when I first set eyes on it during Czechoslovakia's Velvet Revolution in December 1989. Little prepared you for the Prager Strasse with its tower blocks and the Newa Grill, an allegedly smart restaurant. Before the war, this had been the city's main shopping street. I knew it from Otto Dix's famous painting of the crippled beggar. I walked around in bitter cold, looking at the ruins of this one-time Baroque jewel, with Shostakovich's String Quartet No. 8 ringing in my ears. Of course the city was rebuilding, but very slowly. The Opera was up and running again, as were the art gallery and the Zwinger. We found a jazz club in an eighteenth-century crypt. The restaurants served sweet local wine from Meissen.

GHOSTS

The Leipzig tour guide almost certainly regretted the passing of the moral and historical certainties of the Old Regime. Many of the people who showed me round East Germany in the years immediately following the *Wende* had had their careers shortened and their lives blighted by the end of the DDR. My guide on my first day in Erfurt, for example, was a former chemistry master from the local *Gymnasium*. He looked too young to be retired. He knew his stuff, but would not be drawn out when it came to politics. The next day he was replaced by a younger woman, who apologised for him and confirmed that he had left the school under a cloud after someone got access to the Stasi's files on him.

Older people's lives were invariably marked by the past. It was almost impossible to have it any other way. This did not just apply to East Germany. I was taken around the sad Lower Saxon town of Hildesheim by a woman in her early sixties. She explained the process of rebuilding of a city that had burned for two weeks at the end of the war, the flames devouring its quasi-entirety and with it some of the greatest works of Ottonian art and architecture in Germany. Long after the drab new buildings went up, a petition was launched to bring back a few of the magpie, half-timbered houses on the market square that had been such a feature of Hildesheim before the war. She struck me as a cold fish, but when we stopped for a coffee or a beer, she began to talk of the trek she had made from Pomerania with her mother at the age of six. I thought she was going to cry. She had forgotten no detail of this terrifying ordeal.

My escort in Coburg was a former border guard and an amateur historian, who later sent me useful texts on the history of the town. He had been born in East Prussia and was seven when the war ended. He had fled with his mother and had reached Frankfurt an der Oder before the Soviet soldiers caught up with them. He implied that his mother was raped and he and some other boys were put up against a wall to be shot. At the moment when the boys thought their end had come, a rat or a cat jumped on a neighbouring wall. The soldiers swivelled round and fired several rounds at the animal. The boys needed no urging. They scarpered.

In Coburg I also met a youngish woman from Ingolstadt whose mother had escaped from East Prussia in 1945 at the age of three. She had taken a train to Pillau and then a ship.

Fortunately for her, and indeed her daughter, it was not one of those torpedoed in the icy waters of the Baltic. Nor was all terror inflicted by the Soviets. My friend Karl Heinz Bohrer was given hell by US soldiers in the Rhineland because they caught him, aged eleven, fetching milk dressed in a coal-scuttle helmet. At the time the Allied armies were highly paranoid about 'were-wolves', a force promised by Goebbels that failed to materialise.

Coburg has a certain *Residenzgefühl*—the feeling of being in the shadow of the palace and the ruling dynasty. These proud towns and cities are one of the more delightful sides of Germany. Italy can match them easily, but it is hard to imagine them in Britain or even in France, where centralised monarchy has existed for so long. Coburg is both pretty and proud, even if a long brown shadow is cast over its past: with the encouragement of Charles Edward, the last reigning duke of Saxe-Coburg and Gotha, it appointed the first Nazi town council in Germany. It was said there were still plenty of Hitlerites about; the driver who took me off to Bayreuth at the end of my stay was possibly one of them. I asked him if he had known Charles Edward. Yes, he said, '*Er war ein recht netter Mensch!*'; he was a really nice man.

Coburg is really in Thuringia—its sister town Gotha incon-testably so—but in 1919, Bavaria concluded a treaty with the city to bring it under its aegis, and that preserved it from becoming a part of East Germany in 1945. The Americans had to halt the Soviet advance into the town with tanks. Near Coburg, the little walled town of Sesslach has a communal brewhouse making Sesslacher, a traditional red-brown 'Vienna' lager. For a modest price you can take the beer home and bottle it. This was probably close to the original Franconian style of beer, before it was sup-planted by the men of Munich. Sesslach used to be associated with Jewish cattle traders and its Jewish cemetery still stands.

CENTRAL GERMANY

Thuringia and Hesse lie at the core of Germany. The Harz Mountains run somewhere in between. They will tell you that the Americans originally intended to make Kassel their military headquarters after the war, but the British-induced firestorm had wiped out 8 square kilometres of the city, leaving little more than Schloss Wilhelmshöhe on the hill, where the last Kaiser had boarded while at the *Gymnasium*—and that was also hit. In the end, the Americans had to go to Wiesbaden instead. The construction of the palace had apparently been paid for by renting out soldiers to the British to fight their battles for them, particularly during the American War of Independence. I ate Kassler at a restaurant there, and mused that I had also eaten a hamburger on Capitol Hill.

Hofgeismar in North Hesse, now a theological seminary, boasts a royal hunting lodge, where I spent those challenging few days debating Adam von Trott's memory (see Part II). This is indeed Trott country, with the Trottenwald, the family seats at Imshausen and Solz, and the lovely, sheep-scattered rolling hills that Adam loved so much. Celle comes as a surprise to anyone from Britain, as the town is stamped by the Hanover dynasty in a way that modern Hanover itself is not. Visiting Brits soon learn that the Hanoverian kings who took over in Britain in 1714 were two-timing us, simply continuing to lead their merry lives as electors of Hanover. It was not until the accession of George III that they really took the decision to be British first and Hanoverian second.

* * *

The Ruhr and the north-west of Germany are the two parts of the country I know least. At the Trott conference in Hofgeismar was a woman from the 'free city' of Bremen, who kept reminding the others that things were different there—that the liberal traditions of the Hansa cities had somehow managed to tame the wild beast of Nazism. I have never been to Thomas Mann's ancestral free city of Lübeck, but have taken small nibbles at Hamburg occasionally. I once met a man there who wanted to introduce me to Hardy Rodenstock (real name Meinhard Görke), the East Prussian-born manager of a number of German *Schlagersänger* or pop singers with a taste for expensive wine. German pop music is recognisable by its booming beat—a bit like a military tattoo.

Fabulous things used to appear on Rodenstock's table, ancient vintages of top growths in magnums and double-magnums, and the world's wine press used to flock to his soirees. Even in superior Britain, one heard of a lot of 'Hardy this' and 'Hardy that'. There they would sit together: the British wine merchants in their pinstripes and twin-sets, and the German pop stars in their cherry-coloured blazers and tight mini-skirts, quaffing bottles of century-old Margaux and Yquem. I was not keen and never followed up the lead; I always found something rather repellent about people scoring points in this way. You used to see quite a bit of it in Germany. I remember my Hamburg friend—I found him amusing; others didn't—the late Mario Scheuermann, who collaborated with Rodenstock on books. He once expressed incredulity at someone telling him he had not enjoyed the 1928 Château Palmer: 'But has he had it in magnum?'

As it turned out, my nose was right. Although Rodenstock had never appeared to defend himself, in 1992 he settled out of court following a ruling that there was indeed something fishy about his wine. Maybe the stuff he fed Britain's great and good was kosher, but the wines he was selling at home were not always so. Officially he was a wine-lover, not a merchant, but he could always find a bottle if someone really wanted it—but the wine would come at a price. It was at this moment that 'special' bottlings would replace the real wines. A little Lafite of an old—but not necessarily great—vintage would be mixed with inferior, recent wine to look like a wine from before 1870 or so, when the scourge of phylloxera changed the wine map of Europe. Rodenstock's game came to an end when he sold a bottle of 'Thomas Jefferson's' 1787 Château Lafitte to the American collector William Koch. When Koch discovered he'd been duped, there was all hell to pay.[6] I understand that a lot of tasting notes from that time have been excised from websites. Older wine books, however, often contain the telltale phrase 'drunk with Hardy Rodenstock'.

* * *

As it was, ancient wine was the reason I made my only trip to Bremen to date. In 1996 I was invited to taste the oldest wine in the Ratskeller, the Rose Wine, a Rüdesheimer dating from 1653 and still stored in cask. The pretext was the 350th anniversary of Bremen achieving the rank of Imperial Free City. After my arrival, I had a good walk and took in several teashops. Bremen is the centre of the German tea and coffee trade, and the selection from top tea gardens in Darjeeling and Assam put Britain to shame. This is often the case: KaDeWe in Berlin has a far better selection of teas than you would find in a similar emporium in London. Be careful, however: the questionable decaf brand Café HAG comes from Bremen, so no laurels for coffee—stick to tea. The greatest Bremen coffee magnate in recent times was Klaus Jacobs, but he largely built up his business in Switzerland and ended up owning a host of chocolate and coffee companies before being bought out by Philip Morris. He gave €200 million to the International University of Bremen, which is now called the Jacobs University in his honour.[7]

Some shops sell Klaben, the Bremen version of the Dresden Stollen. A few rather Dutch-looking *Bürgerhäuser* have been rebuilt near the Romanesque cathedral and there is a lively restored old quarter in Schnoor. It was May during my visit, and there were plaice and wonderfully fresh *Matjes* herrings. I was looking for *Kükenragout*: a local mix of baby chickens, ox tongue, crab and crayfish, traditionally eaten at the election of a new senator. In the Hansa cities senatorial rank granted huge prestige, a bit like the ducal families of Venice or Genoa. In Hamburg, for example, the patrician families of the port considered themselves far grander than the local nobility.

The British gave Bremen to the US in 1945, because their ally lacked a seaport for unloading supplies. The Ratskeller became an officers' mess and the cellar was severely depleted. Only the Rose Wine remained off limits. The 1653 naturally ullages a bit; when that happens it is topped up from some other casks labelled 'Apostles', dating from the eighteenth century. The Rose Wine was just the cream on the cake that day. The cellarmaster had never been allowed to taste it, mind you; permission had to be given by the mayor. It tasted extraordinary: coffee and cherries and with a huge acidity. We had also been privileged to taste forty-five Riesling wines, ranging from a young 1983 to a mature 1893. The most outstanding were the *Auslesen*: 1948 Wehlener Sonnenuhr from JJ Prüm, a '45 Schloss Johannisberg, a 1933 Hattenheimer Hassel from Schloss Schönborn, and a 1921 Kiedricher Berg from Robert Weil. Of the *Trockenbeerenauslesen*, the star was possibly the 1893 Erbacher Marcobrunn.

When the Catholics of southern and western Germany enjoy a break for Ascension, the northerners celebrate Fathers' Day. I witnessed jolly scenes at Wotersen in Schleswig-Holstein, with little girls in Zille aprons being drawn in carts behind horses and tractors. At the Gutshaus a man was grading asparagus. He explained the distinctions to me. The perfect spears were 'Class A'; then there were the bent ones (B), and finally the broken ones, which were sold to make soup. The German asparagus was by far the most expensive on offer. Market stalls were selling Greek stuff at a third of the price.

BAMBERG

Bamberg is one of the nicest cities in Germany, possibly because only 7 per cent of it was destroyed in the war. It lies on the border between Wine and Beer Germany. The little wine it produces is eagerly mopped up by the locals almost as soon as it is released. The most famous product of the city is smoked beer. Two breweries, Schlenkerla and Spezial, still specialise in this product, which can be an acquired taste. There were sixty-five breweries in 1818; when I went on a beer tour of the city in 2001 that number had already been whittled down to nine, but those nine still managed to make some fifty different beers. The real Bamberg beer is actually a red-brown lager, but as usual there are plenty of variations during the year, from Kellerbier or *Gig* (a picnic beer), to the Lenten bock or *fliessendes Brot* (liquid bread) at the onset of winter.[8]

Like Munich, Bamberg has seasonal brews: a *Doppelbock* is an extra-strong beer for Lent, when you need to compensate for the lack of meat. It is also called 'Salvator' or 'Saviour' for the same reasons. At Christmas, there is a Benediktiner Dunkel-Bock, at a prodigious 6.7%. Once I left London to spend a solitary New Year in Bamberg, sitting alone at festive tables, walking up to the Benedictine monastery at the top of the Michaelsberg—one of the seven hills of the Franconian Rome—for a glass or two of Maisel's Hefe at the brewery tap; it tasted of bananas. I watched Bambergers arriving in droves, with a firework in one hand and a bottle of *Sekt* in the other. A pop and a whoosh, and the year was out. The locals were very friendly and did their best to accommodate the stranger. I came to the conclusion that Bamberg looked best dusted with a little snow, like icing sugar on a Christmas cake.

WINE GERMANY

I came to German wine via Austria, which is sometimes similar, but never the same. I had been commissioned to write a book about Austrian wine shortly after the 1985 Wine Scandal. When I started to write about Germany, I naturally developed an interest in its wine as well. In this I had an excellent mentor in Stuart Pigott, who was living in Berlin at the time, and I often stayed with him and his then wife Ursula Heinzelmann at their flat in Wedding. At the beginning of the new millennium, I was appointed to lead both the German and Austrian juries at the new Decanter World Wine Awards. I continued to perform my German role until 2016. During that time, I was generally invited every August to Wiesbaden by the Association of German Prädikat Wine Estates (VDP), to taste the wines of the previous vintage; most years I'd visit a wine-producing region as well. My office gave me a familiarity with what I consider to be some of the best white wines in the world. In recent years, German red wines have improved beyond measure too. I also think it is true that, in the past fifteen years, I have spent more time in West Germany than I have in the East.

Not all German wines are good. I should not ordinarily recommend the wines of Kreuzberg, Werder or Potsdam, but all three exist. On my first ever visit to Potsdam, I found the wall into the Royal Vineyard collapsed in a number of places and walked in to look at the broken casements that protected the by now long dead vines. On the terrace below Frederick the Great's summer palace, there were little fig trees protected from the fierce northern winter by similar devices. Frederick would have his dream of the south, like Goethe, who laments in his *Italian Journey*, '*Gute Birnen hab' ich gespeist; aber ich sehne mich nach Trauben und Feigen.*'[1] Hopeful Germans grew, have grown, and will grow vines just about everywhere. My late friend, the wine critic Mario Scheuermann, used to rave about a vineyard in which he had an interest in Lauenburg, Schleswig-Holstein. I have often seen vineyard sites near Königsberg in East Prussia on old maps, but the truth is that in most cases, the northern limit for reliable production is 50 degrees of latitude. This would place the borders at Mainz, Wiesbaden and Frankfurt. The Ahr Valley (Bonn), Meissen and Koblenz (Mosel Valley) would all be a little to the north, but exposed south-facing slopes and slate soil can make up for lost heat.

Bonn is a 'small town in Germany', and was a funny place to plant a capital. It was associated with Beethoven and home to a famous university, but its provincialism was a distinct disadvantage for politicians, civil servants and diplomats who were required to live there during the years of the Western republic. Some people did benefit, however, and perhaps none more so than the winemakers of the Ahr Valley. The government's anti-nuclear bunker was actually constructed under the vineyards of the Meyer-Näkel family, who led the revival of Pinot Noir wines in the Ahr some years ago. At the height of the Bonn Republic, however, most winemakers and innkeepers were not required to make too much of an effort, as these were the low-hanging fruit to be picked by politicians and lobbyists. Belgians coming for the day added their whack to the cocktail in the form of streams of tourists liable to go home after lunch with a three-pack of wine.

Needless to say, the wine has come on by leaps and bounds since the Bundestag moved to Berlin. Despite being the country's northernmost vineyard area, the Ahr Valley now produces what is probably the best red wine in Germany. For some reason, I have never been, nor visited such *domaines* as Stodden, Meyer-Näkel, Adeneuer, Kreuzberg and Nelles, whose wines I greatly admire; Pinot Noir of considerable delicacy, with aromas often more floral than fruity.

The Mosel Valley is one of the most traditional parts of Germany. It was bruised by heavy fighting in 1945, but most of it still looks authentic. As it crosses over from Luxembourg, the Mosel is joined by the Saar and Ruwer rivers, which are now lumped together with the Mosel to form one viticultural region, chiefly famous for its Rieslings. Winewise, the Ruwer is dominated by two estates: Maximin Grünhaus in Mertesdorf and the Karthäuserhof in Eitelsbach. Maximin Grünhaus cultivates three great slopes that had belonged to the monastery of St Maximin previously on the site until the monks went baronial under the Kaiser's parvenu Bonn friend von Stumm-Halberg. These three slopes are the Abtsberg (which was reserved for the abbot), the Herrenberg (for temporal princes) and the Bruderberg (for the monks). The last was naturally the least of the wines. As its name suggests, the Karthäuserhof is a former Carthusian monastery, though the present house was rebuilt in Imperial times and has a number of amusing flourishes added to the billiard room. The key to great wines here is slate: blue at the Abtsberg, red at the Karthäuserberg and at the Nies'chen slope in nearby Kasel.

Another tributary of the Mosel is the Saar, which boasts an even greater number of top wines. The most famous Saar producer is Egon Müller IV in Wiltingen; then come Geltz Zilliken, Schloss Saarstein, Van Volxem, von Othegraven, Peter Lauer in Ayl and von Hövel. Other Saar producers are based on the Mosel, and have land at top Saar sites, like Nik Weis, whose

St Urbans-Hof owns parts of Ockfen and the large von Kesselstatt *domaine*, which is more often miss than hit. Where the Saar meets the Mosel, there is a parade of top estates, which produce the class of wines of breed and elegance that can be Germany's best. The beauty of the landscape alone has been enough to bring tourists to the region since Roman times: think only of Turner.

But the Mosel can be a stiff place, despite the sublimity of its great cliff-like slate terraces. I remember a particularly stuffy old chap in Bernkastel whose lip curled when my driver cut into his potatoes with a knife. This is not done in German polite society. Bernkastel, with its touristy Christmas market, belies its nature. The wines remain problematic, as many of the best need a bit of sweetness to cover their acidic skeletons and are preferably drunk when they have a bit of age on them. This makes them hard to accommodate in a modern world, although there are brave attempts to pair them off with Chinese food, because—so they say—Chinese food likes a bit of sweetness. Yes, there are dry Mosels too, but they are often not nearly as good as the sweet *Kabinett* or *Spätlese* version, let alone a top *Auslese*, or *Auslese* Gold Cap, which you would be wary of trammelling with the potentially distracting presence of food.

Any list of top Moselaner would have to contain these names from the stunning Mittelmosel: Heymann-Löwenstein in Winningen, the genial Ernst Loosen or Markus Molitor in Bernkastel, Clemens Busch in Pünderich, Fritz Haag in Brauneberg, Max Ferd (Dirk) Richter in Mülheim, Reinhold Haart in Piesport, Grans-Fassian and St Urbans-Hof in Leiwen, Schloss Lieser, Selbach-Oster in Zeltingen, JJ Prüm in Wehlen and the Batterieberg in Enkirch. Many of the sites have witty names, or commemorate an important usage—I assume the celebrated *Doctor* winery in Bernkastel points to the same idea as the *Apotheke* vineyard in Trittenheim: a pick-me-up. An important caveat must be stressed about the *Doctor*: there are two

Witwe Dr H. Thanisch estates offering almost identical portfolios and labels, but one is much better than the other. The easiest way to determine whether you have bought the best one is to look for the VDP eagle. That one is Erben Thanisch. The slightly less good one is Erben Müller-Burggraef. In Kröv there is Nacktarsch, or 'Bare Bum', a generic wine that commemorates the spanking of a naughty boy who infiltrated a cellar and tippled from a cask. The logo would raise serious eyebrows in Britain. Some vineyard sites are not what they seem: the Juffer (maiden) in Brauneberg is a reference to a convent. As Dirk Richter put it, 'It's the only virgin that improves with age'.

HIC HOCK

The Mittelrhein is hot on history and slightly lukewarm on wine. The previous star, Toni Jost, actually makes better wine in the Rheingau now. The best winemaker these days seems to be Jochen Ratzenberger in Bacharach. The Mittelrhein is a stunning stretch of river for all that, and to date the only bit of the Rhine that I have seen from a boat: I went all the way up to the Lorelei rock from Bingen and saw some of the famous castles perched on the cliffs above me. Bingen is opposte Rüdesheim in the Rheingau. Most of the top Rheingau wines occupy the south-facing vineyards between Assmannshausen and Wiesbaden, with a small clutch in the village of Hochheim opposite Mainz, which gives its name to 'hock', the generic term for Rhine wine. The inevitable, ineffable Goethe came this way from Wiesbaden, where he sketched out his bacchic, Persian-inspired *West-östlicher Divan* and tried to find out what made wine tick, tapping rocks along the way.

From the 1970s, a debate raged in the Rheingau as to whether German wine should be sweet or dry. The notorious German

Wine Law of 1971 had favoured semi-sweet wines and proliferated notorious *Grosslagen* such as Zeller Schwarze Katz,
Niersteiner Gutes Domtal or Piesporter Michelsberg. A movement to reverse or abrogate the law gathered momentum under
the leadership of Bernhard Breuer and Erwein Graf Matuschka-
Greiffenclau of Schloss Vollrads—sadly neither with us today—
and their Charta organisation of top estates. With time, the idea
was enshrined in the new classification of German wines elaborated by the VDP, of which about 95 per cent of the best 250–
300 German vineyards are members. Instead of judging wine by
Prädikat (levels of sweetness), the new system adopted the
French system of *cru*—based on the quality of the soil and expo-
sition. This system was not recently imported from France, but
was earlier used in the nineteenth century to determine which
vineyards should pay the most tax, and is recorded on various old
excise maps. The top category of *Erste Lage* is only awarded to
dry wines. The sweeter styles are only made when a long, hot
autumn makes it possible. The Rheingau went through a bad
patch in the '80s and '90s when it abandoned sweetness but failed
to establish a dry style with sufficient body. This they have
achieved now.

The Rheingau is Riesling, with a bit of Pinot Noir mostly at
the Assmannshausen end, where August Kesseler is king.
Riesling spread slowly from Hochheim after the fifteenth century. The Cistercians at Kloster Eberbach naturally had Pinots
from Burgundy. It was this monastery that made the first special
Kabinett wine (they put it away in a cupboard), and it was Schloss
Johannisberg that created *Spätlese* when the bishop of Fulda's
orders to pick only arrived after the bunches had begun to shrivel
with noble rot. In August 2016, I noted:

> The best in Hochheim was Domdechant Werner's Domdechaney,
> while Toni Jost, whose wine had greatly improved in Bacharach, was
> the best in Walluf. Robert Weil remains, of course, king in Kiedrich

with his Grafenberg. In Erbach, the Staatsweingut had to share the honours with Achim Ritter und Edler von Oetinger for the Marcobrunn, while the laurels for the Wisselbrunnen in Hattenheim were divided between Hans Lang and Josef Spreitzer, who made a marvellous Mittelheimer St Nikolaus as well.

Fritz Allendorf proved yet again that he can make wonderful wines with his Winkeler Hasensprung and Jesuitengarten. In the latter, Geheimrat Wegeler was also a star. Up on the Johannisberg the best wines were from Schloss Johannisberg together with the Hölle from the Johannishof. Wegeler made a wonderful Geisenheimer Rothenberg. The prize for the Berg Roseneck site in Rüdesheim went to Fritz Allendorf. In Berg Rottland the honours were due to Leitz and G H von Mumm. Wegeler made the best Berg Schlossberg.[2]

The often foolishly overlooked Geheimrat Wegeler in Oestrich also has top sites in the Mosel.

As noted above, for a decade and more I was entertained once a year in Wiesbaden, at the gateway to the Rheingau, and about forty-five minutes from Frankfurt on the S-Bahn. It is a lovely spa town, with scaldingly hot waters and Art Nouveau hotels. Wiesbaden owes its wealth and development to patronage by Kaiser William II, who used to come for two weeks a year to the theatre festival, which still runs, and endure the latest outpourings of his court sycophant, 'the festive Lauff'. There is some attractive Biedermeier architecture in the centre, but the real thrill of the place comes from the streets upon streets of Wilhelmine buildings; their spacious flats, I am told, are now mostly occupied by Frankfurt professionals. Walk up the steep Neroberg to the city vineyard, and you come across row after row of massive—and massively attractive—villas.

They say that Wiesbaden was saved by a strong wind that blew the American bombers off target, but nemesis might have come in the shape of the US Army headquarters installed here after 1945. For many years, whole sections of the place were cordoned off, and did not admit Germans. Even today the jazz bar in the Kursaal is generally filled with elderly American ex-servicemen, remembering better times. Wiesbaden may be a satellite town, but it does not feel provincial like a British city in close proximity to London or Manchester; on the contrary, it feels sleek, fashionable and moneyed.

The town at the centre of the Rheingau is Rüdesheim, which sits under the pompous Niederwald Monument up the hill. On the monument are inscribed the verses of the nationalist hymn, *Die Wacht am Rhein*. The hill is steep, and covered with excellent vines. Locally they hold that if a horse can stand up on the slope it is no good for vines. Rüdesheim is part of the itinerary of American tourists and can be a lively place. I once had dinner with Bernhard Breuer there in a hotel he owned. Sensible conversation was rendered impossible by raucous tourists doing the chicken dance. Probably best to stay at the old-world Schwan in Oestrich and eat at Zum Krug in Hattenheim. Of course there are plenty of nice places, including the State Domaine at Kloster Eberbach. I once saw an Elvis lookalike drive up to his table on a big motorbike, sit down at the table and demurely order a glass of Pinot Noir. It's cool to drink red these days.

Despite appearances, Frankfurt is actually quite a nice spot. People who have the choice don't really live in it; they have houses in the Taunus or the Rheingau, or a roomy flat in Wiesbaden. I was in Frankfurt shortly before the launch of the Euro on 1 January 2002 and was due to interview some worthy from the European Central Bank; only I wasn't, or I was delayed, as all the lifts had stalled. Nothing was going up or coming down—a metaphor for financial stability, I suppose. Frankfurt hardly resembles the Imperial city that it was before 1806, but its importance as a banking centre is based on a role that goes back to those times. You can more or less assume that any interesting building you see from that time has been recreated, including

Goethe's house and museum. It was snowing in 2002 and the *Glühwein* in the Christmas Market came into its own. Across the Main in Sachsenhausen, there were relaxed places to eat and drink the local cider or *Apfelwein*. In those days, late-night Frankfurt still jived to its own brand of techno, and revellers went to the underground U60311 bar, a space constructed as an underground station.[3]

* * *

The Nahe region along the river of the same name, which feeds into the Main, is probably the best wine region in Germany. There is a lot of volcanic rock about and the landscape is remarkable. The old Prussian royal copper mine used to be where Prussia and Bavaria met. It is now Gut Hermannsberg, an estate producing starkly mineral wines. The new name is considerably easier to get one's tongue around than the old. A distinguished wine might have been labelled with the lapidary: Staatliche Weinbaudomäne Niederhausen Schloßböckelheim Schlossböckelheimer Kupfergrube—just try adding 'Riesling *Trockenbeerenauslese*' to that. In its time, the Dr Crusius estate used to make incredible wines under the Bastei rock in Traisen, but they have lost their touch. The best grower in the Nahe today is surely Helmut Dönnhoff, who has now largely handed over the reins to his son Cornelius. Dönnhoff has wonderful sites in Norheim, Niederhausen and Schlossböckelheim. The other top estates are Emrich Schönleber, Schäfer-Fröhlich, Joh. Bapt. Schäfer and Kruger-Rumpf.

Rheinhessen was once the land of Blue Nuns. British wine merchants used to travel far and wide with their chequebooks, offering premiums for the sort of fruit liable to make 'good' *Liebfraumilch*. They also encouraged growers to plant early-ripening grape varieties that produced more sugar—things like Kerner, Bacchus, Huxelrebe and Ortega. Most of these have been grubbed up now, but sadly some remain. They are often bottled as *Beerenauslese* or *Trockenbeerenauslese*, but are usually vulgar incarnations. Only the so-called Rhine Terraces were in some way immune to this cheap commercialism, in that the top sites at Nierstein and Offenbach were known to buyers looking for the best Riesling wines. The names to look out for on the Rhine Terraces now are Kühling-Gillot, St Antony, Gunderloch—though I am not wholly convinced—and Schätzel. From elsewhere, Wagner-Stempel and Battenfeld-Spanier are good. In Southern Rheinhessen, or the Wonnegau, the front-runners are Wittmann and Groebe.

The Pfalz is a large region with its head in Rheinhessen and its feet quite literally in France: about half a dozen growers in fact have their land across the border, near French Wissembourg in Alsace. In France at least, Wissembourg is better known for beer. The best of the Pfalz is in the middle: the so-called Mittelhaardt, which centres on the cute old town of Deidesheim. A few years ago, I went to a lovely summer party at the Menger-Krug estate just outside the town, where they specialise in sparkling wines (not to be confused with the other Krug). There was great excitement in the family, as the first male child had just been born for over 100 years. We stayed at the Steigenberger on the edge of the town, and not for the first time. Those who take their breakfast outside are pursued by ravening ducks.

Deidesheim itself is dominated by the 'three Bs': Bürklin-Wolf, Reichsrat von Buhl and Bassermann-Jordan, which have the pick of the best vineyards in Deidesheim and Forst. Most recently I have been disappointed by the three big-hitters, and have preferred wines from Acham-Magin or Georg Mosbacher. They seem to have more of the power that I expect from a Pfalz wine. The von Winning estate also makes waves by using lots of oak to age their wines, as does Christmann, by dint of being severely organic. Some of the northern Pfalz growers make really excellent wines, such as Pfeffingen-Fuhrmann-Eymael and Fitz-Ritter. Increasing amounts of red wine are made in the Pfalz, the best of it from growers like Knipser and Kühn in the north and Rebholz in the south.

When the Pfälzer Helmut Kohl needed to entertain a head of state, he would travel the short distance from his home near the Rhine in Ludwigshafen-Oggersheim and treat them to lunch at the Deidesheimer Hof. Certainly the last time I stayed there, the hotel proudly displayed its collection of photographs of Gorbachev, Mitterrand, Chirac, Queen Elizabeth and Mrs Thatcher.[4] Once they were seated at the table, Kohl did his best to make them sample the local speciality *Saumagen*, stuffed hog's stomach, or at least a smidgen of the black pudding. *Saumagen* is actually rather good—far superior to haggis—but some quailed at the thought, and I suspect Mrs Thatcher was one of them. In compensation, the hotel had some of the best wines of Deidesheim and Forst in its vaults: from vineyards like Hohenmorgen and Langenmorgen, these included the Jesuitengarten and Kirchenstück—both attesting to the fact the Pfalz was won back to Catholicism during the Counter-Reformation—and the suitably Kohl-sized *cru* Ungeheuer.[5]

* * *

Würzburg is at the centre of wine Franconia. The city was horribly smashed in 1945; in its way, the destruction was every bit as bad as Dresden, although it killed fewer people. The magnificent Tiepolo ceiling in the prince-bishop's palace survived by a miracle. The city is well known for the three great institutions that own the city's best vineyards: the Bürgerspital, the Juliusspital and the Staatlicher Hofkeller. There is more Silvaner than Riesling in Franconia, but the Silvaner can be amazingly good, and the bulk of Franconian wines were always dry. There used to be a restaurant somewhere in Würzburg where you could point to a vineyard and the waiter would bring you a bottle of wine from it. It was always my ambition to do this. I have been assured that the restaurant still exists, but I have never learned its name.

There are two-and-a-half parts to the Franconian vineyard. The half revolves around the excellent red wine producer Paul Fürst at Burgstadt in the west; then there are the vineyards of Würzburg; and, finally, those that first follow the Main from Sonnenhausen to the clusters round the little walled town of Iphofen to the south-east, and then around Eschendorf as the river snakes north again. In Escherndorf is the 'Lump' vineyard. *Lump* is something of an insult in German, meaning 'blackguard' or 'toe-rag'. I suspect that this is the reason why, in recent years, the vineyard has been coyly renamed 'Am Lumpen'. The Julius-Echter-Berg vineyard commemorates a famous Renaissance bishop of Würzburg. Away from that city, the names to look out for are Horst Sauer, Fürst Löwenstein, Graf von Schönborn, Schmitt's Kinder and Hans Wirsching. Castell has a great deal of land and vineyard, but is perhaps the smallest *Residenz* of all, and the seat of another Fürst or prince. The Castells had helped their cousins, the zur Lippes from Meissen, when they were finally allowed out of captivity. The one time I was in the principality was during the asparagus season. After six weeks of asparagus, Germany begins to stink of it a bit—especially when some restaurants insist on putting out whole menus of the stuff, starting with soup.

SWABIA

Half of Swabia is in the old Kingdom of Württemberg: Catholic in the south where it borders the Bodensee, and Protestant in Stuttgart and the north. The other half is Baden, which, like Württemberg, had a Protestant ruler (a grand duke), but was

Catholic in its southern reaches. Where Swabia borders Franconia is the Hohenloheland, named after the seven-branch princely dynasty that owns several large Schlösser in the region. It starts at the Imperial city of Schwäbisch Hall. At Langenburg, as in Coburg, there is an air of *Residenzgefühl*. Although the town is the size of a pocket handkerchief, there are still *Hoflieferanten*, or purveyors to the court, making Wibele biscuits for the prince, whose enormous Schloss still dominates the town.

I was shown over the area by a London friend who was the daughter of the house. In London she was Xenia; in Hohenloheland there was much bowing and scraping, and the locals addressed her deferentially as '*Durchlaucht*', Your Serene Highness. Her father, the late Prince Kraft, was a nephew of the Duke of Edinburgh; relations were good with the British, but he had difficulties with the German Imperial family, as he told me on the second day I spent under his roof. The problem was 'Auwi', or Prince August William of Prussia, the Kaiser's fourth son and the only one not to pursue a military career. In the '20s, he threw in his lot with the Nazis, much to his father's fury—which might well have been why he did it. When the Americans caught him, they treated him badly in one of their internment camps; he was eventually released when the Hohenlohes paid some money to the commandant. He now had nowhere to go, so he came to Langenburg, where he lived until shortly before his death in 1949. As Prince Kraft revealed that evening, his remains were still there.

The next day, the prince took me to meet Auwi, who was housed in a little neo-Byzantine mausoleum with Art Nouveau details. It was home to his ancestors, but also, to his fury, to the interloper. Kraft had hated him and admitted having fired his pea-shooter at him as a child. He had wanted to get rid of him, but the former head of the Imperial family, Louis-Ferdinand, wouldn't hear of his being taken to Hechingen, which was joint-owned by both the Prussian and the Sigmaringen Hohenzollerns. Louis-Ferdinand had died since, and my suggestion that the present head of the family might be more receptive made the prince brighten. Since 1989, rather more possibilities had become available: the cathedral in Berlin, or even the Friedenskirche with Kaiser Fritz?

At another Hohenlohe mansion, Schloss Friedrichsruhe, I found Lothar Eiermann, one of the pioneers of modern German cooking. In Eiermann's early days, all eyes were on Paul Bocuse in France, who was turning the kitchen upside town, lightening sauces and trying to eliminate butter and flour. It was the time of the *nouvelle cuisine*: restaurants were going to be healthier places. Not everyone was convinced, of course, but then, food fashion is the oddest thing of all. The Bocuse message was brought back to Germany by Eckhart Witzigmann, who had worked in Bocuse's kitchens in Lyon. Witzigmann went on to win two Michelin stars at Tantris in Munich and three at Aubergine. He was the first German chef to do so—even if he was in fact Austrian, having been born in Bad Gastein. In 1973, Prince Hohenlohe-Ohringen had headhunted Eiermann to run the kitchen. At first, all food had to be ordered from the market at Rungis outside Paris, but by the '90s he could find everything he needed locally, especially Hohenlohe beef and veal. He was anxious to revive some good old German recipes, like Leipziger Allerlei, a dish consisting chiefly of tender young vegetables, to which he added sweetbreads, morels, crayfish and coxcombs.

You quit Hohenloheland at Rothenburg ob der Tauber, much rebuilt after it was shelled by the US Army in 1945 as they tried to destroy the SS headquarters there. It has been one of Germany's greatest tourist traps since the days of German Romanticism, and its medieval allures also appealed to the Nazis, who used it for all sorts of youth festivals and pseudo-medieval sports competitions between rival Hitler Youth groups.

Rothenburg has its attractions off-season, but those who dislike crowds might instead consider Dinkelsbühl or Nördlingen, which are not far away. Stuttgart has little to recommend it; having been the centre of the German motor industry, it was bombed flat. After the war the council, by a majority of one, voted to rebuild the royal palace. This was rare at the time: in Braunschweig they pulled theirs down. It is in a nice position, and there is a 17-hectare vineyard in the centre of the city. There are pretty places nearby, not least the relatively unspoilt university town of Tübingen with its college or 'Stift' and the poet Hölderlin's tower; or Bad Cannstatt, where they also have an Oktoberfest a week after Munich.

* * *

Württemberg also has its vines around Heilbronn and east of Stuttgart, centring on Fellbach. The regional speciality is the black grape Lemberger, known as Blaufränkisch in Austria. The gypsum soils east of Stuttgart are now considered ideal for Sauvignon Blanc, however, and a number of growers have started to make it. Aldinger is the name to conjure with here; the best of the others are Schnaitmann, Drautz-Able, Dautel, Graf Neipperg, Wöhrwag and Ellwanger. If you keep going south-east from Stuttgart, you find yourself in what was the territory of the older branch of the Hohenzollerns. The cadet branch became the rulers of Brandenburg and Prussia. Their little principality was centred on Sigmaringen on the Bodensee, which is another instance of *Residenzgefühl*. Sigmaringen was also the last incarnation of the Vichy Government, when the family were thrown out of their largely nineteenth-century Schloss so that Pétain and Laval could move in following the Allied invasion in 1944. This curious episode in the history of France was documented by the writer Céline in his novel *Castle to Castle* of 1957. By that stage, the late prince had also been ejected from the army, as Hitler feared the growing popularity of the royal families. He suffered the attentions of the Gestapo, but his dossier and the investigating officer were both destroyed when an Allied bomb scored a direct hit on their Stuttgart headquarters.

I interviewed Prince Friedrich Wilhelm in 1996, at the time I was writing my life of Frederick the Great. He was able to give me news of the Hohenzollerns. He had seen Frederick the Great's body when the coffin was brought to Hechingen, and as a child he had had the painful experience of shaking the Kaiser's one good hand. Later I met his cousin, the grand duchess of Mecklenburg-Strelitz, another grandchild of the king of Saxony. She too had vivid memories of the Vichy period in the Schloss, particularly of old Pétain in the lift. Once she trapped him in it for three hours by switching off the electricity; and she recalled Laval, his sleeves rolled up, killing time by helping the local farmers with the harvest. Her husband the grand duke was philosophical about his lack of territory. The Schwerin branch of the family had won out at first, but after 1919 the duchy was wound up altogether.

I got to know the region through the eccentric hotelier Andreas Kleber, whom I met on a train travelling from Wrocław to Dresden. He was a passionate trainspotter and spent all his free time travelling the railways and amassing books of train timetables. In 1992, he invited me to a Prussian festival at the Kleber Post, a hotel that had been in the family for over 300 years. I had to change trains and wait for a friend in Ulm. I realised I hadn't packed a tie and went into the nearest department store I could find: 'Give me the nicest tie you have.' She came back with some of the nastiest ties I'd ever seen. 'You had better show me the nasty ones,' I concluded. I picked out one that looked as if it had been designed by Jackson Pollock. It featured in the programme made that night by the regional broadcaster ZDF, when they asked for my thoughts on Prussia.[6]

I was astonished that evening to find myself sitting opposite the 97-year-old Ernst Jünger, author of the famous First World War memoir *Storm of Steel*, and the last living recipient of the Pour le Mérite. He was naturally the star of the television show, and said all sorts of positive things about Prussia. He told me how much he resented not being able to wear his medal, which had been given him by the Kaiser in 1918. As Andreas was leeching money, his friend Jünger had invested in his hotel. In 1995, when Jünger reached a century, Andreas gave a dinner for him at which both Chancellor Kohl and President Roman Herzog were present. Jünger lived on for another three years. Shortly before he died, he and Andreas drove the local express train all the way to Stuttgart.

* * *

Germany has a border with Austria and Switzerland on the sunny Bodensee. In September 1996, I took in all three countries and ended up landing in Lindau on a well-provisioned boat from Bregenz. Lindau has a hot, littoral feel to it. It was the start of a rapid journey through Friedrichshafen, to see the later Otto Dix pictures in the Zeppelin Museum, then the magnificent pilgrimage churches in Birnau and Meersburg, before we took a ferry to the garden island of Mainau. Our journey ended in Konstanz, where we were welcomed by the *Imperia*: a controversial statue of a courtesan literally holding a pope and an emperor in the palms of her hands.

I stayed in the former Dominican Friary, later home to the Zeppelins, and now a Steigenberger Hotel. This was where the would-be religious reformer Jan Hus was incarcerated at the time of the Council of Constance, and from which he was taken to be executed on 6 July 1415. The ancient conventual buildings had been converted imaginatively. The upper parts of the chapel had been turned into suites and another part was a bar. As for Hus's tower dungeon, the top floor was the hotel's bridal suite, while downstairs served as the kitchen cold store. We had dinner that night in the city's top restaurant, Bertold Siber's Seehotel Siber. The chef was looking peaky: he had been shot by Romanian bandits just two weeks before and discharged himself from hospital to say hello.

Twice in 1996, I tried to procure an interview with Ernst Jünger for the *Financial Times*. In May Andreas had once again promised to track him down. I was still trying to wangle the story in September. The day I left Konstanz, Jünger was dining with the French ambassador at the Kleberpost. He was famously loath to give interviews, and managed to slip out of my clutches, but I travelled up to Saulgau for all that. Andreas distracted me with other local curiosities: a priest who made elaborate displays out of fruit and flowers then fed them to the pigs; the pilgrimage church at Steinhausen; and a walk-on role in a film about the hotel. I never did get the interview.

BLACK FOREST

I once met Gottfried Horcher at his restaurant in Bon Retiro, Madrid. Horcher had once been the grandest place to eat in Germany, yet it had been domiciled in Madrid since 1943. The Horchers still maintained contact with Germany and had a house in the Black Forest, the homeland of Gottfried's grandfather Otto, who had founded Horcher in 1904. It was no accident that someone involved in restaurants and food should have links to the Black Forest: that is where you eat best in Germany, and where the best German produce comes from—not only hams and 'mountain' cheeses, but also fruits and heavenly fruit schnapps. Above all, the Black Forest is famous for fish and game. Plentiful supplies of these allowed Horcher's to remain the top restaurant in Berlin through two world wars, even when there was rationing and many people were starving.

In the old days, winter conditions were harsh for the Forest-dwellers in the south-western corner of Germany; as they tell you, the locals survived by 'counting money, distilling schnapps, killing pigs, curing hams, making clocks and babies.' Baden and the Black Forest also produce good wine. Nowadays when I go there I am mostly bound for the better winemakers on the Kaiserstuhl: the Hegers, Kellers and Salweys, or the Hubers in nearby Malterdingen. The Kaiserstuhl is a range of dead volcanic hills, and the hottest place in Germany. South of the Kaiserstuhl are the two brothers Wassmer, Fritz and Martin. Fritz in particular makes excellent Pinot Noir in a Burgundian idiom. Between Freiburg and the Rhine there is Münster cheese; much of the wine is made from the same grapes as Alsace wine in France, where a few people can still manage an Alemannic dialect that is more or less the same as the Badenese.

The northern part of the Badenese wine region actually nudges Franconia, and a couple of villages are even allowed to use the sacred Bocksbeutel bottle that typifies Frankenwein. The man to look out for near Offenbach is young Andreas Laible in Durbach, which is also a village famous for schnapps. He makes wonderful Rieslings. Apart from trawling through Baden for wine and restaurants, I have attended no fewer than three cookery schools in the Black Forest in my time. The first was at the Hotel Stollen in Gutach. My fellow students were all keen 'Hobbycooks', who led me to believe they spent their weekends perfecting recipes from two-Michelin-star restaurants. Frankly, it wasn't really much of a course: we students watched the chef prepare dishes on the menu, and we were then issued with a teaspoon and allowed to sample them before we went into lunch or dinner. I came to the conclusion that 'hobbycookery was little more than a superior way of exciting a jaded appetite in an advanced consumer society.'[7] Some of those in attendance went on these weekend-long courses regularly. As one told me enthusiastically, that way he was able to learn one-star, two-star and three-star dishes to cook for his friends.

The next one I attended was at the Adler-Post in Titisee-Neustadt. Here we were entrusted to a Herr Lipp, who gave us a number of interesting extempore lectures on crayfish and farmed salmon. I picked up a few tips, particularly about cooking white asparagus. Then we were sent into the kitchen in pairs. My partner was a strong and silent landscape gardener from Nentershausen, North Hesse. Otherwise, my fellow apprentices included an old man who had been in the Danzig police before the war, and who had ended up attached to a Romanian regiment at Stalingrad. He didn't say so, but it is safe to assume he was in some sort of SS unit. He had been captured by the Americans in Passau at the end of the war and interned with members of the Wehrmacht's *Charlemagne* Regiment of French volunteers. 'Imagine,' he said, 'there was just me, and all these Frenchmen!' I thought they had all been killed on the heights before Berlin in 1945, but he said this was not the case.

He told me that he and his wife had been back to Danzig/Gdansk recently, and that they had taken with them the key to their old house in Langfuhr. One day they had even gone to the house and turned the key in the lock. Luckily, he added, the present incumbents were not at home—otherwise the old policeman might have found a Polish policeman feeling his collar.

The third cookery course was in the village of Baiersbronn, which is famous for being the best place to eat in all Germany. There were a one-star, a two-star and a three-star in those days, all within walking distance of one another.[8] Sadly, my course was in the relatively humble one-star, yet we unravelled the secrets of the Black Forest gateau—which was actually invented in Berlin—and were impressed by Joachim Schindler in Lohmühle, who tickled a trout in a local lake for our benefit.

There are some nice towns and cities on the borders of the Black Forest; sadly, Karlsruhe is not one of them, although it is worth a pit-stop for the surviving buildings of the neoclassical architect Friedrich Weinbrenner. The Forest's capital is Freiburg im Breisgau, which the Germans famously bombed themselves at the beginning of the Second World War: the pilots thought they were in Alsace. Of course, the Allies later bombed it too, so that there was little of it left by the time the war came to an end. It is still a pleasant place, particularly in summer, with the open-air market around the Minster, the inns with spacious gardens where you drink local wine or beer, and the many shops selling cuckoo clocks. I have even bought one for my son.

The hills rise high above Freiburg. In the summer of 1984, I drove there with a friend from Paris who fell ill in one of the mountain restaurants; she had to be brought down in a taxi and confined to her bed. I wandered around the hills by myself while she was fussed over by her father and stepmother. I remember finding a curious sort of zoo featuring a caged fox. I had not been conscious of the smell of foxes before then. Now, of course, I smell them every day in London. There were also polite hikers in tweeds saluting the Maker with a cheery, Catholic '*Grüss Gott!*' as they passed. Their greeting had something reassuring about it, a feeling that my presence had been accepted in some way—but then, thinking back on it, maybe they were strangers too.

EPILOGUE

THE FOURTH REICH?

I often hear conspiracy theories about Germany, sometimes even from members of my own extended family: Germany, they tell me, is planning to take over Europe through domination of the EU. This is a well-orchestrated plan to effect economically what the Germans were unable to perform by force of arms. As a result, we other Europeans will become their slaves, in the same way as they intended to enslave us back then and have us working as helots for the Reich. A variation on this idea is the 'Fourth Reich'. Apparently, powerful Nazis put the Third Reich into a coma in 1945 only to revive it once the time was right. In the meantime, they went off to South America, where they could hatch their plans away from the prying eyes of the occupying Allied forces.

Meetings were certainly held prior to German defeat, and documents have been thrust under my nose attesting to the fact that representatives of important German firms were in on the plan. I remember one I was given in the course of a *History Channel* programme in which I featured. The 'important names' mentioned in the document were new to me, but that does not mean that they were necessarily insignificant. It was all a bit like Goebbels's pet werewolves. In the last weeks of the war, Goebbels put a lot of effort into creating a radio station and recruiting men who would keep up the fight against the conquering Allies, but when push came to shove, they failed to materialise. In 1945, Germany was utterly defeated in every sense of the word. All that happened was that a number of teenaged boys who happened to be in the wrong place at the wrong time were shot on suspicion of being 'werewolves'.

In the same programme, they once again tried to convince me that Bormann et al. went off to a happy but active retirement in Bolivia. I was and am quite content with the evidence that shows he was killed fleeing from the Bunker in Berlin. Certainly a lot of Nazis got out, and more either failed to be arraigned before the denazification courts or managed to evade justice for long enough to die in their beds. In this book, we have looked at why this happened. The responsibility lay chiefly with the Adenauer government and the need to have a functioning elite—even if it included old Party members—and to remilitarise in order to satisfy Germany's new friends in the West. In the United States, the Catholic Church is frequently invoked as a body that would help big Nazis to get to South America. I confess that this one mystifies me. When I watched the *History Channel* film, the lanky presenter pointed to various churches along the way to Genoa as if they were evidence of Catholic collusion; one was next to a bar and hotel where a war criminal had apparently lodged one night. He took this as an indication that the priest was involved. There are rather a lot of churches between Germany and Genoa, and many of them are next to bars and hotels.

There are good priests and bad; there are antisemitic priests as well, but their antisemitism is not vouchsafed by dogma. As Bishop Galen made clear in 1933, the Church does not recognise race, and in the Catholic liturgy blood has quite different connotations from Nazi ones. St Paul took Christianity to a wider world and the fact that it was no longer confined to Jewry was one of its particular strengths. If a Jew converts to Catholicism, he becomes a Catholic and is no longer a Jew. One bad egg was Alois Hudal, from Hitler's favourite Austrian city of Graz. Hudal was a low-ranking titular bishop who ran the Anima seminary for Austrians and Germans in Rome. His pro-Nazi views and indirect attacks on Vatican policies led to ostracism by the Holy See as early as 1937. After 1945, he helped Nazis escape, but this received no sanction from the Church. In truth, neither Pius XI nor Pius XII was 'Hitler's Pope', and the latter gave plenty of encouragement to 'Ochsensepp' Müller, who kept him informed of the plot to remove and kill the Führer.[1]

The confusion seems to lie in the idea that the Nazis were pro-Catholic. They weren't. The Church's strength was that it was supernational, and Catholics owed allegiance elsewhere— something that was intolerable to the Nazis. Nazism elaborated its own forms of religion, and where it was Christian it lent towards the 'German Christians' in the Evangelical Church. During the Third Reich, Hitler and Goebbels in particular did their best to discredit the Catholic Church, chiefly by a succession of show-trials in 1935–7, aimed at removing monks and priests from their roles in education. The standard ploy was used: homosexual priests and brothers had been caught molesting children. When the trials were called off, the Nazi hierarchy let it be known that this was only a pause. The Party had other fish to fry for the time being: the Jews, and then there was a war to be won.

The story that German business leaders or politicians are plotting to take over Europe via the EU is strangely reminiscent of the tale of the Elders of Zion. In that forged polemic, it was the Jews who were preparing to conquer the world. *The Protocols of the Elders of Zion* was published in Tsarist Russia in 1903, but it was only at the end of the First World War that it became famous outside its native land, at which point it took in the Kaiser, who was looking for someone to blame for defeat, Hitler, and many others besides. But the Führer was aware of its debunking: 'it is apparently based on a forgery, as the *Frankfurter Zeitung* moans to the entire world: the best proof that it is not a fake.'[2] As these pages have shown, I hope, I have spent much of my life talking to men and women in all walks of German life, from politicians, academics, writers and business people down to ordinary men and women in hotels and bars. Never have I heard anything of this allegedly powerful clique that is so hell-bent on assuming power in Europe through economic hegemony. My suspicion is that the idea of a plot to take over Europe is another instance of negative propaganda.

If Germany succeeds where others fail, there is a reason for it. Germany has been a world-beating manufacturing powerhouse since shortly after reunification. Its phenomenal progress was helped by proficiency in technology and the sciences, as well as its plentiful natural resources. Where manufacturing in Britain, for example, is in terminal decline, Germany's is not only maintained but healthy. Germany practises 'stakeholder capitalism', with assets more equitably shared out between staff and workers; agreement is therefore more easily reached about keeping down wage costs. Germany is also firm in its determination to maintain price stability. As Robert Skidelsky points out, with progressive reform, the EU has begun to mirror the structure of the postwar German state: decentralisation of its institutions and a division of powers between the federal government and the individual *Länder*. Germany also runs many of the more important bodies within the EU. Germany is reluctant to lead, but leads for all that.[3]

There are certainly issues that need to be addressed: Germany seems to be overprotective when it comes to its bondholders, and the Germans do better out of the Euro than the other member states. Germans are cautious by nature. Twice in the past century, their people have starved—such experiences breed a certain hardiness, and also a degree of distrust of those who would squander their resources. Not for nothing, I thought at least, was it the Catholic countries of southern Europe that pleaded for leniency during the Greek debt crisis, while the more Calvinist administration in Germany was keenest to abide by keeping to the terms of the loans. Germany had set a course for 'punitive austerity'—but then, Germany can boast that it started with absolutely nothing in 1945, yet only three years later business-men had crawled out of the ruins and were on their ways to making their first millions.

That German politicians and business folk would be unhappy with the accusation that they intended to conquer Europe—and perhaps the world—is to a large extent down to the sort of ideo-logical training they have received since the closing years of the Adenauer era. All educated Germans have to live with the past, and use their knowledge of it to understand the possible perils of the present. It is significant that the people who challenge this, both in Germany and elsewhere, tend to be both old and less educated. There is a danger, however, of the new grand coalition trying to win back right-wing support by stealing right-wing policies. Some have now claimed that the time of 'expiation' is over, and that a more self-indulgent, 'normal' right will emerge in German politics. That remains to be seen. The Germans are observed not only from within, but also by a world that is all too ready to throw the book at them should they ever slip up; they have all been taught that there is a beast at their hearts, and that the fox needs to be secured in its cage.

FURTHER READING

This book has been written from my own travels, experiences, articles and diaries, together with a deep reading of texts and literature, mostly in German. It largely begins with the creating of the two republics in 1949, but anyone interested in the subject of the postwar military occupation might like to look at my book *After the Reich* (John Murray, 2007). For English readers, a good starting-point for the history of the Western republic is Charles Williams's *Adenauer: The Father of the New Germany* (Little Brown, 2000). Adenauer dominated West German politics until the mid-60s, and has had just eight successors as chancellor to date. I have not read any of the books in English on the first socialist postwar chancellor, Willy Brandt, but I recommend the German-language life by Peter Merseburger: *Willy Brandt 1913–1992: Visionär und Realist* (DVA, 2002). On Helmut Schmidt, I have chiefly used Hans Joachim Noack's *Helmut Schmidt: Die Biographie* (Rowohlt, 4th ed., 2010).

The following are also in German. On the Bavarian politician Franz Josef Strauss, there are his own memoirs (Siedler, 2nd ed., 1989) as well as a useful life by Horst Möller, *Franz Josef Strauss: Herrscher und Rebell* (Piper, 2015), and the highly negative biography by Bernt Engelmann, *Das neue Schwarzbuch: Franz Josef Strauss* (Kiepenheuer & Witsch, 1980). Again, Helmut Kohl's memoirs (Droemer, 2007) are informative and written in a clipped, matter-of-fact style; there are also biographies by Herbert Schwan and Rolf Steininger's *Helmut Kohl: Virtuose der Macht* (Artemis & Winkler, 2010) and Hans-Peter Schwarz's *Helmut Kohl. Eine politische Biographie* (DVA, 2nd ed., 2012). I have also found Richard von Weizsäcker's memoirs *Vier Zeiten* (Siedler, 1997) helpful for the events of 1989. On Angela Merkel, there is a biography in French by Baudouin Ballaert (Editions du Rocher, 2006), as well as German-language books by Jacqueline Boysen (Ullstein, 2001), Gerd Langguth (DTV, 2005) and Wolfgang Stock (Olzog, 2000). Ralf Georg Reuth and Günther Lachmann's *Das erste Leben der Angela M.* is a biography of the dirt-dishing sort (Piper, 2013).

There is more in English on the DDR. Mary Fulbrook has written a solid history in *The People's State* (Yale UP, 2005), and more recently Hester Vaizey has come to grips with it in *Born in the GDR* (OUP, 2014); Anna Funder's *Stasiland* (Granta, 2003) is slightly older, but it is still a ripping read. There is also Anne McElvoy's *Saddled Cow: East Germany's Life and Legacy* (Faber, 1992). In German, a useful textbook is Dietrich Staritz's *Geschichte der DDR* (Suhrkamp, revised ed., 1996).

For an autobiography that describes the time of the 1968 student revolt, I would also add my friend, the German literary critic Karl Heinz Bohrer: *Jetzt: Geschichte meines Abenteuers mit der Phantasie* (Suhrkamp, 2017). On the eradication of Nazism from German art, the important Gilkey report is to be found in John Paul Weber's *The German War Artists* (Cerberus, 1979).

I hope the sections on literature and cinema will also yield some starting points for further reading and viewing.

NOTES

PREFACE

1. Giles MacDonogh, *A Good German: Adam von Trott zu Solz*, Quartet Books, London, 1989.

PART I: GERMANY SINCE 1945

1. Josef von Nowak, *Mensch auf den Acker gesät: Kriegsgefangenen in der Heimat*, Sponholtz Verlag, Hameln, 1956. I am grateful to Werner Pfeiffer for directing me to this book.

2. See, for example, Miriam Gebhardt, *Crimes Unspoken: The Rape of German Women at the End of the Second World War*, Polity, Cambridge/ Maldon, MA, 2017.

3. Gerhard Ziemer, *Deutscher Exodus: Vertreibung und Eingliederung von 15 Millionen Ostdeutschen*, Stuttgart, 1973, p. 94. The figures given in Ziemer derive from the Statistisches Bundesamt (Federal Statistical Office) in Wiesbaden from 1958. Of course, exact numbers for deaths are elusive, and vulnerable to manipulation according to political allegiances.

4. See Michael Neiberg, *Potsdam: The End of World War II and the Remaking of Europe*, Basic Books, New York, 2015.

5. Marion Gräfin Dönhoff, 'Polen annektiert die Ostgebiete', in Marion Gräfin Dönhoff, *Weit ist der Weg nach Osten: Berichte und Betrachtungen aus fünf Jahrzehnten*, DTV, Munich 1988.

6. Herbert Schwan and Rolf Steininger, *Helmut Kohl: Virtuose der Macht*,

Artemis & Winkler, Munich, 2010, pp. 15, 18. See also Oliver Zimmer, *Remaking the Rhythms of Life: German Communities in the Age of the Nation-State*, OUP, Oxford, 2013.

7. Hans-Peter Schwarz, *Helmut Kohl. Eine politische Biographie* (2nd ed.), DVA, Munich, 2012, p. 17.

8. Jacqueline Boysen, *Angela Merkel: Eine deutsch-deutsche Biographie*, Ullstein, Berlin, 2001, p. 7.

9. See Mark Riebling, *Church of Spies: The Pope's Secret War Against Hitler*, Basic Books, New York, 2015.

10. Franz Josef Strauss, *Die Erinnerungen* (2nd ed.), Siedler, Berlin, 1989, p. 77.

11. Dietrich Staritz, *Geschichte der DDR. Erweiterte Neuausgabe*, Suhrkamp, Frankfurt/Main 1996, pp. 66–7.

12. Hester Vaizey, *Born in the GDR: Living in the Shadow of the Wall*, OUP, Oxford, 2014, p. 163; Anna Funder, *Stasiland*, Granta, London, 2003, p. 57.

13. Funder, *Stasiland*, p. 5.

14. Giles MacDonogh, *After the Reich: From the Liberation of Vienna to the Berlin Airlift*, John Murray, London, 2007, pp. 372–74.

15. Horst Möller, *Franz Josef Strauss: Herrscher und Rebell*, Piper, Munich 2015, p. 308.

16. Staritz, *Geschichte der DDR*, p. 96.

17. Strauss, *Die Erinnerungen*, pp. 181–2. In fact, the Soviets were happy to go one step further and allow Austria to regain its sovereignty—see Staritz, *Geschichte der DDR*, p. 90.

18. Staritz, *Geschichte der DDR*, p. 105.

19. Marion Gräfin Dönhoff, 'Die Flammenzeichen rauchen...', in Gräfin Dönhoff, *Weit is der Weg nach Osten*.

20. Staritz, *Geschichte der DDR*, p. 127.

21. Ibid., p. 179.

22. Mathias Grefrath, *Die Tageszeitung*, 27 September 2017.

23. Strauss, *Die Erinnerungen*, p. 137.

24. Helmut Kohl, *Erinnerungen 1990–1994*, Droemer, Munich, 2007, p. 11.

25. Schwarz, *Helmut Kohl*, p. 78.

26. Annette Weinke, *Gewalt, Geschichte, Gerechtigkeit: Transnationale Debatten über deutsche Staatsverbrechen im 20. Jahrhundert*, Wallstein, Göttingen, 2016, pp. 212–13.

27. Marion Gräfin Dönhoff, 'Nach der Explosion', in *Weit ist der Weg nach Osten*.

28. Strauss, *Die Erinnerungen*, p. 381.

29. Peter Merseburger, *Willy Brandt 1913–1992: Visionär und Realist*, DVA, Stuttgart/Munich, 2002, p. 356.

30. Information from Ned Richardson-Little.

31. Merseburger, *Willy Brandt*, p. 393.

32. Ibid., p. 396.

33. Ibid., p. 397.

34. Staritz, *Geschichte der DDR*, p. 230.

35. The stage was built by the Nazis and first named after their favourite playwright, Dietrich Eckhart.

36. John F. Kennedy, '*Ich bin ein Berliner*' speech, 26 June 1963, footage available at https://www.youtube.com/watch?v=56V6r2dpYH8 [last accessed 13 February 2018].

37. Richard von Weizsäcker, *Vier Zeiten: Erinnerungen*, Siedler, Berlin, 1997, p. 158.

38. Marion Gräfin Dönhoff, 'Versöhnung: ja—Verzicht: nein...', in *Weit ist der Weg nach Osten*.

39. Karl Heinz Bohrer, *Jetzt: Geschichte meines Abenteuers mit der Phantasie*, Suhrkamp, Berlin, 2017, pp. 22–3.

40. Weizsäcker, *Vier Zeiten*, p. 156.

41. Hans-Joachim Noack, *Helmut Schmidt. Die Biographie* (4th ed.), Rowohlt, Hamburg, 2010, p. 108.

42. Weizsäcker, *Vier Zeiten*, p. 189.

43. Merseburger, *Willy Brandt*, pp. 615–16.

44. Martin Kölbel, ed., *Willy Brandt und Günter Grass: Der Briefwechsel*, Steidl, Göttingen, 2013, p. 415.

45. Möller, *Franz Josef Strauss*, p. 395.

46. Merseburger, *Willy Brandt*, p. 7.

47. Boysen, *Angela Merkel*, p. 16.

48. Gerd Langguth, *Angela Merkel*, DTV, Munich, 2005, p. 49.

49. Ralf Georg Reuth and Günther Lachmann, *Das erste Leben der Angela M.*, Piper, Munich/Zurich, 2013, p. 56.

50. Boysen, *Angela Merkel*: 'das schadet niemandem' (p. 28).

51. 'Walter Ulbricht: "Das Ding muss weg!"', Mitteldeutsche Rundfunk, 30 November 2017, http://www.mdr.de/damals/archiv/artikel91872. html [last accessed 13 February 2018].

52. Boysen, *Angela Merkel*, p. 33.

53. Wolfgang Stock, *Angela Merkel: Eine politische Biographie*, Olzog, Munich 2000, pp. 14–15.

54. Boysen, *Angela Merkel*, p. 53.

55. Staritz, *Geschichte der DDR*, p. 276.

56. 1919–2016. Chiefly rememebered now for singing the song 'Hoch auf dem gelben Wagen'; available at https://www.youtube.com/watch?v= s3HvMnYnGcA [last accessed 13 February 2018].

57. Noack, *Helmut Schmidt*, p. 179.

58. Karl-Heinz Baum, '"Ich bin jetzt wie mein Vater, der SS-Mann"', *Frankfurter Rundschau*, 20 October 2017, http://www.fr.de/kultur/raf-in-der-ddr-ich-bin-jetzt-wie-mein-vater-der-ss-mann-a-1371812? GEPC=s3 [last accessed 13 February 2018].

59. This policy originated at a conference in Sonthofen, Bavaria. The Union parties would do nothing to help the West German government.

60. Bernt Engelmann, *Das neue Schwarzbuch: Franz Josef Strauss*, Kiepenheuer & Witsch, Cologne, 1980, p. 7.

61. Möller, *Franz Josef Strauss*, p. 18.

62. Schwan and Steininger, *Helmut Kohl*, p. 108.

63. Ibid., pp. 108–9.

64. Ibid., p. 136.

65. A source of heavy irony today, given the closed-door policy of Viktor Orbán's Hungary.

66. The author received a small piece, a present from the winemaker Willi Opitz, in Illmitz on the Hungarian border.

67. Schwan and Steininger, *Helmut Kohl*, p. 134.

68. Ibid., pp. 138–9.

69. Ibid., p. 139.

70. Ibid., p. 142.

71. Weizsäcker, *Vier Zeiten*, p. 363. The wordplay is on 'Krenz' and 'Grenze'—in many German dialects, 'G' and 'K' sound virtually identical: 'unbounded freedom', or un-Krenz-ed freedom.

72. Schwan and Steininger, *Helmut Kohl*, p. 160.

73. 'Wende', in ibid., p. 155.

74. The old term 'milliard', meaning 'one thousand million' (one billion), has been used in this book to avoid ambiguity.

75. Schwan and Steininger, *Helmut Kohl*, pp. 166–7.

76. Ibid., p. 167.

77. Weizsäcker, *Vier Zeiten*, p. 363.

78. Ibid., p. 364.

79. Schwan and Steininger, *Helmut Kohl*, pp. 171, 174.

80. Kohl, *Erinnerungen*, p. 20. That Christmas, the DDR released its political prisoners.

81. Ibid., p. 24.

82. Kohl, *Erinnerungen*, pp. 59–61.

83. Kohl, *Erinnerungen*, p. 243.

84. Ibid., p. 152.

85. Quoted in Kohl, *Erinnerungen*, p. 242.

86. Schwarz, *Helmut Kohl*, pp. 622–3.

87. Author's diary, 20 August 1991.

88. *Tagesspiegel*, 8 August 1995.

89. Author's diary, 21 August 1997.

90. I could not eat as much as I should like to throw up.

91. Kohl, *Erinnerungen*, p. 354.

92. Still the only KZ I have ever visited.

93. Author's diary, 14 August 1992. The Gauck Commission looked into activities of the Stasi. It was chaired by the future president Pastor Joachim Gauck.

94. Hagen Elchler, 'Historiker fordert Umbenennung: Viele Oststrassen immer noch mit DDR-Namen', *Mitteldeutsche Zeitung*, 19 October 2017, http://www.mz-web.de/sachsen-anhalt/historiker-fordert-umbenennung-viele-oststrassen-immer-noch-mit-ddr-namen-28615060 [last accessed 13 February 2018].

95. In a Prague nightclub in 1989, I asked an East German man why he

was allowed to drink beer while I was only offered expensive drinks like 'whisky cola'. 'Weil du nach Geld stinkst,' was his rude reply—you stink of money.

96. Baudouin Bollaert, *Angela Merkel. Portrait*, Editions du Rocher, Monaco, 2006, p. 7.

97. Schwarz, *Helmut Kohl*, p. 869; this is in Kohl's dialect.

98. Bollaert, *Angela Merkel*, p. 23.

99. Stock, *Angela Merkel*, p. 24.

100. Ibid., p. 28.

101. Kohl, *Erinnerungen*, p. 240.

102. Schwarz, *Helmut Kohl*, p. 881. Kohl was known to describe himself as an 'old warhorse'.

103. Schwan and Steininger, *Helmut Kohl*, p. 313.

104. *Süddeutsche Zeitung*, 2/3 October 2017.

105. Bohrer, *Jetzt*, pp. 514–15.

106. *Frankfurter Allgemeine Zeitung*, 25 September 2017.

107. *Die Zeit*, 25 September 2017.

108. Claus Offe, 'Germany: What Happens Next?', *Social Europe*, 3 October 2017, https://www.socialeurope.eu/germany-happens-next [last accessed 7 March 2018].

109. Mathias Greffrath, *Die Tageszeitung*, 27 September 2017. The Bad Godesberg Conference defined the SPD as a party seeking limited social democratic aims, rather than a radical change to society.

PART II: THE GERMAN PEOPLE

1. Author's diary, 17 August 1991.

3. James Stern, *The Hidden Damage* (2nd ed.), Chelsea Press, London, 1990, p. 222, quoted in Giles MacDonogh, *Prussia: The Perversion of an Idea*, Sinclair-Stevenson, London 1994, p. 4.

4. Idem, p. 241.

5. The song that accompanied the chimes of the Garrison Church in Potsdam. It is actually Mozart's *Ein Mädchen oder Weibchen* from *The Magic Flute*.

6. Baudouin Bollaert, *Angela Merkel. Portrait*, Editions du Rocher, Monaco, 2006, pp. 12, 19.

7. I have also seen the ungainly translation 'testifier'.

8. Karl-Heinz Janssen, 'Als Soldaten Mörder wurden', *Zeit Online*, 17 March 1995, http://www.zeit.de/1995/12/Als_Soldaten_Moerder_wurden [last accessed 7 March 2018].

9. Georg Bönisch, 'Kämpfer gegen das Vergessen', *Der Spiegel*, 19 March 2008.

10. Annette Weinke, 'Alliierter Angriff auf die nationale Souveränität? Die Strafverfolgung von Kriegs- und NS-Verbrechen in der Bundesrepublik Deutschland, der DDR und Österreich', in Norbert Frei, ed., *Transnationale Vergangenheitspolitik*, Wallstein, Göttingen, 2006, p. 56.

11. Norbert Frei, 'Nach der Tat, Die Ahndung deutscher Kriegs- und NS-Verbrechen in Europa—eine Bilanz', in Frei, ed., *Transnationale Vergangenheitspolitik*, p. 11.

12. Weinke, 'Die Strafverfolgung', p. 48.

13. Andreas Eichmüller, 'Die Strafverfolgung von NS-Verbrechen durch west-deutsche Justizbehörden seit 1945. Eine Zahlenbilanz,' *Vierteljahrshefte für Zeitgeschichte*, 56/4 (2008), pp. 624–5.

14. Ibid., pp. 635–6.

15. One has only to think of Harry Lime in the 1949 film *The Third Man*.

16. Norbert Frei, 'Erinnerungskampf: Zur Legitimationsproblematik des 20. Juli 1944 im Nachkriegsdeutschland', in Christian Jansen, Lutz Niethammer and Bernd Weissbrot, eds, *Von der Aufgabe der Freiheit*, Berlin, 1995.

17. Clarita Müller-Plantenburg, 'Frauen bestehen auf Recht und Würde nach 1945. Am Beispiel von Clarita von Trott zu Solz', in *Der unsichtbare Teil des Widerstands—Auf dem Weg zu Frieden, Verständigung und Rechtstaat (1917–2013)*, Imshausen, 2017, p. 108.

18. Müller-Plantenburg, 'Frauen bestehen auf Recht und Würde nach 1945'.

19. Giles MacDonogh, *After the Reich: From the Liberation of Vienna to the Berlin Airlift*, John Murray, London, 2007, p. 350.

20. Obituary of Marion Gräfin Yorck von Wartenburg, *The Times*, 19 April 2007.

21. Norbert Frei, 'Erinnerungskampf', pp. 665–6.

22. Annette Weinke, 'Strafverfolgung', p. 60.

23. Ibid., p. 73.

24. See Rheingau, '42.500 Stolpersteine und drei Morddrohungen. Aktionskünstler Gunter Demnig verlegte in Oestrich-Winkel Gedenksteine für im Nazi-Regime getötete Juden' (42,500 stumbling blocks and three death threats: Political artist Gunter Demnig lays down memorial stones for Jews killed under the Nazi regime in Oestrich-Winkel), Facebook post, 24 April 2014, https://www.facebook.com/rheingau/posts/10152361003703390 [last accessed 15 March 2018].

25. Author's diary, 1 July 1991.

26. Volker Bach, *The Kitchen, Food, and Cooking in Reformation Germany*, Rowman and Littlefield, Lanham, MD/Boulder, CO/New York/London, 2016.

27. George has eaten the entire goose.

28. Hester Vaizey, *Born in the GDR: Living in the Shadow of the Wall*, OUP, Oxford, 2014, pp. 111, 128.

29. Ibid., p. 123.

30. Ibid., p. 142.

31. There are exceptions: the Prussian Hohenzollerns were Calvinists, their people Lutheran; while the Saxon kings converted to Catholicism to win the crown of Poland. The Saxon people, however, remained Lutheran.

32. Eichmann's family moved from Solingen to Linz. He grew up in Austria.

33. Kevin Hagen, 'Donald Trumps deutsche Wurzeln: Pfalz im Blut', *Spiegel Online*, 20 January 2016, http://www.spiegel.de/politik/deutschland/donald-trump-besuch-in-seiner-heimat-kallstadt-a-1072487.html [last accessed 15 March 2018].

34. SWR1 Rheinland-Pfalz, 'Freinsheimer Bäckerei spielte Trumpf aus. Die Trump-Schnitte—suss oder unerhört?', 9 February 2017.

35. The present chief conductor since 2016, Jakub Hrůša, is Czech.

36. Author's diary, 24 May 1992.

37. Since rebuilt.

38. Author's diary, 24 May 1992.

39. Obituary of Karl Diehl, *The Times*, 7 February 2008.

40. Ulrike Hermann, *Die Tageszeitung*, 16 June 2017.

41. Ibid.

42. Lidl is pronounced 'liddle' in its British advertisements, making its products sound homegrown.

43. Obituary of Rudolf Oetker, *The Times*, 20 January 2007.

44. Karl Schmidt-Rotluff, *Rote Düne*, 1913, for example.

45. Vaizey, *Born in the GDR*.

46. See, for example, Alex Preston, 'The man who sleeps in Hitler's bed', *The Guardian*, 24 June 2015, http://www.theguardian.com/world/2015/jun/24/the-man-who-sleeps-in-hitlers-bed?CMP=share_btn_tw [last accessed 7 March 2018]. In one of this article's pictures, Conrad Hommel's 1940 portrait of Adolf Hitler is clearly visible.

47. Berthold Hinz, *Die Malerei im deutschen Faschismus—Kunst und Konterrevolution*, Hanser, Munich, 1974, introduction.

48. In November 2015, a marble head of Hitler by Thorak was unearthed near the museum in Danzig/Gdansk. The head was dated 1942. It had not been exhibited in the Great German Art Exhibition for 1942 or 1943 and was almost certainly a private commission, possibly for Danzig-West Prussia Gauleiter Albert Forster, and was presented to the Danzig city museum, located on the same site.

49. Cora Goldstein, 'Purges, Exclusions and Limits: Art Polices in Germany 1933–1949', n.d., Cultural Policy Center, University of Chicago, http://culturalpolicy.uchicago.edu/sites/culturalpolicy.uchicago.edu/files/goldstein.pdf [last accessed 15 March 2018].

50. Ibid.

51. Ibid.

52. Email to author, 18 June 2015.

53. Mortimer G. Davidson, *Kunst in Deutschland 1933–1945: Wissenschaftliche Enzyklopädie der Kunst im Dritten Reich, vol. 1: Skulpturen*, Grabert, Tübingen, 1988, passim.

54. In the words of Brecht, '*Erst kommt das Fressen, dann kommt die Moral.*'

55. Joan M. Lukach, *Hilla Rebay: In Search of the Spirit in Art*, George Braziller, New York, 1983, p. 276.

56. Goldstein, *Purges*.

57. Carl J. Friedrich, quoted in Goldstein, *Purges*.

58. Ulrike Stoll, *Kulturpolitik als Beruf—Dieter Sattler (1906–1968)*, Ferdinand Schöningh, Paderborn, 2005, p. 131.

59. Goldstein, *Purges.*

60. Ibid.

61. J. LeRoy Davidson and William Benton, 'Advancing American Art', *Art News* 45/8 (1946).

62. Goldstein, *Purges.*

63. Cora Sol Goldstein, *Capturing the German Eye, American Visual Propaganda in Occupied Germany,* University of Chicago Press, Chicago, IL, 2009, p. 77.

64. Manfred Thiel, *Werner Peiner, Ein Künstler in Sturm und Stille,* Elpis, Heidelberg, 2004, pp. 151–2, 158.

65. Davidson, *Kunst in Deutschland, vol. 2: Malerei,* p. 366.

66. Dominique Egret, *Arno Breker—Ein Leben für das Schöne,* Grabert, Tübingen, 1996–7, p. 26.

67. Arno Breker, *Im Strahlungsfeld der Ereignisse,* KW Schütz, Preussisch Oldendorf, 1972, p. 334.

68. Egret, *Breker,* plates 127 and 195.

69. Egret, *Breker,* plate 210.

70. Ingeborg Bloth, *Adolf Wissel: Malerei und Kunstpolitik im Nationalsozialismus,* Gebrüder Mann, Berlin, 1994, p. 172.

71. Anja Hessen, *Malerei des Nationalsozialismus, der Maler Werner Peiner (1897–1984),* Georg Olms Verlag, Hildesheim/Zürich/New York, 1995, p. 137.

72. See *Vernetztes Gedächtnis,* 'Bilder-Zyklus aus acht Sgraffiti', n.d., http://www.vernetztes-gedaechtnis.de/dom_bilderzyklus.htm [last accessed 7 March 2018].

73. Gavriel D. Rosenfeld, *Munich and Memory: Architecture, Monuments, and the Legacy of the Third Reich,* University of California Press, Berkeley, CA/Los Angeles, CA/London, 2000, p. 79.

74. John Paul Weber, *The German War Artists,* with an introduction by Robert Mills, Cerberus, Columbus, SC, 1979, p. 15.

75. Goldstein, *Capturing the German Eye,* p. 106.

76. Ibid., p. 107.

77. Rosenfeld, *Munich and Memory,* p. 79; Weber, *German War Artists,* p. 30.

78. Weber, *German War Artists,* p. 22.

79. Ibid., pp. 25, 29.

80. Ibid., p. 15.

81. Ibid., pp. 16–17.

82. Ulrike Stoll, *Kulturpolitik*, p. 158.

83. Rosenfeld, *Munich and Memory*, p. 80.

84. Ibid., p. 99.

85. Ibid., p. 88.

86. Stoll, *Kulturpolitik*, pp. 167–8.

87. Rosenfeld, *Munich and Memory*, p. 92.

88. Carl Zuckmayer, 'Deutschland, Sommer 1948: Jüngstes Gericht oder Stunde Null?', in Carl Zuckmayer, *Deutschlandbericht für das Kriegsministerium der Vereinigten Staaten von Amerika*, Wallstein, Göttingen, 2004, p. 227.

89. Rosenfeld, *Munich and Memory*, p. 94.

90. Ibid., p. 95.

91. Weber, *German War Artists*, p. 82.

92. Ibid., p. 85

93. MacDonogh, *After the Reich*, p. 382.

94. 'M1941 Records Concerning the Central Collections Points ("Ardelia Hall Collection")', OMGUS Headquarters Records, 1938–1951, National Archives and Records Administration, Washington DC, 2004.

95. 'The Monuments Men: Edith A. Standen', Monuments Men Foundation for the Preservation of Art, n.d., http://www.monumentsmenfoundation.org/the-heroes/the-monuments-men/standen-capt.-edith-a.-wac [last accessed 7 March 2018].

96. 'M1941 Records'.

97. Cited in Weber, *German War Artists*, p. 38.

98. Weber, *German War Artists*, p. 38.

99. Ibid., p. 39

100. Goldstein, *Capturing the German Eye*, p. 107.

101. Weber, *German War Artists*, p. 11.

102. Ibid., p. 44.

103. Goldstein, *Capturing the German Eye*, p. 107.

104. Weber, *German War Artists*, p. 41.

105. Ibid.

106. Ibid., p. 53.

107. Ibid., pp. 62–3.

108. *Der Spiegel*, 15 September 1949. Author's translation.

109. Weber, *German War Artists*, pp. 92, 99.

110. Ibid., p. 99.

111. Ibid., p. 8.

112. Hessen, *Malerei des Nationalsozialismus*, p. 6.

113. 'U.S. Army Documents Concerning Holdings of WW2-era Nazi/German Artworks, 1993–2002', available at http://www.governmentattic.org/8docs/USarmyNaziArtworks_1993-2002.pdf [last accessed 7 March 2018].

114. Obituary of Heinz Berggruen, *The Times*, 1 March 2007.

115. Karl Heinz Bohrer, *Jetzt: Geschichte meines Abenteuers mit der Phantasie*, Suhrkamp, Berlin, 2017, p. 49.

116. Author's diary, 5 April 1996.

117. Since reconstructed in a modern idiom.

118. Giles MacDonogh, 'Refined Tastes in Art and Apple Strudel', *Financial Times*, 26 October 2002.

119. Staritz, *Geschichte der DDR*, p. 73.

120. Johannes R. Becher, *Danksagung* (1956), cited in Staritz, *Geschichte der DDR*, p. 74: 'Think of him Germany, your friend—the best./O thank Stalin, no one as great as he/The East so deeply part of the West/United in him. He bestrode the sea...' (Author's translation.)

121. Author's diary, 8 June 1991.

122. Wolfgang Jacobsen, Anton Kaes and Hans Helmut Prinzler, *Geschichte des deutschen Films*, J.B. Metzler, Stuttgart/Weimar, 1993, p. 324.

123. Michael Rauhut, *Beat in der Grauzone: DDR-Rock 1964–1972—Politik und Alltag*, BasisDruck, 1993, p. 27.

124. Ibid., p. 7.

125. A pun both on punk (German As are open) and on the favoured ghetto of the East German elite.

126. Max Raabe, 'Der Mann mit dem Palast Orchester', Stern, 1 December 2005, http://www.stern.de/kultur/musik/max-raabe-der-mann-mit-dem-palast-orchester-3499166.html [last accessed 7 March 2018].

PART III: THE THREE GERMANYS

1. Giles MacDonogh, *After the Reich: From the Liberation of Vienna to the Berlin Airlift*, John Murray, London, 2007, p. 347.

SCHNAPPS GERMANY

1. The house liqueur in the excellent East Prussian restaurant Marjellchen in Charlottenburg.

2. Andreas Kurtz, 'Siegfried Rockendorf, 50, starb nach der Geburtstagsfeier seines Vaters in Bad Sachsa im Harz: "Der Avantgardist der gehobenen Berliner Gastronomie" ist tot', *Berliner Zeitung*, 15 December 2000, http://www.berliner-zeitung.de/siegfried-rockendorf—50—starb-nach-der-geburtstagsfeier-seines-vaters-in-bad-sachsa-im-harz—der-avantgardist-der-gehobenen-berliner-gastronomie—ist-tot-16294408 [last accessed 9 March 2018].

3. Although I recorded a quite wretched meal there on my forty-first birthday.

4. Author's diary, 3 June 1991.

5. Now, sadly, it is no more.

6. See Mary Fulbrook, *The People's State: East German Society from Hitler to Honecker*, Yale UP, New Haven/London, 2005; Hester Vaizey, *Born in the GDR: Living in the Shadow of the Wall*, OUP, Oxford, 2014.

7. Fulbrook, *The People's State*, p. 75.

8. Giles MacDonogh, 'The Spy's the Limit', *The Guardian*, 7 June 2003.

9. Karsten Krampitz, 'Andere Wende', *Der Freitag* 34 (2017), https://www.freitag.de/autoren/karsten-krampitz/andere-wende [last accessed 9 March 2018].

10. Author's diary, 23 May 1991.

11. Klaus Peters, 'Mercure-Abriss wird Fall für das Gericht', *Märkische Allgemeine*, 1 March 2017, http://www.maz-online.de/Lokales/Potsdam/Mercure-Abriss-wird-Fall-fuer-das-Gericht [last accessed 15 March 2018].

12. There is a well-known story about the trooper who sodomised his horse. The king's response was: 'The man is a pig—transfer him to the infantry!'

13. See Kevin McManus, 'Pursuing a Cool Profit After a Good War', *The*

Washington Post, 26 August 1996, https://www.washingtonpost.com/archive/business/1996/08/26/pursuing-a-cool-profit-after-a-cold-war/581372d7-c2d3-438e-9fb4-676f26d1cd87/?utm_term=.837ec 7647c0e [last accessed 9 March 2018].

14. Author's diary, 8 April 1996.
15. Giles MacDonogh, *Brillat-Savarin: The Judge and His Stomach*, John Murray, London, 1992.
16. Author's diary, 4 June 1991.
17. 'Misery' and 'Anxiety'.
18. Vaizey, *Born in the GDR*, p. 59.

BEER GERMANY

1. The title is permitted if it becomes part of the former noble's name, hence Georg Freiherr von Ehrwürdig zu Karstadt, or Herlind Gräfin von Strohbundl.
2. 'Ochsensepp' was a name that distinguished him from the other Josefs (Sepps), in that he was in charge of the oxen.
3. People often ask for Hitler's suite at the Hotel Imperial in Vienna. The hotel assured me once that the suite (which had eleven rooms) did not exist anymore, but they always did their best to please customers.
4. 'Over all the summits, there is peace.'
5. Author's diary, 30 December 1989.
6. Patrick Radden Keefe, 'The Jefferson Bottles', *The New Yorker*, 3 September 2007, https://www.newyorker.com/magazine/2007/09/03/the-jefferson-bottles [last accessed 9 March 2018].
7. Obituary of Klaus Jacobs, *The Times*, 17 September 2008.
8. Giles MacDonogh, 'A True Place of Pilgrimage for Beer Lovers', *Financial Times*, 23 June 2001.

WINE GERMANY

1. 'I have eaten good pears, but I long for grapes and figs.' Written on 1 September 1786. Christophe Michel and Johann Wolfgang Goethe, eds, *Italienische Reise*, Insel, Frankfurt am Main, 1976, p. 15.
2. Giles MacDonogh, 'The 2015 Vintage in Germany', *Wine & Food Diary*, 1 September 2016, www.MacDonogh.co.uk/wineandfoodarchive.htm [last accessed 9 March 2018].

3. Giles MacDonogh, 'Out to Play in One of Europe's Great Money Centres', *Financial Times*, 19 January 2002.

4. Kohl records entertaining Gorbachev and his wife Raisa there soon after reunification: Helmut Kohl, *Erinnerungen 1990–1994*, Droemer, Munich, 2007, p. 264.

5. 'Monster'. Bismarck said of it, 'This Monster is monstrously good.' It is believed to be named after a Herr Ungeheuer, who once owned the land.

6. My sister watched the programme uncomprehending, as she speaks no German. At the end of it she said, 'Where did you get that dreadful tie?'

7. Giles MacDonogh, 'The Black Forest Without Gateau', *Financial Times*, 30 May 1992.

8. At the time of writing, it boasts two three-stars and one two-star.

EPILOGUE: THE FOURTH REICH?

1. See Mark Riebling, *Church of Spies: The Pope's Secret War Against Hitler*, Basic Books, New York, 2015.

2. Adolf Hitler, *Mein Kampf* (2 vols), Zentralverlag der NSDAP, Munich, 1936, p. 337; see also Walter Laqueur, *Russia and Germany: A Century of Conflict*, Weidenfeld & Nicolson, London, 1965.

3. Robert Skidelsky, 'Germany's Hour', *Social Europe*, 22 September 2017, https://www.socialeurope.eu/germanys-hour [last accessed 9 March 2018].

INDEX

INDEX

INDEX

INDEX

INDEX

INDEX

INDEX

INDEX

INDEX

INDEX

INDEX

INDEX

INDEX

INDEX

INDEX

INDEX

INDEX

INDEX

INDEX

INDEX

INDEX

INDEX

INDEX

INDEX

INDEX

INDEX

INDEX

INDEX

INDEX

INDEX

INDEX

INDEX

INDEX

INDEX

INDEX

INDEX

INDEX

INDEX

INDEX

INDEX

INDEX

INDEX